Hate Crimes

Books in the **Contemporary World Issues** series address vital issues in today's society such as genetic engineering, pollution, and biodiversity. Written by professional writers, scholars, and nonacademic experts, these books are authoritative, clearly written, up-to-date, and objective. They provide a good starting point for research by high school and college students, scholars, and general readers as well as by legislators, business-people, activists, and others. Each book, carefully organized and easy to use, contains an overview of the subject, a detailed chronology, biographical sketches, facts and data and/or documents and other primary source material, a forum of authoritative perspective essays, annotated lists of print and nonprint resources, and an index. Readers of books in the Contemporary World Issues series will find the information they need in order to have a better understanding of the social, political, environmental, and economic issues facing the world today.

Hate Crimes

A REFERENCE HANDBOOK

THIRD EDITION

Donald Altschiller

An Imprint of ABC-CLIO, LLC

Santa Barbara, California • Denver, Colorado

Library of Congress Cataloging-in-Publication Data

Altschiller, Donald.
    Hate crimes : a reference handbook / Donald Altschiller. — Third Edition.
        pages cm. — (Contemporary world issues)
    Includes bibliographical references and index.
    ISBN 978-1-61069-946-4 (alk. paper) — ISBN 978-1-61069-947-1 (ebk)   1. Hate crimes—United States.   I. Title.
    HV6773.52.A47 2015
    364.15—dc23   2015018857

ISBN: 978-1-61069-946-4
EISBN: 978-1-61069-947-1

19 18 17 16 15   1 2 3 4 5

This book is also available on the World Wide Web as an eBook. Visit www.abc-clio.com for details.

ABC-CLIO
An Imprint of ABC-CLIO, LLC

ABC-CLIO, LLC
130 Cremona Drive, P.O. Box 1911
Santa Barbara, California 93116-1911

This book is printed on acid-free paper ∞
Manufactured in the United States of America

While the national media occasionally highlight notorious hate crimes and diligently record the number of people the perpetrators kill, the names of the victims are rarely remembered. On August 5, 2012, six Sikhs praying at their Oak Creek, Wisconsin, temple were murdered by Wade Michael Page, a white supremacist gunman. Four others were wounded in the neck. The murder victims were Paramjit Kaur, 41; Satwant Singh Kaleka, 65, the founder of this Sikh temple (known as a *gurdwara*); Prakash Singh, 39, an assistant priest; Sita Singh, 41; Ranjit Singh, 49; and Suveg Singh, 83. All of the male victims wore turbans as part of their Sikh faith.

Almost two years later on April 13, 2014, three individuals who were walking near the Jewish Community Center in a Kansas City, Missouri suburb, were murdered by Frazier Glenn Miller, a longtime violent anti-Jewish and white supremacist racist. The victims included a 14-year-old boy, Reat Griffin Underwood, and his 69-year-old grandfather, Dr. William Lewis Corporon. Both were Christians who worshipped at a local Methodist church. A 53-year-old woman, Terri LaManno, of Kansas City was killed at the parking lot of Village Shalom, where her mother resides. LaManno was also a Christian, who attended a Catholic church in Kansas City. Unbeknownst to the bigoted gunman at that time, only one person targeted by his gunfire was Jewish. The uninjured person's name was not reported.

In the last few decades, there have been many hate crime incidents throughout the United States and the aforementioned violent incidents were widely publicized on TV, radio, and newspapers. When these horrific murders are later recalled, the victims of these tragic incidents—some of whom were not even the intended targets—should not be described solely as nameless members of a racial, religious, or other minority group or recorded mainly as a statistic in the FBI annual hate crime statistics report. Any discussion about the prevalence and dangers of hate crimes aimed at specific minority groups should include the names of individual victims. In this book, I have tried to include their personal names, whenever available, because it offers a crucial human dimension to these dehumanizing murders.

The first edition of this book was published 16 years ago and since that time, much has changed in the national understanding of hate crimes. Sadly, though, a lot hasn't changed. First, the bad news: some individuals throughout the United States are still victimized because of their race, religion, ethnicity, skin color, sexual orientation, gender, or other immutable characteristics. But there is much encouraging news: all three branches of government—legislative, executive and judicial—have become more involved in combating these crimes. The U.S. Congress, state legislatures, and municipal governments have passed national and local hate crime legislation. Law enforcement agencies ranging from the FBI to local police have become more vigilant in enforcing these statutes. Finally, the courts have been empowered to stipulate enhanced penalties for crimes that target individuals because of their membership (or perceived membership) in particular minority groups.

A revised and updated version of the 2005 second edition, the present work includes significant new material and two new chapters. The first chapter provides a background and history of hate crime legislation while the second chapter, a new addition, discusses the ongoing controversies about the passage of such laws and related discussions and debates about the gathering and accuracy of hate crime statistics. Chapter 3, another new feature, provides divergent and eclectic viewpoints on hate-crime statutes, the problem of hoax hate crimes, and the impact of these crimes on some affected groups, among other topics. Experts on hate crimes along with noted civil and human rights organizational authorities are profiled in the following chapter. The Data and Documents chapter offers important statistical reports and studies on hate crimes directed at particular groups, including gays, lesbians and transgendered, and the homeless, among other data. The sixth chapter provides annotated bibliographies of books and journal and magazine articles; this section also offers the most extensive detailed listing of congressional hearings and reports on hate crimes currently available. This chapter is followed by a Chronology providing an annotated listing of hate crime incidents beginning with the birth of the modern civil rights movement in the mid-1950s. Since the book contains some terms many readers have not heard before, the concluding section is a Glossary.

Despite media coverage of hate crime incidents, there are still widely held misperceptions about who perpetrates these crimes. Too much of American history has been soiled by centuries of slavery, antireligious, and anti-immigrant prejudice and violence carried out predominantly by white Christians who defended and championed often violent horrendous bigotry toward those they did not view as their equals. Given this dark historical backdrop, it may be understandable to assume all of the victimizers are white, even though this is not currently accurate. In fact, in multicultural America, the perpetrators occasionally resemble the diverse racial, ethnic, and religious spectrum of our society. The Chronology chapter of this book specifically documents several incidents that disprove the prevailing perception that these crimes are almost solely committed by white racists: On a few occasions, African Americans have harassed and abused Asian Americans; American Muslims have torched synagogues and physically attacked American Jews; Hispanics have beaten up African Americans; and gays, lesbians, and transgendered individuals have been harassed and assaulted by members of different minority groups. Fortunately these incidents are isolated but nevertheless, it is important to note that membership in a racial or religious minority does not immunize a person against harboring poisonous hatred and bigotry. The incidents cited in the Chronology chapter are statistically recorded (without names) in the annual FBI national hate crime charts and these statistics also indicate the multicultural range of hate crime perpetrators.

If there is any solace derived from the terrible hate crimes, mentioned above, in Wisconsin and Kansas City, the surrounding communities expressed both their intense grief and outrage and showed fervent concern for their fellow citizens so affected by these tragedies. Following the Wisconsin tragedy, President Obama along with many religious and civic groups rallied around the Sikh community. A year after the Kansas City murders, more than 3,000 participants engaged in a week-long three-mile walk titled "Seven Days: Make a Ripple, Change the World" to promote "faith, love and kindness." While the topic of this book is depressing, one should never lose perspective about the basic goodness and humanity of our fellow citizens.

I am indebted to several individuals for their invaluable assistance in writing this book. Michael Lieberman, the ADL Washington Counsel and the preeminent national expert on hate crimes, kindly and generously provided me important information and contacts. Kenneth Marcus, the president and general counsel of the Louis D. Brandeis Center for Human Rights Under Law offered excellent advice and support. I also want to thank the several contributors to the Perspectives chapter for providing their diverse and important viewpoints on hate crimes and hate crimes legislation. Robin Tutt, the ABC-CLIO editor, shepherded the manuscript throughout the process and very promptly answered my questions and addressed my publishing concerns.

While I can't say that writing a book on this topic has been enjoyable, the love of my wife, Ellen, has always helped me to focus on the precious aspects of life.

Hate Crimes

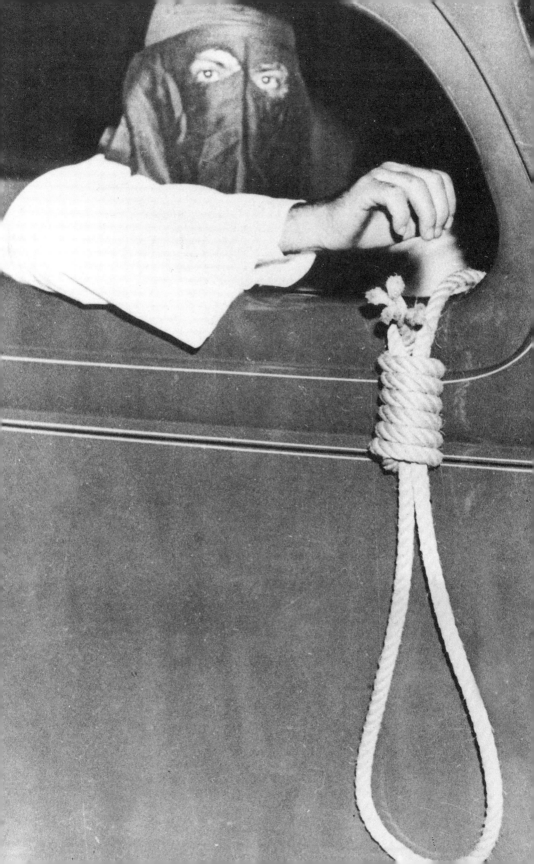

Introduction

Alan Berg, Vincent Chin, Matthew Shepard, James F. Byrd Jr., Balbir Singh Sodhi. During the past two decades, these names—previously unknown to the public—were in the news. They were all mentioned in newspapers and magazines; a few were noted in books, television documentaries, and even a theatrical performance. Although these five individuals came from different regions of the country and had vastly different professional, ethnic, and family backgrounds, they all had one terrible experience in common: they were killed because of their affiliation—or perceived affiliation—with a minority group.

On June 18, 1984, Alan Berg, a popular Denver radio talk show host, was murdered in a machine gun attack in the driveway of his home. His assailants—members of a neo-Nazi group—were convicted three years later of murder. According to trial testimony, the murderers stalked him for several days because they were enraged by his frequent on-air attacks against white supremacists and neo-Nazis. "They killed him because of his job, and they did it because he was a Jew," asserted Thomas O'Rourke, an assistant U.S. attorney (*Los Angeles Times*, 1987). During the economic downturn of the early 1980s, two

---

A hangman's noose dangling from an automobile driven by a hooded Ku Klux Klan member is among the grim warnings to blacks to stay away from the voting places in the municipal primary election at Miami, Florida, on May 3, 1939. In spite of the threats, more than 500 blacks exercised their right to vote. (AP Photo)

3

unemployed Detroit autoworkers bludgeoned Vincent Chin to death, blaming this Chinese American—who looked Japanese to them—for their lost jobs. More than 15 years later, on October 6, 1998, Matthew Shepard, a University of Wyoming student, was beaten, tortured, tied to a fence, and left for dead by local teenagers because he was gay. Only a few months earlier, James F. Byrd Jr., an African American from Jasper, Texas, was found decapitated and dismembered on a road near his hometown. His assailants, who had connections with the Ku Klux Klan (KKK), had tied him up and dragged his body with their truck. Two days after the Arab terrorist attacks on September 11, 2001, Balbir Singh Sodhi, a Sikh gas station owner in Arizona, was viciously murdered by an assailant who thought that because the victim wore a turban, he was a follower of Osama bin Laden. Although these tragic incidents are relatively infrequent, they nevertheless represent the disturbing phenomenon of hate crimes occurring throughout the United States.

What is a hate crime? How does it differ from other crimes directed at individuals or property? "For the purpose of collecting statistics, Congress has defined a hate crime as a 'criminal offense committed against a person or property that is motivated in whole or in part by the offender's bias against a race, religion, ethnic/national origin group or sexual orientation group,'" according to the Federal Bureau of Investigation (2015). In short, hate crimes are directed against members of a specific group largely because of their membership in that particular group.

Hate crimes take many forms: a swastika scrawled on a grave in a Jewish cemetery; racist and threatening telephone messages against African Americans; physical assaults against gay men and lesbians. Many of these so-called nonviolent crimes rarely make the news. Although the aforementioned murders did receive media attention, many violent incidents do not receive such coverage. (See Chapter 7, "Chronology.")

Few people would dispute the odious nature of hate crimes, but should they be punished differently from other criminal activities? Advocates of hate crime legislation directly address the rationale for special punishment. Kent Greenawalt, a

Columbia law professor, noted that "harm caused by violence that is motivated by bias can be greater than the harm done by ordinary acts involving the same amount of violence. The victim may suffer special injury because he or she is aware that race is the basis for an attack. Such crimes can frighten and humiliate other members of the community; they can also reinforce social divisions and hatred. For our society at this time, crimes of bias present particular dangers. That is a sufficient justification in principle to warrant special treatment under the criminal law" (Greenawalt, 1992–93, 627).

History of Hate Crimes Legislation

Although bias crimes have occurred throughout U.S. history, it is only in the past few decades that specific legislation has been enacted in response to violent bigotry directed at specific groups. (For clarification, bigotry is the state of mind of a bigot, a person voicing intolerant opinions and prejudices; these views are protected under the First Amendment as long as they are not accompanied by violence.)

According to New York University law professor James B. Jacobs, the term *hate crime* was popularized by three members of the U.S. House of Representatives who cosponsored a bill in 1985—which was later passed in 1990—requiring the federal government to collect and publish statistics on the increasing number of violent crimes motivated by ethnic, religious, and racial hatred. Jacobs noted that only 11 articles on hate crimes appeared in national newspapers that year; a few years later, more than 1,000 stories were published (Jacobs and Potter, 1998, 4).

A century ago, bias-related crimes were prosecuted under a variety of laws, including the Civil Rights Act of 1866, the Enforcement Act of 1870, the Ku Klux Klan Act of 1871, and the Civil Rights Act of 1875. These federal laws were specifically intended to stop both the violent rampages directed against southern African Americans and the curtailment of their rights during Reconstruction. (For a more detailed historical discussion of each of these laws, see Lawrence, 1999, 110–160.) Of course, it must be noted that federal and state statutes had previously legalized slavery and state-sanctioned violence in the United States. Under legislation in many southern states, African Americans were enslaved and suffered innumerable human rights violations. Almost 80 years later, the modern civil rights movement successfully lobbied for legislation to ensure the full civil rights of black Americans and to strengthen the already existing statutes prohibiting racially based violence.

However, it wasn't until the early 1980s that the concept of bias-motivated crimes expanded to include other religious and racial minority groups. In 1981, the Anti-Defamation League (ADL), the most prominent Jewish civil rights organization in the United States, drafted model hate crimes legislation to cover not only anti-Jewish crimes but all types of hate crimes aimed at minority groups. Almost all states and the District of Columbia have enacted laws similar to or based on the ADL model. The majority of states have at least one or more hate crime laws (consult the ADL Web site at www.adl.org for more information).

These laws establish a number of rules:

- They penalize criminal vandalism against religious institutions, including synagogues, churches, mosques, and other houses of worship.
- They prohibit bias-motivated violence and intimidation against individuals.
- They require state governments to compile hate crime statistics.
- They enact "penalty-enhancement" statutes for crimes motivated by hate.
- They mandate special training for law enforcement personnel.

As the ADL notes, the Bill of Rights protects expressions of hate, but criminal actions motivated by hate should receive more stringent punishment than actions stemming from other motivations. (See Chapter 2 for arguments both pro and con on the enactment of hate crime laws.) A convicted criminal is subject to an enhanced penalty if the victim is chosen because of race, religion, national origin, sexual orientation, or gender. The ADL model statute includes criminal penalties for vandalism aimed at houses of worship, cemeteries, schools, and community centers. This legislation allows for victims to recover punitive damages and attorneys' fees, and holds parents liable for the criminal actions of their children. In 1996 the ADL added the category of gender to its model hate crimes legislation, because gender-based crimes are similar in nature to race- or religion-based hate crimes.

The federal government also has many civil rights statutes that cover a range of activities, including the exercise of rights provided by special laws and the U.S. Constitution, the exercise of religious freedom, housing-related rights, and federally protected activities such as voting or the right to use public accommodations.

The following are descriptions of significant federal laws and pending legislation on hate crimes, largely adapted from the Anti-Defamation League Web site (Anti-Defamation League, 2015) and the U.S. Department of Justice (2015).

Civil Rights Act of 1968

In response to the growing power of the civil rights movement (and also the national shock in reaction to the 1963 murders of civil rights workers Andrew Goodman, Michael Schwerner, and James E. Cheney), the U.S. Congress enacted this omnibus law, which greatly expanded protections against all types of discrimination. The protections include:

- voting or qualifying to vote, qualifying or campaigning as a candidate for elective office, or qualifying or acting as a poll watcher, or any legally authorized election official, in any primary, special, or general election;

- participating in or enjoying any benefit, service, privilege, program, facility, or activity provided or administered by the United States;

- applying for or enjoying employment, or any perquisite thereof, by any agency of the United States;
- serving, or attending upon any court in connection with possible service, as a grand or petit juror in any court of the United States;
- participating in or enjoying the benefits of any program or activity receiving federal financial assistance; and
- allowing any person regardless of his race, color, religion or national origin to enroll in or attend any public school or public college.

The Federal Bureau of Investigation (FBI) claims that its jurisdiction over hate crimes is mainly predicated on this Section 245 of Title 18 of the United States Code.

Interference with the Exercise of Religious Beliefs and Destruction of Religious Property

First enacted in 1988, this statute provides federal jurisdiction for religious vandalism cases in which the destruction exceeds $10,000. Since the enforcement of the statute is restricted by the interstate commerce clause of the U.S. Constitution and the requirement that the vandalism exceed the stipulated amount of money, some federal officials have been somewhat hampered in their ability to invoke this statute.

Federal Explosives Statute

In 1982, Congress added the word "fire" to previous legislation on explosives, thus creating the federal crime of arson. The Bureau of Alcohol, Tobacco, and Firearms (ATF) branch of the U.S. Treasury is empowered to enforce this statute.

According to Maj. Gen. Reynold N. Hoover, an expert on explosives and ordnances,

Title XI, as originally enacted, established federal jurisdiction in those cases where property was damaged or destroyed by means of an explosive. Congress sought to relieve these restrictions through the Anti-Arson Amendment. At hearings on the amendment, ATF officials estimated that 30 percent of the significant arson investigations were discontinued because proof that the arson was caused by means of an explosive was too difficult. The House Committee considering the amendment also found that fire was used extensively for criminal purposes such as extortion, terrorism, revenge, homicide, and fraud against insurance companies. The addition of "fire" to Title XI indicated congressional intent to provide a comprehensive definition of explosives that encompassed a combination of ingredients that could explode when assembled. (Hoover, 1995)

Federal arson legislation simplified federal prosecution by eliminating the need to prove that an explosive was used to damage property. Although there have been additional amendments to Title XI following the adoption of the Anti-Arson Act of 1982, there have been no substantive changes made to the federal explosives law since that time.

This statute has been used by the U.S. Department of Justice (DOJ) to prosecute cross burnings.

Hate Crimes Statistics Act

On April 23, 1990, Congress passed the Hate Crime Statistics Act, which requires the attorney general to collect data "about crimes that manifest evidence of prejudice based on race, religion, sexual orientation, or ethnicity." The attorney general delegated the responsibilities of developing the procedures for implementing, collecting, and managing hate crime data to the director of the FBI, who in turn, assigned the tasks to the Uniform Crime Reporting (UCR) Program. Under the direction of the attorney general and with the cooperation and assistance of many local and state law enforcement agencies, the UCR Program created a hate crime data collection to comply with the congressional mandate.

The UCR Program's first publication on the subject was *Hate Crime Statistics, 1990: A Resource Book* (Federal Bureau of Investigation, 1992), which was a compilation of hate crime data reported by 11 states that had collected the information under state authority in 1990 and were willing to offer their data as a prototype. The UCR Program continued to work with agencies familiar with investigating hate crimes and collecting related information so that it could develop and implement a more uniform method of data collection on a nationwide scale. *Hate Crime Statistics, 1992* (U.S. Department of Justice, 1993) presented the first published data reported by law enforcement agencies across the country that participated in the UCR Hate Crime Statistics Program.

The hate crime data in this Web publication comprise a subset of information that law enforcement agencies submit to the UCR Program. The types of hate crimes reported to the program (i.e., the biases that motivated the crimes) are further broken down into more specific categories. As collected for each hate crime incident, the aggregate data in this report include the following: offense type, location, bias motivation, victim type, number of individual victims, number of offenders, and the race of the offenders.

- Incidents and offenses—Crimes reported to the FBI involve those motivated by biases based on race, religion, sexual orientation, ethnicity or national origin, and disability. Forthcoming system changes will also allow the reporting of crimes motivated by biases based on gender and gender identity, as well as crimes committed by, and crimes directed against, juveniles.
- Victims—The victim of a hate crime may be an individual, a business, an institution, or society as a whole.
- Offenders—Law enforcement specifies the number of offenders and, when possible, the race of the offender or offenders as a group.

- Location type—Law enforcement may specify one of 30 location designations (e.g., residence/home, school/college, and parking lot/garage, camp/campground, gambling facility/casino/race track, industrial site, park/playground, and shopping mall).
- Hate crime by jurisdiction—Includes data about hate crimes by state and agency (Federal Bureau of Investigation, 2013).

According to the ADL, many law enforcement agencies were gratified by this legislation, which offers them the ability to chart the national distribution of these crimes and thus discern patterns and forecast possible racial and ethnic tensions in different localities. Ideally, the act helps foster better police–community relations, allowing police to demonstrate their concern for the welfare of citizens victimized by hate crimes by vigorously pursuing the criminal activities of violent bigots. This special reporting system also encourages victims to file charges. Nevertheless, the means of collecting such data and the lack of comprehensive reporting by law enforcement agencies throughout the United States has been criticized.

In September 1994, lawmakers amended the Hate Crime Statistics Act to include bias against persons with disabilities by passing the Violent Crime Control and Law Enforcement Act of 1994. The FBI started gathering data for this additional bias type on January 1, 1997.

The Church Arson Prevention Act, which was signed into law in July 1996, mandated that the collection of hate crime data become a permanent part of the UCR Program.

In 2009, Congress further amended the Hate Crime Statistics Act by passing the Matthew Shepard and James Byrd Jr. Hate Crime Prevention Act. The amendment includes requiring the collection of data for crimes motivated by bias against a particular gender and gender identity, as well as for crimes committed by, and crimes directed against, juveniles.

The FBI approved a recommendation by the Criminal Justice Information Services Division's Advisory Policy Board to expand the bias types in the religious category to include all the religions identified by the Pew Research Center and the U.S. Census Bureau. Also, the hate crime data collection procedures were modified to include an anti-Arab bias motivation. The collection of both types of data began on January 1, 2015.

Hate Crimes Sentencing Enhancement Act

Originally introduced in the U.S. Senate, this measure was enacted into law as Section 280003 of the Violent Crime Control and Law Enforcement Act of 1994. The provision defined a hate crime as "a crime in which the defendant intentionally selects a victim, or in the case of a property crime, the property that is the object of the crime, because of the actual or perceived race, color, religion, national origin, ethnicity, gender, disability, or sexual orientation of any person." This provision required the U.S. Sentencing Commission to increase the penalties for these crimes. This measure also applies to attacks and vandalism which occur in national parks and on federal property.

In May 1995, the United States Sentencing Commission announced its implementation of a three-level sentencing guidelines increase for hate crimes, as directed by Congress. The amendment took effect on November 1, 1995.

Violence against Women Act of 1994 (VAWA)

Enacted as Title IV of the Violent Crime Control and Law Enforcement Act of 1994, this act covers the increasing problem of violent crime against women. Under this law, "persons within the United States shall have the right to be free from crimes of violence motivated by gender."

Passed in September 1994, the law includes the following provisions:

- education and training programs for police and prosecutors,
- support for domestic violence and rape crisis centers, and

- a "Civil Rights Remedy" for victims of gender-based violent crimes, including punitive and compensatory damage awards.

The provision for a Civil Rights Remedy has been challenged in several state court cases. On May 15, 2000, the U.S. Supreme Court, in *United States v. Morrison*, ruled that Congress had no legal authority to provide victims of gender-motivated violence access to federal courts. In a 5–4 ruling, the Court decided that the VAWA's Civil Rights Remedy was unconstitutional and that Congress could not regulate intrastate criminal conduct under the commerce clause. Rather, this matter must be left to the states to decide. The Court declared that the Civil Rights Remedy strayed beyond Congress's authority to enforce the Fourteenth Amendment because it was directed against private individuals, not state jurisdictions.

In 2003, Rep. John Conyers Jr. (D-MI) introduced the Violence against Women Civil Rights Restoration Act. The bill responds to the Supreme Court's decision in *United States v. Morrison* and restores the ability of victims of gender-motivated violence to sue their attackers in federal court, where there is a connection to interstate commerce. This bill was sent to committee but was never submitted for a full vote by the House of Representatives.

Church Arson Prevention Act of 1996

A series of arson attacks against churches from 1995 through 1997 created a great deal of alarm among law enforcement agencies and the general public. Despite the widespread nature of these incidents, neither the government nor human rights organizations were able to document a national domestic terror conspiracy orchestrated by violent extremists. The large number of these incidents—committed by individuals in different parts of the country acting independently—was nevertheless a worrisome phenomenon.

Sponsored by Sen. Edward Kennedy (D-MA), Sen. Lauch Faircloth (R-NC), Rep. Henry Hyde (R-IL), and Rep. John Conyers (D-MI), the Church Arson Prevention Act was introduced to facilitate federal investigation and prosecution of crimes against houses of worship and to amend an earlier statute enacted by Congress in 1988 that mandated federal prosecution for religious vandalism incidents exceeding $10,000 in property damage. (See the earlier discussion, "Interference with the Exercise of Religious Beliefs.") In an unusual bipartisan effort, both the U.S. House of Representatives and the U.S. Senate unanimously approved legislation broadening criminal prosecutions for attacks against houses of worship and establishing a loan guarantee for rebuilding them. The legislation also authorized additional personnel for several agencies. The law was enacted on July 3, 1996.

The National Church Arson Task Force notes that of the 308 persons arrested, 254 were white, 46 were African American, and eight were Hispanic. One hundred nineteen people arrested were juveniles. Of the 106 suspects arrested for arsons at African American churches, 68 were white, 37 were African American, and 1 was Hispanic. Of the 197 suspects arrested for arsons at non–African American houses of worship, 181 were white, 9 were African American, and 7 were Hispanic. Five of the white suspects were arrested for arsons at both African American and non–African American churches (National Church Arson Task Force, 1998).

Between January 1, 1995, and September 8, 1998, federal, state, and local prosecutors successfully obtained convictions of 235 defendants in connection with 173 arsons or bombings of houses of worship. These successes included the first convictions under provisions of the Church Arson Prevention Act of 1996. Of the 61 defendants who have been convicted of federal charges, 29 defendants were convicted of hate crimes arising from 24 incidents. Another four defendants were convicted of, or were allowed to plead guilty to, lesser federal charges in cases in which hate-based motives were alleged. Of 171 defendants convicted of state criminal charges, 25 defendants were convicted for 13 incidents connected to hate crime motives.

The National Church Arson Task Force report acknowledges that some crimes "were motivated by multiple factors, including racism and religious hatred. Arsonists have burned churches for other reasons, including opportunistic and random vandalism, pyromania, mental health disturbances, feuding with ministers, retribution against religious authorities, parking or neighborhood disputes, covering up of burglaries, and financial profit. In some cases, the arsonists claimed they believed the church to be an abandoned building" (National Church Arson Task Force, 1998).

The report concludes, however,

> when actual or perceived racial hatred has sparked the arson of a church, the crime is even more egregious. In the African American community, the church historically has been a primary community institution. It was the only institution that was permitted during the years of slavery. It was the institution that enabled people to read. It has been the institution that formed the backbone for a tremendous amount of political activism. Critical events of the civil rights movement, such as the Montgomery bus boycott, had their genesis in the church. Many leaders within the African American community grew up in the church or remain ministers of the church. So, for the African American community, it was decidedly disturbing to see the number of churches being burned. (National Church Arson Task Force, 1998)

U.S. Armed Forces and Hate Crime Prevention

In 1997, Congress included a provision in the National Defense Authorization Act requiring the Secretary of Defense to provide ongoing human relations training for armed forces personnel that would cover "race relations, equal opportunity, opposition to gender discrimination, and sensitivity to 'hate group' activity."

Campus Hate Crimes Right to Know Act of 1997

This law amended the Higher Education Act of 1965 to include a requirement to report all crimes "based on race, gender, religion, sexual orientation, ethnicity, and disability." This act does not include the classes of color and national origin. Under this law, all colleges and universities that receive federal funds must collect and report hate crime statistics to the Office of Postsecondary Education for crimes in which the victim was targeted because of race, gender, religion, sexual orientation, ethnicity, or disability. Since the Department of Education used broader categories of hate crimes than the FBI, a coalition of civil rights and religious groups successfully helped enact an amendment to the *Higher Education Opportunity Act* to expand the hate crime data mandate and thus make the collection policies of all these government agencies uniform.

Local Law Enforcement Enhancement Act

On June 15, 2004, the U.S. Senate approved legislation by a 65–33 vote that would expand federal hate crime protection to include sexual orientation, gender, and disability. Offered as an amendment to a Department of Defense authorization bill, this legislation, which would also increase federal assistance to local and state officials in the investigation and prosecution of hate crimes, was introduced by Sen. Edward Kennedy (D-MA) and Sen. Gordon Smith (R-OR) and was identical to provisions approved by the Senate in June 2000 and by the U.S. House of Representatives in September 2000. In both pieces of legislation, however, the hate crimes provisions were not inserted in the final version of the bill. This legislation was later incorporated in different form into the Matthew Shepard–James Byrd statute.

Matthew Shepard and James Byrd Jr. Hate Crimes Prevention Act

On October 28, 2009, President Barack Obama signed this act into law. The Matthew Shepard and James Byrd Jr. Hate

Crimes Prevention Act of 2009 gives the FBI authority to investigate violent hate crimes, including violence directed at the gay, lesbian, bisexual, and transgender community.

This federal civil rights law criminalizes willfully causing bodily injury (or attempting to do so with fire, a firearm, or other dangerous weapon) when:

(1) the crime was committed because of the actual or perceived race, color, religion, national origin, of any person; or

(2) the crime was committed because of the actual or perceived religion, national origin, gender, sexual orientation, gender identity, or disability of any person, and the crime affected interstate or foreign commerce, or occurred on federal property.

This law broadens federal jurisdiction over hate crimes by authorizing the attorney general to provide assistance, when requested by federal or state officials. Prior to enactment of this law, hate crimes were not considered separate and distinct offenses under federal law; federal jurisdiction over hate crime was limited to only certain civil rights offenses.

On the fourth anniversary of the passage of this law, the U.S. Justice Department issued a press release hailing its ability now to prosecute crimes motivated by race, color, religion, and national origin without having to show that the defendant was engaged in a federally protected activity. The Shepard–Byrd Act also empowers the department to prosecute crimes committed because of a person's sexual orientation, gender identity, gender, or disability as hate crimes.

The law also marked the first time that the words, "lesbian, gay, bisexual, and transgender" appeared in the U.S. Code (U.S. Department of Justice, 2013).

In the fall of 2013, the Civil Rights Division of the U.S. Justice Department brought federal hate crimes charges against two Latino men associated with the Compton 155 street gang in California. These men attacked a 17-year-old African American who was walking down a street in the city of

Compton—striking him in the head with a metal pipe—and pointed a gun at another African American juvenile who was present. Both attackers admitted their actions were substantially motivated by race and color (U.S. Department of Justice, 2013).

In an earlier crime, a Justice Department investigation and prosecution in response to the beating of an Atlanta man resulted in the first conviction in Georgia under the sexual orientation provision of the Shepard–Byrd Act. In this case, two men pleaded guilty to assaulting a 20-year-old gay man as he left a grocery store in an Atlanta neighborhood. Video footage of the incident showed not only physical violence but also the use of antigay epithets. The two men were sentenced to serve 10 months in prison on federal hate crimes charges as well as five years on state charges for aggravated assault, robbery by force, and theft by receiving stolen property and obstruction.

The Civil Rights Division has held trainings for thousands of law enforcement officials—federal, state, and local—to ensure that first responders to an assault or other act of violence know what questions to ask and what evidence to gather at the scene to allow prosecutors to make an informed assessment of whether a case should be prosecuted as a hate crime under this recent statute.

Emmett Till Unsolved Civil Rights Crime Act of 2007

In an incident that is often cited as the beginning of the modern civil rights movement, Emmett Till, a 14-year-old African American from Chicago was brutally murdered in 1955 while visiting his relatives in the Mississippi Delta region. The murder was allegedly sparked by Till's conversing with Carolyn Bryant, a white woman who worked in a store in the area that he was visiting. Some accounts claimed he "whistled" at her. Till's reported conversation with a white southern woman so enraged her husband, Roy, and his half-brother J.W. Milam that they pistol-whipped him and they later forced him to tie a heavy cotton gin fan to his body just before he was murdered and dumped into the Tallahatchie River. Bryant and Milam were indicted for the murder and tried in September 1955. After only a little more than an hour of deliberation, the jury unanimously acquitted them of capital murder. However, both Roy Bryant and J.W. Milam admitted to the murders in a 1956 interview with *Look* magazine. After being acquitted, however, no charges could legally be brought against them again. According to the author of the book *Death in the Delta*, "the crime and the exoneration later affected writers and musicians as important and diverse as novelists Toni Morrison and James Baldwin (both of whom wrote plays about it), scenarist Rod Serling (who wrote a television drama), singer Bob Dylan (who wrote a song), and poet Gwendolyn Brooks (who wrote a ballad)" (Whitfield, 1988).

On May 10, 2004, the DOJ reopened the Till case for further investigation. The FBI sent an 8,000-page file to Mississippi officials on the August 1955 slaying of Till, which included among other items, the gruesome photos of Till's body lying in an open coffin, which evoked national outrage.

Although the confessed killers were dead, some civil rights lawyers thought a case could have been made against others who might have played a role before or after the killing. A local grand jury, however, failed to return any indictments, and the case was officially closed in December 2007.

Soon after the 2004 reopening of the Till case, there was political pressure to re-examine many of the unsolved murders of the civil rights era. The Emmett Till Unsolved Civil Rights Crime Act of 2007 was introduced in Congress in 2007. Representatives Kenny Hulshof (R-MO) (retired) and John Lewis (D-GA) introduced the act in the House; and senators Christopher Dodd (D-CT) and Patrick Leahy (D-VT) introduced the act in the Senate. The act had bipartisan support in Congress. The House of Representatives passed it on June 20, 2007, by a vote of 422 to 2; only representatives. Lynn Westmoreland (R-GA) and Ron Paul (R-TX) voted against it. The Senate passed the act unanimously on September 24, 2008, and it was signed into law by President George W. Bush on October 7, 2008 (Civil Rights and Restorative Justice Project, 2010).

The act directed the DOJ and the FBI to coordinate the investigation and prosecution of civil rights era homicides that occurred on or before December 31, 1969. The act also directed the DOJ and FBI to coordinate their activities with state and local law enforcement and to make annual reports to Congress on the progress of investigations and prosecutions falling under the auspices of the act. The act is in effect until 2017 (Civil Rights and Restorative Justice Project, 2010).

For fiscal years 2008 through 2017, the act authorized grants to state or local law enforcement agencies for costs associated with their investigation and prosecution of civil rights era homicides; and to DOJ's Community Relations Service (CRS) to bring together law enforcement agencies and communities to further the investigation of these homicides. However, since the Till Act has been in effect, the amount of funds actually appropriated to DOJ for these grants have been minimal (Civil Rights and Restorative Justice Project, 2010).

Executive Branch

As a result of the aforementioned legislation, the executive branch of the U.S. government has been involved in the following ongoing activities and initiatives:

- In November 2014, the DOJ launched a new Interagency Initiative on Hate Crimes coordinated by the White House Domestic Policy Council that will promote cross-agency collaboration and will address prevention of violent hate crimes, as well as effective responses to hate crimes. The DOJ also announced several actions to strengthen and improve the federal government's ability to prevent and respond to hate crimes, including a new series of trainings on the Shepard–Byrd Act around the country for state, local, and tribal law enforcement agencies and community leaders.

- The Civil Rights Division, FBI, and CRS committed to conducting a series of trainings on the Shepard–Byrd Act around the country for state and local law enforcement agencies and community leaders. DOJ did a series of these trainings across the country shortly after the Act was passed. In many cases, the relationships grew in the years after the training through inclusion in police chief's roundtables and regular community meetings. These trainings helped local law enforcement agencies identify cases that should have been investigated as a hate crime.

- Since statistical data is critical to understanding hate crimes and to understanding what works in terms of responding to and preventing hate crimes, the National Crime Statistics-Exchange (NCS-X), FBI, and Bureau of Justice Statistics (BJS) are working to increase the participation of a sample of law enforcement agencies in the National Incident Based Reporting System (NIBRS) in order to create a nationally representative system of incident-based crime statistics of crimes known to the police. Unfortunately, too many jurisdictions fail to report or under-report hate crimes data, preventing law enforcement officials, government leaders, and community members form working effectively to prevent and respond more effectively to hate violence. The Obama administration and DOJ are continuing to collaborate and identify new ways to expand state and local law enforcement agencies' use of NIBRS.

- In the years 2009–2013, the DOJ charged 201 defendants on federal hate crimes or hate crimes–related charges, including the Shepard–Byrd Act and other federal hate crimes provisions—an increase of almost 50 percent from the prior five fiscal years (2004–2008). The Department also convicted almost 50 percent more defendants on federal hate crimes or hate crimes-related charges, compared to the prior five fiscal years.

- The CRS, an arm of the U.S. DOJ, is a specialized federal conciliation service available to state and local officials to help resolve and prevent racial and ethnic conflict, violence, and civil disorders. When governors, mayors, police chiefs, and school superintendents need help to defuse racial crises, they turn to CRS. CRS helps local officials and residents tailor locally defined resolutions when conflict and violence threaten community stability and well-being. CRS conciliators assist in identifying the sources of violence and conflict and utilizing specialized crisis management and violence reduction techniques that work best for each community. CRS has no law enforcement authority and does not impose solutions, investigate or prosecute cases, or assign blame or fault. CRS conciliators are required by law to conduct their activities in confidence, without publicity, and are prohibited from disclosing confidential information.

- The Office of Juvenile Justice and Delinquency Prevention (OJJDP) provided $100,000 for a study to identify the characteristics and types of juveniles who commit hate crimes (Office of Juvenile Justice and Delinquency Prevention, 1996). The OJJDP also provided funding for a "Healing the Hate" curriculum to assist the prevention and treatment of hate crimes committed by young people.

- In addition, the U.S. DOJ, the U.S. Department of the Treasury, and the U.S. Office of Education have been involved in hate crime enforcement, education, and prevention. The ADL and other human rights organizations and professionals have assisted in a model hate-crime training curriculum for use by the federal Law Enforcement Training Centers, a program of the U.S. Department of the Treasury.

- As a result of the church arson attacks in the 1990s, the Department of Housing and Urban Development (HUD) organized seminars to discuss a $10 million loan guarantee rebuilding fund for houses of worship devastated in hate-motivated arson attacks. Under the National Rebuilding Initiative program of HUD, more than 100 institutions have received assistance.

U.S. Supreme Court Decisions

Most legislation on hate crimes was enacted during the early to mid-1990s, but some court cases have challenged the constitutional and legal grounds of these statutes. During a 10-year period, a few major cases were eventually argued in the U.S. Supreme Court. (For a more detailed discussion, please refer to *Hate Crime Laws: The ADL Approach* [ADL, 2015] from which some of the following summaries were derived and the *Policymaker's Guide to Hate Crimes* [U.S. Department of Justice, 1997].)

Apprendi v. New Jersey

On December 22, 1994, Charles C. Apprendi Jr. fired several shots into the home of an African American family. While in custody, Apprendi made a statement, which he later retracted, that he did not want the family in his neighborhood because of their race. Apprendi was charged under New Jersey law with second-degree possession of a firearm for an unlawful purpose, which carries a prison term of 5 to 10 years. The count did not refer to the state's hate crime statute, which provides for an enhanced sentence if a trial judge finds, by a preponderance of the evidence, that the defendant committed the crime with a purpose to intimidate a person or group because of race. After Apprendi pleaded guilty, the prosecutor filed a motion to enhance the sentence. The court found, by a preponderance of the evidence, that the shooting was racially motivated and sentenced Apprendi to a 12-year term on the firearms count. In upholding the sentence, the appeals court rejected Apprendi's claim that the due process clause requires that a bias finding be proved to a jury beyond a reasonable doubt. The New Jersey State Supreme Court affirmed that decision.

On June 26, 2000, the U.S. Supreme Court held in an 5–4 opinion delivered by Justice John Paul Stevens held that the due process clause requires that any fact that increases the penalty for a crime beyond the prescribed statutory maximum, other than the fact of a prior conviction, must be submitted to a jury and proved beyond a reasonable doubt. Justice Stevens wrote for the Court that "the New Jersey procedure challenged in this case is an unacceptable departure from the jury tradition that is an indispensable part of our criminal justice system."

Besides its impact on hate crime laws, the decision has wider implications for future criminal justice cases. The *Apprendi* case did not reject penalty enhancement for hate crime cases but did assert that a hate crimes charge must be established during the trial, and not afterward.

Barclay v. Florida

In this case brought before the Supreme Court in 1983, defendant Elwood Barclay, an African American, was convicted of murdering a white man on June 17, 1974. He had pinned a racist note to the victim's body with a knife. In assessing several aggravating factors at the penalty phase, a Florida trial judge considered Barclay's membership in the Black Liberation Army and the group's mission to kill white people indiscriminately and instigate a race war.

Barclay claimed that the trial judge's consideration of his racist beliefs and group membership violated his First Amendment rights. A plurality of the Supreme Court disagreed. The Black Liberation Army's desire to start a race war, the Court concluded, was relevant to three of Florida's statutory aggravating factors.

As summarized in the Southern Poverty Law Center Web site (Southern Poverty Law Center, 2004), the Court majority stated that Barclay selected five other victims to kill for being white before settling on his ultimate victim which demonstrated that the defendant posed a "great risk of death to many persons."

Second, the evidence of his beliefs and group affiliation was relevant to his intent to "disrupt or hinder the lawful exercise of a governmental function"; the notion of a race war threatened the foundation of American society, the Supreme Court said.

Finally, the sentencing judge's comparison of the racist murder to Nazi concentration camps was relevant to weighing the "especially heinous, atrocious and cruel" aggravating circumstance of the crime.

R.A.V. v. City of St. Paul

An important early challenge to hate crime laws involved a group of white skinheads who burned a cross in the yard of a black family in St. Paul, Minnesota, on June 21, 1990. Soon after, 17-year-old Robert A. Viktora was charged and later convicted of violating the municipal bias-motivated crime ordinance, which banned cross burning and displaying the swastika. The statute stipulated that these actions "arouse anger, alarm, or resentment in others on the basis of race, color, creed, religion or gender." Appealing the conviction to a Minnesota district court, the lawyer for Viktora claimed the law violated his client's First Amendment right of free speech. The district court ruled in favor of the defendant, overturning the conviction and declaring the law unconstitutional. The court claimed that the St. Paul ordinance was too broad in its application and violated First Amendment rights of freedom of expression.

In a counter appeal brought by the City of St. Paul, the Minnesota Supreme Court ruled that the local ordinance was valid because cross burning was similar to "fighting words"—a phrase used in a 1942 landmark U.S. Supreme Court decision—that incited violence and hence was not protected by the First Amendment of the Constitution.

R.A.V. v. City of St. Paul was finally brought before the U.S. Supreme Court on June 22, 1992. In an opinion written by Justice Antonin B. Scalia, a majority of the U.S. Supreme Court reversed the Minnesota Supreme Court's ruling, finding that the ordinance unconstitutionally restricted speech on the basis of its content. Applying its free speech precedents to the St. Paul ordinance, the majority concluded that the ordinance applied only to "fighting words" that insult or provoke violence "on the basis of race, color, creed, religion, or gender." A jurisdiction may proscribe unprotected speech on the basis of its content, the Court held, but it may not select one area of speech to criminalize while leaving other areas unrestricted, unless the selection is content-neutral. Therefore, Scalia wrote, a jurisdiction may criminalize unprotected speech in a selective manner, as long as the selectivity is not "conditioned upon the government's agreement with what the speaker may intend to say."

The Court noted that words that expressed hostility toward a person because of his or her sexual orientation or political affiliation were not prohibited by the city ordinance. The Court wrote that because the ordinance restricted biases of a particular nature, it barred only those viewpoints that the city council found distasteful. Scalia asserted that the ordinance unconstitutionally allowed persons on one side of a debate to speak freely while restricting the other side's response. The majority held that a law prohibiting all fighting words communicated in a threatening manner, instead of proscribing all fighting words that convey messages of racial intolerance, would be constitutional. In this case, the Court ruled, the Minnesota ordinance went beyond permissible regulation and infringed upon the free speech rights of the defendant.

The decision declared that pure or symbolic bias-motivated speech, no matter how damaging to the intended target, cannot be outlawed solely on the basis of its effect on the victim. In 2003, the Supreme Court in *Virginia v. Black*, reasserted the government's authority to punish cross burning aimed at intimidating minority groups or others.

Wisconsin v. Mitchell

This landmark case decided in 1993 involved a racial assault committed against a white boy by a group of young black men. According to the Supreme Court summary:

> On the evening of October 7, 1989, a group of young black men and boys, including Mitchell, gathered at an apartment complex in Kenosha, Wisconsin. Several members of the group discussed a scene from the motion

picture "Mississippi Burning," in which a white man beat a young black boy who was praying. The group moved outside and Mitchell asked them: "Do you all feel hyped up to move on some white people?" Shortly thereafter, a young boy approached the group on the opposite side of the street where they were standing. As the boy walked by, Mitchell said: "You all want to fuck somebody up? There goes a white boy; go get him." Mitchell counted to three and pointed in the boy's direction. The group ran toward the boy, beat him severely, and stole his tennis shoes. The boy was rendered unconscious and remained in a coma for four days. (*Wisconsin v. Mitchell*, 1993)

After a jury trial in the Kenosha County Circuit Court, Mitchell was convicted of aggravated battery. Although the offense generally carries a maximum sentence of two years' imprisonment, the jury found that the defendant intentionally selected his victim because of the boy's race and increased his sentence to seven years based on the Wisconsin hate penalty enhancement statute. (The Wisconsin statute, modeled after the ADL's proposed hate-crime law, mandates increased penalties for a crime when the victim is targeted because of "race, religion, color, disability, sexual orientation, national origin or ancestry of that person.") Mitchell's attorney claimed that the additional punishment violated his client's right to free speech, and the Wisconsin Supreme Court concurred by reversing the judgment and held that the penalty enhancement statute "violates the First Amendment directly by punishing what the legislature has deemed to be offensive thought." The decision also stated that "the Wisconsin legislature cannot criminalize bigoted thought with which it disagrees."

The supporters of the Mitchell case, including defense lawyers and constitutional scholars, argued that the Wisconsin statute punished thoughts. The friend-of-the-court brief issued by the Wisconsin Association of Criminal Defense Lawyers asserted: "the right of all people to assert their opinion, regardless of how unpopular or odious, must be preserved . . . the Wisconsin statute does not even attempt to punish one for the harm caused by the expression of hurtful opinions. Such expression, however, is absolutely protected by the First Amendment, regardless of the pain or fear it may engender."

The State of Wisconsin appealed the decision of the Wisconsin Supreme Court. On June 11, 1993, the U.S. Supreme Court, in *Wisconsin v. Mitchell*, reversed the Wisconsin court ruling. In a unanimous decision, the justices agreed that the hate penalty enhancement ordinance does not violate the First Amendment. The Court held that the enhanced penalty is appropriate "because this conduct is thought to inflict greater individual and societal harm." Furthermore, the justices argued that the statute would not stifle free speech because the bias motivation would have to be connected with a specific act; the law focused on a person's actions, not on an individual's bigoted ideas.

Chief Justice William Rehnquist, who wrote the *Mitchell* court's unanimous opinion, found that the St. Paul ordinance targeted expression, which is protected by the First Amendment, while the Wisconsin statute is aimed at conduct not protected by the Constitution. Wisconsin's enhanced-penalty law created an increased penalty for illegal conduct inspired by the defendant's "bigoted motivations," according to the Court. While a particular bias was an element of the crime itself under the Minnesota ordinance, it was a factor to be considered during sentencing under the Wisconsin statute, said the Court. The chief justice said that, although a sentencing judge may not take into account the defendant's beliefs, however offensive to most people, the Constitution does not preclude the admission of evidence concerning one's beliefs and associations at sentencing if those beliefs and associations are in some way related to the commission of the crime. Rehnquist explained that sentencing judges often consider many factors in addition to evidence bearing on guilt, including a defendant's motive for committing the offense. The judges noted that, for example, murder, if committed for financial gain, can be considered an aggravating factor under many states' sentencing statutes. According to the judges, the First Amendment allows admission of a defendant's statements to prove intentions or motive, as long as they are relevant and fairly described. Especially noteworthy, the Court ruled that the statute has no "chilling effect" on free speech. Rehnquist said that it would be highly unlikely that an individual would withhold his "bigoted" beliefs for fear that evidence of those beliefs would be used against him at trial if he committed a serious offense.

Other state appellate and high courts considering the constitutionality of hate crime legislation since *Mitchell* have followed either *Mitchell* or *R.A.V.* without expressing difficulty in reconciling the two decisions. These courts generally have upheld state statutes that punish specific behavior motivated by bias, and the U.S. Supreme Court has denied appeals of these state courts have ruled that there is no meaningful difference between such statutes and the penalty-enhancement statute upheld in *Mitchell*. Both types of statutes punish a crime motivated by bias, the courts asserted. Based on this legal jurisprudence, the Maryland appellate court, upheld a statute making it a crime to "harass or commit a crime upon a person . . . because of that person's race, color, religious belief or national origin." The Supreme Court of Missouri summarized with regard to a similar statute, "While [the statute] admittedly created a new motive-based crime, its practical effect is to provide additional punishment for conduct that is already illegal but is seen as especially harmful because it is motivated by group hatred" (American Prosecutors Research Institute, 2000, 12). Thus, these state court decisions, in line with the U.S. Supreme Court decision in the *Mitchell* case uphold the concept that enhanced punishment for criminal conduct on account of a defendant's motives of bias or hatred toward a protected group is consistent with the U.S. Constitution.

Hate Crimes Legislation at the State Level

Shortly after the ADL drafted the model hate crime statutes in 1981, Oregon and Washington passed similar legislation. By 1994, 34 states and the District of Columbia enacted hate crime laws with penalty enhancements. As of 2014, only five states have not enacted any hate crime laws (Human Rights Campaign, 2015).

The ADL initiative garnered the support of other human and civil rights organizations, lobbying many states to enact local and municipal penalty enhancement statutes for bias-motivated crimes inspired by this important model legislation. These statutes do not establish a separate category for these crimes; the perpetrators, however, are subject to enhanced punishment if their crimes were motivated by bias.

The earlier sections detail federal hate crime laws, but many states have also enacted some form of ethnic intimidation or bias-motivated sentence-enhancement laws in attempts to curtail hate crimes. In some instances, state statutes afford broader protection to include sexual orientation, mental or physical disability, age, and/or marital status.

States have various statutory provisions covering hate crimes. These provisions include ones that:

- criminalize destruction of religious institutions;
- criminalize bias-motivated violence and intimidation;
- mandate reporting of hate crimes;
- mandate training for state police officers in recognizing and reporting hate crimes; and
- prohibit infringement on another person's civil rights.

State hate crime statutes vary in the protection offered to victims. The ADL (2012) provides a superb detailed chart of state hate crime laws, including the statutes covering penalty enhancement, the categories for penalty enhancements (race/religion/ethnicity, sexual orientation, gender, gender identity, disability), and separate columns noting the state statutes for civil action, police training, institutional vandalism, and cross burning.

A few state statutes include other protected characteristics such as age (California, District of Columbia, Florida, Hawaii, Iowa, Kansas, Louisiana, Maine, Minnesota, Nebraska, New Mexico, New York, and Vermont) and political affiliation (California, District of Columbia, Iowa, Louisiana, and West Virginia). The District of Columbia law covers the widest range of categories, including prejudice based on "actual or perceived race, color, religion, national origin, sex, age, marital status, personal appearance, sexual orientation, family responsibility, physical handicap, matriculation or political affiliation." In Vermont, a defendant convicted of an offense punishable by one year of imprisonment may receive double the sentence if the crime was motivated by bias. Even though the court must consider the motivation of the perpetrator in the sentencing, the judge is not required to enhance the punishment. Most surprisingly, as of 2015, the state legislature in Wyoming, where Matthew Shepard was murdered, still refuses to pass legislation to punish hate crimes against gay men and lesbians.

The actions of the states where hate crimes statutes have been declared constitutional are especially significant because most prosecutions of bias-motivated violence occur at the state level.

The state of Washington has a bold and uncompromising policy that echoes concerns held by some other state legislatures: "The legislature finds that crimes and threats against persons because of their race, color, religion, ancestry, national origin, gender, sexual orientation or mental, physical or sensory handicaps are serious and increasing. The legislature also finds that crimes and threats are often directed against interracial couples and their children or couples of mixed religions, colors, ancestries or national origins because of bias and bigotry . . . The legislature finds that protection of those citizens from threats of harm due to bias and bigotry is a compelling state interest" (Revised Code of Washington, 2014).

Other state measures and policies include the following:

- Prohibiting particular acts that have traditionally been associated with racial hatred, such as burning crosses or wearing masks or hoods. In 1951, for example, the state of Georgia passed an antimask law because of the violence and intimidation carried out by mask-wearing members of the KKK. (These laws, however, exempt holiday costume masks or other "innocent activities.")
- Enacting statutes that provide compensation to the victims of hate crimes. These laws specify monetary damages (including damages for emotional distress and punitive damages), attorneys' fees, and other costs of litigation.
- Providing funding to school districts to implement programs designed to reduce and prevent hate motivated incidents.

Conclusion

In the last few decades, several bias-motivated crimes were widely reported in the media. Yet the phrase "hate crime" only gained currency in the mid-1980s. Throughout American history, these crimes were mostly described by the victims ethnicity or other group membership, for example, antiblack, anti-Chinese, antihomosexual (the earlier term), or "racist." In the wake of the social and political ferment of the 1960s, federal and state legislators began introducing legislation to protect the rights of African Americans. But the growing number of hate crimes directed at a variety of groups inspired the enactment of additional and broader statutes to protect other victims. In 1981, the ADL, the prominent Jewish civil and human rights organization, drafted model legislation to cover all types of hate crimes aimed at minority groups. This legislative initiative soon became the basis for major hate crime laws throughout the United States. All three branches of the federal government are now involved in hate crime issues: the legislative branch enacts the legislation; the executive branch administers these statutes and the judiciary weighs in when these laws are challenged or need further interpretation. In addition, state and local governments are greatly involved in this chronic societal problem.

References

American Prosecutors Research Institute. 2000. "Local Prosecutor's Guide for Responding to Hate Crimes." https://www.ncjrs.gov/pdffiles1/Digitization/182629NCJRS.pdf.

Anti-Defamation League. 2012. State Hate Crime Statutory Provisions. http://www.adl.org/assets/pdf/combating-hate/ADL-hate-crime-state-laws-clickable-chart.pdf.

Anti-Defamation League. 2015. Hate Crime Laws: The ADL Approach. http://www.adl.org/combating-hate/hate-crimes-law/c/adl-approach-hate-crimes-laws.html.

Civil Rights and Restorative Justice Project. 2010. "Emmitt Till Act." Northeastern University School of Law. http://nuweb9.neu.edu/civilrights/emmett-till-act/.

Federal Bureau of Investigation. 1992. *Hate Crime Statistics, 1990: A Resource Book*. Washington, DC: Federal Bureau of Investigation.

Federal Bureau of Investigation. 2013. "About Hate Crime Statistics." http://www.fbi.gov/about-us/cjis/ucr/hate-crime/2013/resource-pages/about-hate-crime.

Federal Bureau of Investigation. 2015. "Hate Crimes Overview." http://www.fbi.gov/about-us/investigate/civilrights/hate_crimes/overview.

Greenawalt, Kent. 1992–1993. "Reflections on Justifications for Defining Crimes by the Category of Victim." *1992/1993 Annual Survey of American Law*. New York: New York University School of Law, 617–628.

Hoover, Reynold N. 1995. "Learning from Oklahoma City: Federal and State Explosives Laws in the United States." *Kansas Journal of Law and Public Policy*, Fall.

Human Rights Campaign. 2015. "Maps of State Laws." http://www.hrc.org/state_maps.

Jacobs, James B. and Potter, Kimberly. 1998. *Hate Crimes, Criminal Law and Identity Politics*. Oxford: Oxford University Press.

Lawrence, Frederick M. 1999. *Punishing Hate: Bias Crimes under American Law*. Boston: Harvard University Press.

Los Angeles Times. 1987. "2 Supremacists Guilty in Death of Jewish Radio Host." November 18. http://articles.latimes.com/1987–11–18/news/mn-14825_1_neo-nazi.

National Church Arson Task Force. 1998. "Report for the President." http://www.justice.gov/crt/church_arson/arson98.php.

Office of Juvenile Justice and Delinquency Prevention. 1996. *Report to Congress on Juvenile Hate Crime*. Washington, DC: Government Printing Office.

Revised Code of Washington. 2014. "Malicious Harassment-Finding." Volume 2, 9A.36.078.

Southern Poverty Law Center. 2004. "Hate on Trial." Intelligence Report, Winter, Issue 116. http://www.splcenter.org/get-informed/intelligence-report/browse-all-issues/2004/winter/hate-on-trial.

U.S. Department of Justice. 1993. *Hate Crime Statistics, 1992*. Washington, DC: Government Printing Office.

U.S. Department of Justice. 1997. *Policymaker's Guide to Hate Crimes*. https://www.ncjrs.gov/pdffiles1/bja/162304.pdf.

U.S. Department of Justice. 2013. "Commemorating the Fourth Anniversary of the Shepard-Byrd Hate Crime Prevention Act." http://www.justice.gov/opa/blog/commemorating-fourth-anniversary-shepard-byrd-hate-crime-prevention-act.

U.S. Department of Justice. 2015. "Statutes-Hate Crimes."
http://www.justice.gov/crt/about/crm/statutes.php.

Whitfield, Stephen J. 1988. *Death in the Delta: The Story of Emmett Till*. Baltimore: Free Press.

Wisconsin v. Mitchell, 1993, 508 U.S. 476. https://supreme.justia.com/cases/federal/us/508/476/case.html.

Criticism and Defense of Hate Crime Laws

As noted in the previous chapter, the enactment of laws specifically directed to punish and prevent hate crimes dates back only to the last few decades. Since their inception, these laws have been criticized on a number of grounds: constitutional, philosophical, political, and even methodological (regarding the collection of statistical data).

Professor Susan Gellman summarizes the stance of many critics of hate crime legislation: "Those who oppose ethnic intimidation laws, or at least who question them most vigorously, do not disagree that bigotry (and certainly bigotry-related crime) is a serious problem. In fact, many such critics are civil rights and civil liberties advocates. These critics, however, focus on threats to constitutional liberties under the First and Fourteenth Amendment and the enactment of statutes that 'create thought crimes'" (Gellman, 1991, 334).

In addition, these critics question the wisdom of enacting such laws; even if they can be drafted in a way that does not offend the Constitution, they may ultimately undercut their own goals more than they serve them. James B. Jacobs and

---

Texas lawmakers form a prayer circle to support a bill to toughen the state's hate crimes law. The prayer was held in the Texas Capitol Rotunda on May 14, 1999. (AP Photo/Harry Cabluck)

Kimberly A. Potter raise questions about the sociological and criminological consequences of hate crime legislation:

> The concept of hate crime is easy to grasp as an ideal type, but it is difficult to effectuate in a workaday criminal justice system. Most putative hate crimes are not ideologically motivated murders, although some of those do occur. . . . Whether it aids understanding of their conduct and of our society to brand them as bigots as well as criminals is not an easy question to answer. . . . Beyond the problem of definition, labeling particular incidents as hate crimes bristles with subjectivity and potential for bias. Nevertheless, the very existence of the term, the attempt to measure the incidence of hate crime, and the prosecution and sentencing of some offenders under different types of hate crime statutes have already changed how Americans think about the crime problem. At a minimum, the new hate crime laws have contributed further to politicizing the crime problem . . . Rather than Americans pulling together and affirming their common ground by condemning criminal conduct, they may now increasingly see crime as a polarizing issue that pits one social group against another, thereby further dividing an already fractured society. (Jacobs, 1997, 41–42)

Other arguments often invoked against hate crime statutes:

- The diversity of hate crime laws creates problems in identifying, investigating, and reporting the incidents.
- Hate crimes are no more harmful to society than other criminal activity and hence do not merit a separate category of criminal law.
- A key argument of hate crime law proponents is that the bias of the perpetrators necessitates an enhanced punishment but critics, however, claim that isolating a bigoted motivation is often difficult to assess since many crimes are frequently inspired by multifarious factors.

- Hate crime legislation does not confront the most socially destabilizing types of violence, for example, gang and drug-related violence, so their impact on the general society does not warrant this form of extra punishment.
- The laws punish thoughts and beliefs and are no more deserving of enhanced punishment as are other human traits such as greed or cruelty.
- The selection of protected groups to be covered by hate crime statutes are political decisions, resulting from the unfair influence and power of advocates who are able to enact these laws.

Hate crime law proponents cite the following justifications for these laws:

- While many victims of violent crimes may suffer from psychological and sometimes, traumatic reactions to these assaults, there is some anecdotal evidence indicating that hate crime victims suffer from greater depression and anxiety than other victims (Herek and Berrill,1992, 212).
- Hate crimes have an impact on the wider community. Recent widely publicized incidents (the murder of Sikhs in Wisconsin; attacks on the Jewish Community Center in Missouri, etc.) have had a chilling effect on the lives of Sikhs and Jews, especially when they visit their houses of worship or community centers.
- Hate crime laws demonstrate societal concern for the rights of vulnerable minority communities. Some social scientists praise the symbolic values of these laws in guaranteeing safety and respect for all citizens. Legal scholars also have supported these laws for affirming traditional American values of ensuring justice under law.
- According to some legal experts, hate crime laws are analogous to civil rights statutes that prohibit discrimination based on race, religion, gender, ethnicity, among other immutable factors. Similarly, hate crime legislation punishes

the intentional selection of targeted individuals based on these similar traits.

- Many criminal codes stipulate that so-called status crimes committed against police officers, young children, and teachers, to name only a few groups, provide enhanced penalties for assaults directed against these members of these groups. Similarly, hate crime laws also provide extra legal protection for identified groups who require this special legal status because of their historic vulnerability.

- Motivation often determines the punishment for convicted criminals. In those states with capital punishment, for instance, the defendant's motivation in committing a homicide is of special concern to both judges and juries, because certain factors may contribute to the imposition of the death sentence. Similarly, the motivation of hate crime perpetrators is also relevant to the court in deciding what sentence to impose for this type of crime.

Methodology

Besides the philosophical and legal arguments raised against hate crime legislation, several critics—including even law proponents—have raised questions about both how the data is collected and even the accuracy of hate crime statistics.

In a July 2011online report entitled *Assessing the Validity of Hate Crime Reporting: An Analysis of NIBRS Data*, the authors of the report identified the following problems and issues (Haas, 2011):

- "Classification errors can, and in fact do, impact the statistical accuracy of hate crime statistics. Our findings show that the true number of hate crimes in the population is likely much greater than official crime reports suggest. A vast majority of the error found in this study related to the undercounting of hate crimes in official records." (Classification error refers to incidents where police officers record an incident but don't fully classify the crime, e.g., an African-American woman asks a white man walking two large dogs to keep the animals away from her. He refused and then assaults the woman; the police report classified the incident solely as a felony, even though the man uttered a racial slur against the woman.)

- Some police officers had a specific—but arbitrary definition—of hate crimes. "When you see a hate crime, it is the type that makes national headlines"—it is a "clear-cut case." The officers were reticent to solely rely on the victim statements to assess whether bias was the motivating factor of the perpetrator.

- In a focus group with police officers, one policeman said that we hear "racial slurs all the time but that doesn't make it a hate crime." Other officers "do not consider most situations involving racial slurs as hate crimes but rather just the way people talk."

- The large number of undercounts in this study found that many officers fail to recognize "bias indicators" in some incidents. Furthermore, some police assume only severe criminal incidents can be classified as hate crimes, even though a large number of bias-motivated crimes do not necessarily fit this extreme definition.

- Some undercounted hate crimes can be classified as "response/retaliation offenses," which are not initially triggered by bias, but soon devolve into a crime motivated by the prejudice of a perpetrator. These incidents often go unrecorded in hate crime statistics.

Frederick Lawrence, a prominent hate crime laws proponent and former dean of the George Washington University Law School, has written that: "(t)here is reason to believe that, despite increased bias crime reporting by police agencies, a majority of bias crime victims do not report incidents at all. Victims' distrust of the police, language barriers, and fear of either retaliation by the offender or public exposure generally may well lead to systemic underreporting of bias crimes" (Lawrence, 2002, 776).

Some state government agencies have expressed concern about convincing victims to report hate crime incidents. The California attorney general issued a hate crimes report that listed some reasons why victims were reticent to report these crimes to law enforcement or other government agencies:

The reasons include, but are not limited to the following:

* Lack of knowledge about what hate crimes are and how the laws are applied
* Denial by the victim(s) that a hate crime was perpetrated
* Fear of retaliation by the perpetrator for reporting
* Fear of being revictimized by law enforcement or a belief that law enforcement does not want to address hate crimes
* Shame for being a victim of a hate crime
* Cultural or personal belief that one should not complain about misfortunes
* Fear of being exposed as being gay, lesbian, bisexual, or transgendered to one's family, employer, friends, or the general public
* Lack of English language proficiency and knowledge of how to report hate crimes
* Fear of being identified as an undocumented immigrant and being deported
* Fear on the part of people with disabilities who use caregivers that the caregivers who have committed hate crimes against them will retaliate and leave them without life supporting assistance
* Inability of some people with disabilities to articulate when they have been a victim of a hate crime (California Attorney General, 2001, 11)

The underreporting of hate crimes also results from the lack of comprehensive data collection from the major U.S. law enforcement agencies. "Unfortunately, this FBI data does not necessarily mean that there are fewer hate crimes in the U.S.," according to the *Newsweek* online edition (Bekiempis, 2014). The FBI receives its numbers from other law enforcement agencies participating in the Uniform Crime Reporting (UCR) program. But these agencies voluntarily tell the FBI how many of these crimes have been reported in their jurisdictions. In 2013, for example, 18, 415 city, county, rural and other local agencies participated in UCR but only 15,016 of these law enforcement agencies reported hate crime data to the FBI in 2013—demonstrating a wide gap in comprehensive hate crime coverage. In fact, Hawaii and Puerto Rico didn't submit any hate crime data for that year. Even more troubling, the Justice Department's Bureau of Justice Statistics (BJS) indicates that some 60 percent of hate crimes go unreported.

The FBI data are based on police reports; BJS data are based on yearly interviews of some 160,000 people in 90,000 U.S. households. The findings from this survey group are then extrapolated to the rest of the population.

Mark Potok, a senior fellow at the Southern Poverty Law Center and editor-in-chief of its journal, *Intelligence Report*, told *Newsweek* that the FBI numbers "don't tell us much of anything at all" (Bekiempis, 2014).

Some human and civil rights organizations also dispute the accuracy of the official annual FBI hate crime statistics audit. "Even with record high participation, underreporting remains a problem," said Barry Curtiss-Lusher, ADL national chair, and Abraham H. Foxman. "Thousands of police departments did not report data to the FBI, and of those that did, only about 12 percent reported one or more hate crimes to the Bureau. Over 80 cities with over 100,000 in population either did not participate in the reporting program, or affirmatively reported zero hate crimes to the FBI—which would be welcome news, but seems unlikely" (Leadership Conference, 2014).

More than 250,000 Americans over the age of 12 are victimized every year by hate criminals, according to a 2013 Department of Justice study that puts the number some 50,000 higher than the best earlier analyses. At the same time, the study found that in recent years only about one in three hate crimes are ever reported to law enforcement officials. The study, conducted by the Department of Justice's BJS, was based primarily on the annual National Crime Victimization Survey, which employs detailed questionnaires that are widely considered the most accurate measure of U.S. crime available and includes data for the years 2003–2011. Like other analyses, the new study also showed that a vastly higher percentage of hate crimes are violent than are crimes overall. About 92 percent of all hate crimes between 2007 and 2011 were violent, up from 84 percent in the 2003–2006 period. By comparison, the latest FBI statistics (from 2011) show that just 13 percent of all crime is violent. Experts also have long noted the extreme violence that characterizes hate crimes, with many murder victims, for instance, showing signs of suffering "overkill" (Potok, 2014).

Hate Crime Hoaxes

A growing number of hate crime hoaxes have been committed by misguided or ill-intentioned individuals who believe that by staging these incidents they might heighten public awareness about bigotry and prejudice. But their actions may instead provoke a critical response from some in the public who resent deliberate deception (see Chapter 3). As a result, future reports of hate crimes may be greeted with much skepticism, even though they were genuine incidents.

Bias Crimes and Violence before Hate Crime Laws

Since the terrorist attack on the United States on September 11, 2001, Americans have become understandably fearful for their personal safety and security, resulting in a regrettable rise in prejudice against Middle East immigrants and others not considered "real" Americans. Unfortunately, during other stressful times in U.S. history, some Americans were scapegoated or discriminated against because of their national, religious, or ethnic background. During the 19th century, many immigrants were subjected to prejudice, and even violent assaults. Chinese Americans were killed in mob violence; the Know-Nothing Party whipped up crowds to attack Catholics; the Irish were subjected to much prejudice in Boston; an Atlanta mob lynched a Jewish man who was wrongly charged with committing a murder. In the 20th century, Japanese Americans were interned because they were deemed a security threat. Few Americans know that German Americans were subjected to discrimination during World War I or that American Jews were accused of dragging the United States into World War II and were also subjected to much prejudice during that war. And, of course, throughout American history, African Americans who were brought to this country as slaves and then treated as second-class citizens until the rise of the civil rights movement in the 1960s, have been longtime victims of brutal violence and prejudice.

Even during peacetime, many U.S. citizens have been subjected to harassment, discrimination, and occasionally physical violence because of their religion, race, skin color, ethnic origin, economic class, or sexual orientation. The targets of this hatred have included Spanish and other non-English speakers; Italian, Jewish, and other European immigrants; and peoples from Asia, Africa, and the Middle East. Sadly, the list of such groups is too large to enumerate.

Hate Crimes against Selected Groups: A Recent Overview

This section surveys the recent history of hatred and violence directed against some of the major groups that—according to FBI annual crime statistics—are most frequently targeted: African Americans, Asian Americans, gay men and lesbians, and Jewish Americans. As a result of the September 11 attacks, this section will also include a survey of hate crimes committed against Sikhs, Muslims and Arab Americans. Americans with disabilities and Native Americans will also be briefly discussed, even though the government statistics indicate they are victims of a relatively small number of hate crimes.

African Americans

Since the passage of the Hate Crime Statistics Act of 1990, official government statistics indicate that the vast majority of hate crimes motivated by racial bias have been committed against black Americans.

The most recent FBI hate crime statistics covering the year 2013 reported that racial bias incidents represented the largest percentage of all bias-motivated incidents. Among single-bias hate crime incidents in 2013, there were 3,563 victims of racially motivated hate crime: 66.5 percent (2,371) were victims of crimes motivated by their offenders' antiblack or African American bias. (The term victim refers to a person, business, or institution.)

Hate crime laws are not always employed when prosecuting violence committed against individual African Americans. Sometimes prosecutors don't use the hate crime penalty enhancement provision for a variety of reasons, including an inability to prove that racism was the motivating factor in the homicide or lesser crime.

This law enforcement issue arose when Alonzo Bailey, a homeless man, was found chained to a fence in an Oklahoma City industrial park on May 5, 2002. The body of this 33-year-old African American had been set on fire and covered with wooden pallets. The suspected murderer, Anthony Lee Tedford, had Ku Klux Klan (KKK) tattoos on his body. Although the FBI planned to investigate whether the murder was a hate crime, the Oklahoma County District Attorney Wes Lane asserted that a police investigation did not support racism as the motive.

This grisly murder—regardless of whether it was racially motivated—recalled the tragic history of violence directed against African Americans throughout U.S. history. From 1882 to 1968, 4,743 people were reportedly lynched; of those, the vast majority were black. Long before hate crime statutes were enacted, black Americans have been the most frequent victims of hate violence in the United States.

While such violent incidents were generally ignored by the public during the 19th and 20th centuries, antiblack violence is now met with outrage and shame. When James Byrd Jr., a 49-year-old black man in Jasper, Texas, was dragged along an asphalt road for almost two miles by white supremacist attackers on June 7, 1998, this barbaric murder was condemned by President Bill Clinton. The accused perpetrators were later found guilty of the crime and executed by the state of Texas. The incident was reported and analyzed in a few books, and it received widespread media coverage. In partial reaction to this dastardly crime, Congress passed the *Matthew Shepard and James Byrd Jr. Hate Crimes Prevention Act* in 2009.

While much attention in 2014 has been focused on the police officer murders of unarmed African American males in Missouri, New York and Ohio, the most widely publicized racial incidents in the last few decades involved the burning of southern black churches in the 1990s. In June 1996, President Clinton established the National Church Arson Task Force (NCATF) to better coordinate the efforts of federal, state, and local law enforcement to combat such crime. The NCATF opened investigations into 945 arsons, bombings, and attempted bombings that occurred at houses of worship between January 1, 1995, and August 15, 2000. Since January 1995, federal, state, and local authorities have arrested 431 suspects and 305 defendants have been convicted. An NCATF report asserted that the arsons at both African American and other houses of worship "were motivated by a wide array of factors, including not only blatant racism or religious hatred but also financial profit, burglary, and personal revenge" (U.S. Department of Justice, 1998).

Although the NCATF report findings do not indicate a national conspiracy against black churches, this widespread criminal violence warranted the concern of law enforcement officials and the public. Although newspapers and other media extensively covered the rash of church bombings, it wasn't until *USA Today* published 12 articles over a three-day period that examined the nature of these crimes in great detail (*USA Today*, 1996). However, investigative journalist Michael Fumento, writing in the *Wall Street Journal*, argued that *USA Today* was partially responsible for wrongly charging, in his view, that African American church arsons constituted an epidemic (Fumento, 1996).

Epidemic or not, attacks against black churches have a long and tragic history. Reportedly, the first recorded arson against a black church occurred in South Carolina in 1822. After the civil war, the KKK targeted African American churches; almost a century later, four black children were killed in the Sixteenth Street Baptist Church bombing in Birmingham, Alabama in 1963. It is worth noting that former secretary of state Condoleezza Rice was the kindergarten classmate of Denise McNair, who was killed in the bombing.

Recent hate crimes committed against African Americans include the following:

- Steven Sandstrom and Gary L. Eye, both of Kansas City, Missouri, were sentenced to multiple life sentences on September 9, 2008, for the racially motivated murder of William L. McCay on March 9, 2005. While McCay was walking to work one morning, Eye attempted to shoot McCay with Sandstrom's gun as they were driving in a stolen car. He missed and McCay fled. Eye and Sandstrom, afraid that McCay would report them to the police, pursued him. At the next block, Eye got out of the car and fatally shot him.

- In the early-morning hours after Obama's election on November 4, 2008, 27-year-old Michael Jacques and several accomplices used gasoline to torch the Macedonia Church of God in Christ's nearly completed $2.5 million worship center in Springfield, Massachusetts. Nobody was in the building at the time. After a lengthy investigation, police ultimately secured confessions from the participants indicating that the fire was racially motivated. Jacques "was angry that the country was going to have an African American president and that the blacks and Puerto Ricans would now have more rights than whites," according to court documents. After a three-week trial, Jacques was convicted of numerous federal civil rights charges, including destruction of religious property and conspiracy against civil rights. In addition to serving almost 14 years in federal prison, followed by four years of supervised released, he must pay nearly $1.6 million in restitution.

- Timothy Flanagan, a former member of the Church of the National Knights, a KKK affiliate—admitted that on the night of April 30, 2012, he and two other individuals devised a plan to burn a cross in the yard of an African American man in Minor Hill, Tennessee. Flanagan's co-conspirator, Timothy Stafford, constructed a wooden cross in a workshop behind his house. Using Flanagan's credit card, Stafford and co-conspirator Ivan "Rusty" London then purchased diesel-fuel with which to soak the cross. Flanagan and the other co-conspirators then drove the cross to the victim's residence and upon arriving at the residence, Flanagan and London exited the truck. The cross was placed in the driveway leading up to the house and was ignited. According to the local authorities, the co-conspirators burned the cross with the purpose of intimidating the African American male who resided at that residence (U.S. Department of Justice, December 2014).

- In July 2014, the acting assistant attorney general Jocelyn Samuels for the Justice Department's Civil Rights Division and U.S. Attorney Gregory K. Davis for the Southern District of Mississippi announced that a federal grand jury had indicted several individuals for their alleged roles in a conspiracy to commit federal hate crimes against African American people in Jackson, Mississippi.

○ Some defendants were additionally charged with a racially motivated hate crime resulting in the death of a victim run over by a truck and two additional racially motivated hate crimes involving alleged assaults, and with carrying a firearm in relation to one of those assaults including soliciting others to commit hate crimes against African-Americans.

○ The indictment alleges that, beginning in the spring of 2011, the defendants and others conspired with one another to harass and assault African-American people in and around the Jackson area. According to the indictment, on numerous occasions, the co-conspirators used dangerous weapons, including beer bottles, sling shots and motor vehicles, to cause, and attempt to cause, bodily injury to African-American people. The co-conspirators are alleged to have specifically targeted African-American people they believed to be homeless or under the influence of alcohol because they believed that such individuals would be less likely to report an assault. The co-conspirators would often boast about these racially motivated assaults. The indictment details several such assaults, including the fatal assault on a victim who was intentionally run over (U.S. Department of Justice, July 16, 2014).

• In September 2014, the Department of Justice announced that Robert Keller, 70, pleaded guilty in the U.S. District Court for the District of Utah to a federal civil rights crime related to interfering with the housing rights of three members of an interracial family because of the family member's races and because the family members were living in a home while associating with an African American family member in Hurricane, Utah. During the plea proceedings, Keller admitted that on December 30, 2013, he wrote a note to two Caucasian family members of an interracial family threatening to kill them if they did not make their African American family member leave their home. Keller admitted that he used threats of force to willfully intimidate and interfere with the two Caucasian family members because they were occupying a dwelling while associating with their African American family member.

The above incidents sadly demonstrate that W.E.B. DuBois's famous statement about racism in America still resonates, although it is now more than a century later. "The problem of the twentieth century is the problem of the color-line," wrote the eminent African American scholar in 1900. While there is much to be optimistic about in American race relations—the election of the first African American president, a growing black middle class and the large increase of black students in colleges and universities, among other good news—the persistence of racist violence against blacks remains a festering problem. When Barack Obama was elected president, there was much fear about a possible large increase in bias-motivated incidents against African Americans, but fortunately, the number of such hate crimes has not greatly expanded. One can only hope that it will decrease in the coming years.

Asian Americans

Following the September 11 terrorist attacks, some Asian Americans were targeted in violent and deadly hate crimes. Some incidents were ostensibly aimed at "Muslim-looking" individuals but were mostly perpetrated against recent Asian non-Muslim U.S. citizens or recent immigrants, especially Sikhs.

Many Asian Americans have succeeded in achieving the much-vaunted American dream in the last few decades; They are highly represented in many professions (science, business, and the professoriate), their children often attend the top colleges and universities, and some Asian Americans earn the highest median incomes in the country. But the picture has not always been so rosy for immigrants from Asia who started arriving on these shores in the mid-19th century. Unfortunately, there is a long history of violence against Asian immigrants due to their race, dating back to the Gold Rush of the 1840s and 1850s when whites confronting competition from Chinese miners resorted to violence against these recent immigrants. Anti-Asian sentiment, accompanied by numerous anti-Chinese riots, culminated in a notorious massacre in Rock Springs, Wyoming, against Chinese miners resulting in 28 deaths on September 2, 1885. A few years earlier, Congress passed the Chinese Exclusion Act of 1882 which barred virtually all immigration from China and prevented almost all Chinese within the United States from becoming U.S. citizens.

This law was the first time in U.S. history that a specific ethnic group was excluded from entering the United States. Filipino workers, many of whom had been educated by American teachers and already spoke English, were also met with violence and denied U.S. citizenship As a result of white resentment against Japanese farmers developing agricultural tracts from the fertile soil of the Golden State, the state of California lobbied the federal government to stop all immigration from Japan soon resulting in the Asian Exclusion Act in 1924.

During World War II, the U.S. government forcibly removed over 120,000 Japanese Americans–the vast majority of whom were U.S. citizens–from their homes and incarcerated them in internment camps for periods of up to four years. The government claimed they represented a security risk to the nation. But in 1983, more than 40 years after the evacuation order, the Federal Commission on Wartime Relocation and Internment of Civilians determined that one of the primary causes for the Japanese American internment was racial prejudice.

In more recent times, a widely publicized anti-Asian hate murder occurred in 1982. Vincent Chin, a Chinese American from Detroit, was beaten to death by two white autoworkers, while celebrating his upcoming wedding. This deadly incident arose at the height of anti-Japanese sentiment in reaction to the growing import of Japanese automobiles. The workers who killed him were worried about their job security and assumed Mr. Chin was Japanese.

Other notorious crimes in earlier years include the following:

- On April 28, 2000, Anil Thakur, 31, a customer at the India Grocers store in Pittsburgh, Pennsylvania, was murdered and Sandip Patel, the store manager, was paralyzed from the neck down. The assailant was Richard Baumhammers, a white immigration attorney who professed hatred of minorities. He began his murderous rampage by killing Anita Gordon, his 63-year-old Jewish neighbor. Later, he went to a Chinese restaurant and killed Thao Q. Pham, 27, a Vietnamese American, and Ji-Ye Sun, 34, a Korean American. His final victim was Garry Lee, a 25-year-old African American man. Although Baumhammers was initially sent to a psychiatric facility, a jury found him guilty of five murders and he was sentenced to death.

- Thung Phetakoune, a 62-year-old U.S. citizen of Laotian ancestry, was murdered by Richard Labbe in Newmarket, New Hampshire, on July 14, 2001. Witnesses overheard Labbe uttering anti-Asian racial comments before the attack, and Labbe reportedly told the arresting police officer, "Those Asians killed my brother and uncle in Vietnam. Call it payback." Although the defendant was originally charged with a hate crime, the state later dropped the charge, and Labbe pleaded guilty only to manslaughter. The dropping of the hate crime indictment evoked outrage among Asian American organizations (*Asian Week*, 2001).

- Mizanor Rahman, a Bangladeshi immigrant, was beaten to death in Brooklyn, New York, in a racially motivated mob attack on August 10, 2002. The 37-year-old journalist was attacked by a local Hispanic gang when he stumbled into a violent confrontation between local Dominican and Bangladeshi youths over a stolen bicycle.

- While working at a part-time job delivering pizzas in New Bedford, Massachusetts, Saurabh Bhalerao, 24, was robbed, beaten, burned with cigarettes, stuffed in a trunk, and stabbed twice on June 23, 2003. He was later dumped along a road. His assailants shouted anti- Muslim slurs at Bhalerao, even though he is Hindu. Police and community leaders described the attack as a hate crime.

According to the FBI's 2013 hate crimes statistics, there were 164 incidents of hate crimes aimed at Asian Americans, constituting 4.6 percent of racially motivated hate crimes that year.

The now-defunct National Asian Pacific American Legal Consortium (NAPALC), formerly compiled a very useful itemized annual audit of bias-motivated crimes against Asian Americans but their successor group Asian Americans Advancing Justice doesn't currently compile such a list. The Leadership Conference, however, does list some incidents since before 2009 (Leadership Conference, 2009).

Violence against Sikhs

Sikhism is a monotheistic religion with over 25 million followers worldwide, including an estimated 700,000 adherents in the United States. It is the world's fifth largest religion. Although Sikh men wear turbans and are erroneously perceived as Muslims, the Sikh religion is not related to Islam. In the wake of the September 11 terrorist attacks of 2001, South Asians, primarily Sikhs, were targets of violence and hatred. The following selective list highlights some of the violent and deadly hate crime incidents against this community.

- On September 15, 2001, Balbir Singh Sodhi, a 52-year-old, was the first Sikh American targeted in the wake of 9/11 Sodhi was murdered outside his Chevron gas station in Mesa, Arizona, by a man wanting to "kill a Muslim" in retribution for the terror attacks. Frank Silva Roque, a machinist, was convicted of this first-degree murder and sentenced to death on October 9, 2003. During his 25-minute rampage, Roque also fired on the home of an Afghan family and shot multiple times at a Lebanese American clerk without injuring him.

- On September 17, 2001, the fires of hatred were further stoked when U.S. congressman, John Cooksey (R-LA), referred to Arab Americans and South Asians as "towel heads" and suggested racial profiling of these groups. The Louisiana representative said, "If I see someone [who] comes in that's got a diaper on his head and a fanbelt wrapped around the diaper on his head, that guy needs to be pulled over" (Leadership Conference, 2001).

- On December 12, 2001, Surinder Singh Sidhi, a liquor store owner in Los Angeles who wore a turban embroidered with an American flag after 9/11 for fear of being attacked, was beaten in his store by two men who accused him of being Osama bin Laden.

- On July 12, 2004, Sikhs Rajinder Singh Khalsa and Gurcharan Singh were viciously beaten by an intoxicated group of white males in their twenties began to taunt them, referencing September 11th and making fun of their turbans. Rajinder Singh Khalsa attempted to explain the significance of their headgear to the attackers, who responded by assaulting him. He was beaten unconscious and was found to have multiple broken bones.

- On January 30, 2009, Jasmir Singh was attacked by three men around 4 a.m. outside a grocery store in Queens, New York, with a glass bottle. Jasmir's friend who was with him the morning of the attack, told the police that while Jasmir was being attacked, the criminals made racist slurs about Jasmir's beard and turban. His father was attacked on the subway two years later (See the incident discussed later.) (Burton, Summer Anne, 2012).

- On May 30, 2011, a Sikh man lost three of his teeth after being sucker-punched in a New York subway car by a man who accused him of being related to Osama bin Laden. Jiwan Singh, who came to America 30 years earlier and was an employee of the Metropolitan Transportation Authority (MTA), was attacked by a black passenger who grabbed him by the shirt collar, picked him up and threw him into a subway seat in the mostly empty train. The father of five said his son, Jasmir, 23, had also lost an eye after being stabbed by attackers in 2009 who targeted him because of his turban and traditional beard. (See the incident described earlier.)

- On August 5, 2012, 40-year-old Wade Michael Page, a white supremacist, fatally shot six people and wounded four others at a Sikh temple (*gurdwara*) in Oak Creek, Wisconsin. The worshippers were: a woman Paramjit Kaur, 41; and five men: Satwant Singh Kaleka, 65, the founder of the *gurdwara*; Prakash Singh, 39, an assistant priest; Sita Singh, 41; Ranjit Singh, 49; and Suveg Singh, 84. The assailant later took his own life by shooting himself in the head after he was shot in the stomach by a responding police officer.

Despite these disturbing incidents, many Americans were heartened that President George W. Bush issued a strong statement on September 17, 2001, condemning violent incidents against U.S. immigrants and citizens. The U.S. Department of Transportation employees who had been subjecting Sikhs to rigorous searches at airports because of their turbans and other garb were issued formal guidelines that prohibited inspection of an individual based on his manner of dress (U.S. Department of Transportation, 2001). Another encouraging development was the congressional resolution to condemn "bigotry and violence against Arab-Americans, Muslim-Americans, South Asian-Americans, and Sikh-Americans." This resolution urged federal and local officials to fully prosecute hate crime perpetrators in their respective jurisdictions. The U.S. Senate unanimously agreed to the resolution on May 22, 2003, and the U.S. House of Representatives agreed to its version of the resolution on October 7, 2003. As of January 1, 2015, the FBI has expanded its hate crime statistics collecting to include Sikh, Hindu, and Arab categories.

In April 2011, the California state legislature took an admirable stance on deadly hate crimes committed against Sikhs in the earlier months: Darrell Steinberg, the California state Senate president, donned a turban in the Senate building to demonstrate solidarity with the Sikh community. This gesture was inspired by the King of Denmark who reportedly wore a yellow star to show solidarity with the Jewish community in Nazi-occupied Denmark so Jews would not feel alone (American Turban, 2011).

In 2013, Stanford University's Peace and Innovation Lab partnered with Sikh American Legal Defense and Education Fund (SALDEF) and published the first national survey of the public perception of Sikh Americans and their religious headwear, *Turban Myths: The Opportunities and Challenges for Reframing Sikh American Identity in Post-9/11 America*. This study corroborates the existence of a specific cultural bias against the Sikh American community. Key findings of the research include the following:

- Bias exists against the Sikh American articles of faith, including the turban, beard, and uncut hair.
- Seventy percent of the American public cannot identify a picture of a Sikh man as a Sikh.
- About half of the public associates the turban with Islam and believes that Sikhism is a sect of Islam.
- Anti-turban bias exists even among people with a greater knowledge of Sikhs.
- The media contributes to and fuels the bias against the Sikh articles of faith.

- Bias is unconscious, charged by emotion, and reinforced by the environment.
- The Sikh American community and experience remain an understudied population (SALDEF, 2013).

Americans with Disabilities

In the first reported hate crime case involving a person with a disability to go on trial in the United States, eight people were charged with kidnapping, harassing, and torturing Eric Kroch-maluk, a mentally retarded 23-year-old living in Middletown, New Jersey, in 1999. Seven of the eight perpetrators were convicted of bias assault and sentenced to prison. Most sadly, the victim who had limited mental capacity was unable to describe the torture or understand the brutal nature of the crime—he simply wanted to make friends with the perpetrators who had lured him to a party (Perry, 2008, v. 3, 172).

In January 2013, a grand jury in Philadelphia indicted several individuals for holding four mentally disabled people in virtual bondage and depriving them of food among other offenses. Two people died as a result of the imprisonment aimed at funneling social security funds to the perpetrators. This horrifying incident received national and international coverage and is one of the most publicized cases where government prosecutors invoked the hate crime statutes to prosecute on behalf of individuals with disabilities (*Los Angeles Times*, 2013).

Disability was the last protected class to be included in the reauthorization of the Hate Crime Statistics Act in 1996. Although advocacy groups lobbied for inclusion of gender and sexual orientation protections at that time, only disability was included in this act. Nevertheless, this important legal protection may be misleadingly misunderstood because FBI statistics indicate that persons with disabilities are 350 times less likely to be the victim of a hate crime than a victim selected because of race. Since there are an estimated 50 million Americans with disabilities, the authors suggest that poor data collection and the underreporting of such crimes may account for the vast omission of recorded incidents (McMahon et al, 2004, 70).

The 2013 FBI report cited 99 victims of hate crimes, resulting from the offender's bias against a disability: 75 were targets of anti–mental health disability bias and 24 were victims of anti–physical disability bias. These numbers account for 1.4 percent of all single-bias crimes reported that year. From 1996 to 2004, only 257 cases were reported from various state agencies but apparently there was no follow-up study on later years (Perry, 2009, 193). Sociologists and social workers advocate a more rigorous review of the underreporting of hate crimes. Most tragically, many hate crimes are committed by family members or caregivers, who are employed to assist individuals with disabilities (Sherry, 2010, 127). Perhaps, these close relationships may be a great inhibiting factor preventing the victims from reporting such crimes.

Jewish Americans

Hatred of Jews—commonly known by the semantically misleading term *anti-Semitism*—has a very long and bitter history. In 1991, British television aired a documentary series on the subject, aptly titled *The Longest Hatred*. In the United States too, anti-Jewish hatred and violence has flared periodically. One of the most notorious anti-Jewish incidents in the United States during the 20th century occurred in Atlanta, Georgia. Leo Frank, a Jew who was part owner of a pencil factory, was wrongfully accused of murdering a 14-year-old employee, Mary Phagan. In July 1915, encouraged by widespread community anger and the anti-Jewish invective of Tom Watson, a southern populist politician, a mob lynched Frank. This murder stirred immense fear among southern Jews and precipitated a massive exodus of Jews from the region. Despite this incident and the rise of anti-Jewish hatemongers like Father Coughlin, Gerald L. K. Smith, and pro-Nazi groups during World War II, the virus of anti-Semitism has fortunately never exhibited a major strain in U.S. life. "No decisive event, no deep crisis, no powerful social movement, no great individual is associated primarily . . . with anti-Semitism (in America)," once wrote historian John Higham (Dinnerstein, 1971). Nevertheless, anti-Jewish incidents continue to occur, ranging from swastikas being spray-painted at synagogues and Jewish cemeteries to harassment, intimidation, and violent assaults.

According to the FBI's 2013 Hate Crime Statistics tabulations, Jews were the largest religious group victimized by hate crimes accounting for 60.3 percent of all bias-motivated religious crimes and numbered 737 victims. For many years, FBI statistics frequently indicate that between 60 and 70 percent of these crimes are directed at Jews; anti-Muslim incidents usually range from 5 to 15 percent of the total.

According to the 2014 ADL Audit of Anti-Semitic Incidents in the United States, the total number increased by 21 percent in 2014 in a year marked by a violent anti-Semitic shooting attack targeting Jewish community buildings in Kansas and anti-Jewish expressions linked to the war in Gaza. The Anti-Defamation League's (ADL) Audit counted a total of 912 anti-Jewish incidents across the United States during the 2014 calendar year. This represents a 21 percent increase from the 751 incidents reported during the same period in 2013, and is the first time in nearly a decade of declines where the overall number of incidents has substantially risen. Despite the increase in incidents, the total number of anti-Jewish acts still represents one of the lowest totals of anti-Semitic acts reported by ADL.

More than a decade before the FBI began tallying hate crime statistics, the ADL began issuing an annual audit of anti-Jewish incidents first beginning in 1979. As mentioned earlier, there is often a discrepancy between statistics compiled by the U.S. government and the tallies compiled by different human rights and ethnic organizations.

Although the most recent ADL report will be released after this book is completed, it will probably indicate a rise in the number of anti-Jewish incidents in the United States in wake of the Gaza war in the summer of 2014. European Jews have experienced numerous attacks on individuals, synagogues, and community centers, arousing great fear in communities in France, Great Britain, Belgium, Denmark, and Ukraine, among other countries.

While there is often much discussion about whether one can distinguish anti-Israel from anti-Jewish statements and actions, the ADL has a useful and succinct response:

> While the Audit does not categorize criticism of Israel or Zionism as an anti-Semitic incident, such reports are included if they cross the line from legitimate criticism to anti-Semitism by invoking classic anti-Jewish stereotypes or inappropriate Nazi imagery and/or analogies. Public expressions of anti-Israel sentiments that demonize Jews or create an atmosphere of fear or intimidation for U.S. Jews are counted. (ADL Audit, 2014)

The distinction between anti-Jewish and anti-Israel actions and statements, however, has become increasingly blurry, especially in the last few years. Martin Luther King Jr. was aware of it many years ago when he said, "When people criticize Zionists, they mean Jews. You're talking anti-Semitism." Criticism of Israel is increasingly displayed through violent means and on occasion blatantly offensive, evoking Holocaust images against Jews worldwide, erasing the line between the two "anti" ideologies. On college campuses, Jewish students have been subjected to particularly virulent hatred and occasional violence. Daniel Vessal, a member of a Jewish fraternity and an active pro-Israel supporter, was assaulted at Temple University's main campus in Philadelphia in the summer of 2014 (Jewish Exponent, 2014). On many college campuses that year, Jewish students faced hostile rallies, threats on social media, and placards, which make obscene comparisons of Jews and Israel to Nazis in several reported incidents (Louis D. Brandeis Center, 2014).

An Orthodox synagogue in Florida was spray-painted with the word "Hamas" and swastikas on its entrance; a Jewish summer camp in Malibu was vandalized with the words, Jews=Killers. On July 17, 2014, about two dozen anti-Israel protesters targeted the Florida Holocaust Museum with graphic images of dead Palestinians and slogans charging Israel with genocide. Earlier that month, the Chabad of Southern Nevada in Las Vegas (a Hasidic Jewish group) was spray-painted with graffiti that read "Free Palestine" and "Free Gaza" (ADL Blog, 2014).

Anti-Jewish incidents were more violent in Europe during the summer of 2014. French and German synagogues and Jewish community centers were firebombed. In Berlin, an Israeli tourist was attacked and in Britain, a rabbi was attacked near a Jewish boarding school. In Australia, a bus carrying Jewish schoolchildren was targeted by teenagers shouting "Heil Hitler" and threatening to slit the children's throats. In July, the Community Security Trust in Britain, which monitors anti-Jewish incidents, received five times the monthly average of reports. In Paris, an anti-Semitic protest following the start of the recent Gaza conflict resulted in violent threats against Jews and destruction of Jewish-owned businesses reminiscent of Kristallnacht, the notorious night in November 1938 when Jews were attacked and killed and their businesses were burned and destroyed.

Other major incidents in the United States since 1990 and including the Gaza war were the following:

- The most serious anti-Jewish incident in the early 1990s occurred in the Crown Heights neighborhood of Brooklyn, New York, following a traffic accident. On August 19, 1991, the driver of a car that was part of a motorcade for Rabbi Menachem M. Schneerson (the spiritual leader of the Lubavitcher Hasidic movement) accidentally hit Gavin Cato, a seven-year-old African American boy, and his cousin, resulting in his death and the injury of his cousin. A riot ensued over the following three days, during which crowds roamed the streets yelling, "Get the Jews." Jewish homes, cars, and property were attacked. On the night of the accident, 20 black youths assaulted Yankel Rosenbaum, an Australian Jewish scholar, stabbing him and leaving him bleeding on the hood of an automobile. He later died. Lemrick Nelson, age 16, was charged with the murder. On October 29, 1992, Nelson was found not guilty of the murder because the prosecution did not prove that the attack had caused Rosenbaum's death. Defense lawyers did not deny that Nelson had stabbed the 29-year-old Jewish scholar. His attorneys contended the slaying had nothing to do with the fact that the victim was Jewish—a crucial element needed for a hate crimes conviction. Amidst angry protests by the public and the media about an unfair verdict, the U.S. government subsequently charged the defendant with violating Rosenbaum's civil rights. In 1997, Nelson was convicted of these charges and was sentenced to 21 years in prison. The U.S. Second Circuit Court of Appeals, however, overturned the verdict on the grounds of an improper race-based jury selection. Nelson was then sentenced to a maximum of 10 years in prison and was released on June 2, 2004.

- On March 1, 1994, Rashid Baz, a Lebanese immigrant, shot at a van carrying 15 Hasidic Jewish students over the Brooklyn Bridge. One student, 16-year-old Aaron Halberstam, died in the attack. Three other students were wounded; one of them, 18-year-old Nachum Sasonkin, fell into a coma and had few prospects for a normal life. Although he still had a bullet lodged in his brain, Sasonkin has had a miraculous recovery. He later married, became a father, and was ordained as a rabbi. The murderer once vowed to "kill all Jews" (*New York Times*, 1994).

- In another violent incident, a Jewish store owner in Harlem wanted to expand his clothing store, Freddy's Fashion Mart, to a space occupied by a black-owned record store. The owner of the record store didn't want to move, and some community activists supported his decision. For several weeks, they picketed Freddy's Fashion Mart, occasionally shouting anti-Jewish slurs and rhetoric, including the term "bloodsuckers"—a phrase that Nation of Islam leader Louis Farrakhan had used only a few weeks earlier in a widely publicized interview to describe Jews. On December 8, 1995, Roland Smith, one of the protesters, entered Freddy's brandishing a revolver and shot four people. He then doused the store with lighter fluid. Eight people—including Smith—died in the blaze. Although none of the victims were Jewish, anti-Jewish hatred was nevertheless an underlying factor of the crime.

- On June 10, 2009, James W. von Brunn, an 88-year-old white supremacist and anti-Jewish racist walked into the United States Holocaust Memorial Museum, and began shooting, fatally wounding a security guard and sending tourists scrambling before he himself was shot. The gunman and the security guard were both taken to nearby George Washington University Hospital, with von Brunn handcuffed to a gurney. The 39-year-old guard Stephen T. Johns, died a short time later. Museum officials said he had worked there for six years. Von Brunn was incarcerated in North Carolina and died of natural causes on January 6, 2010.

- On August 10, 1999, Buford O. Furrow Jr., a member of the Aryan Nations, entered the North Valley Jewish Community Center in Los Angeles and wounded several people, including a small child. Furrow later claimed that his action was a "wake-up call to white America to start killing Jews." Furrow also killed Joseph Ileto, a Filipino American postal worker.

- On November 4, 2009, three teenagers broke into the Chabad Jewish Center in Hyannis, Massachusetts, and significantly vandalized it by defacing its walls and by throwing religious objects on the floor. In addition, during the break-in the three teenagers downloaded images of Adolf

Hitler and anti-Semitic symbols using the rabbi's computer. The three suspects were arraigned in the Barnstable Juvenile Court (Trends in Hate).

- On April 13, 2014. Frazier Glenn Miller, a neo-Nazi and former KKK member, killed three people at the Jewish Community Center of Greater Kansas City and Village Shalom, a Jewish retirement community, both located in Overland, Kansas. The victims were a 14-year-old boy, Reat Griffin Underwood, and his 69-year-old grandfather, Dr. William Lewis Corporon, who were killed at the Jewish Community Center. Both individuals were Christians and attended a Methodist church. A 53-year-old woman, Terri LaManno, also a Christian was killed at the parking lot of Village Shalom, where her mother resides. Unbeknownst to the gunman, only one person targeted by gunfire was Jewish.

Lesbians, Gay Men, Bisexuals, and Transgendered People (LGBT)

In a 1988 case involving the beating death of a gay man, a circuit court judge in Broward County, Florida, jokingly asked the prosecuting attorney, "That's a crime now, to beat up a homosexual?" The prosecutor replied, "Yes, sir. And it's also a crime to kill them." The judge reportedly replied, "Times have really changed" (Jenness, 1997, 50).

Prior to the passage of the Hate Crime Statistics Act in 1990, no federal statute had addressed the problem of antigay violence. Similarly, very few laws at the state and local levels had specifically addressed these types of crimes. Only recently has violence against gay men and lesbians been considered a hate crime by the federal government and by most state and local law enforcement agencies. Despite a tide of new legislation concerning the issue, the number of reported crimes against gays has continued to increase in some years. On October 9, 1986, the U.S. House of Representatives Judiciary Subcommittee on Criminal Justice convened the first congressional hearings on antigay violence throughout the United States. Physicians, psychologists, sociologists, and other health professionals offered testimony on the nature, extent, and consequences of antigay violence.

The first national study focusing exclusively on the topic of antigay violence was conducted by the National Gay and Lesbian Task Force in 1984. Interviewing almost 1,500 gay men and 654 lesbians in eight U.S. cities (Boston, New York, Atlanta, St. Louis, Denver, Dallas, Los Angeles, and Seattle), the respondents reported the following:

- Nineteen percent of the respondents reported having been punched, hit, kicked, or beaten at least once in their lives because of their sexual orientation.
- Forty-four percent had been threatened with physical violence.
- Ninety-two percent of those who had been targets of antigay verbal abuse had experienced such harassment "more than once or many times" (Herek and Berrill 1992, 19–25).

These survey results also highlight another issue involving bias crimes against homosexuals: Statistics on antigay crimes vary greatly in reports issued by gay rights activists and law enforcement authorities. The National Coalition of Anti-Violent Programs (NCAVP) later assumed this duty in 1997. From 1985 to 1989, the National Gay and Lesbian Task Force (NGLTF) gathered statistics from a wide range of community groups and media sources. Since 1990, these reports have focused on major metropolitan areas, including Boston, Chicago, Denver, Minneapolis, St. Paul, New York City, and San Francisco and many other cities throughout the country. Gay rights organizations have consistently claimed that antihomosexual hate crimes are vastly underreported and that this is true for several reasons. The primary explanation is that lesbians and gay men are often reluctant to report these incidents, fearing that such publicity would adversely affect their employment or relations with family members who are unaware of their sexual orientation. "While victims may want to prosecute their assailants, they are too vulnerable as homosexuals in American society to be exposed in this manner," asserts law scholar Teresa Eileen Kibelstis. She cites a 1994 incident in Los Angeles in which eight men were arrested for assaulting two others with baseball bats. Although the police termed the incident "a gay bashing" and arrested the assailants with the aid of witnesses, the victims quickly left the scene of the crime and were never located. "Gay bashing crimes involve gay victims, and for some lesbians and gay men, that label can have too many repercussions," Kibelstis concludes (Kibelstis 1995).

Many gays and lesbians have been distrustful of police departments nationwide, both historically and in recent times. The Stonewall riot, which occurred at a gay bar in New York's Greenwich Village in 1969 and considered the founding event in the birth of the modern gay liberation movement, involved a police assault against gay and transgendered men. Violent hate crimes committed against gays and lesbians are also notable in another respect: These incidents are especially brutal. According to one study, "an intense rage is present in nearly all homicide cases involving gay male victims. A striking feature . . . is their gruesome, often vicious nature. Seldom is the homosexual victim simply shot. He is more apt to be stabbed a dozen or more times, mutilated, and strangled." A hospital official in New York City remarked, "Attacks against gay men were the most heinous and brutal I encountered. . . . They frequently involved torture, cutting, mutilation . . . showing the absolute intent to rub out the human being because of his (sexual) preference" (Winer 1994).

In 2001, the NCAVP recorded 2,210 attacks on gay men and lesbians; the FBI, however, cited 1,555 incidents in its annual report. Phyllis B. Gerstenfeld notes that the "actual discrepancy is actually much greater because the FBI data purport to include almost all of the United States, whereas the NCAVP report included only a dozen reporting regions with a combined population of about 51 million" (Gerstenfeld 2004).

When comparing the FBI figures with those from nongovernmental monitoring groups, it is important to remember that the private advocacy groups have been monitoring hate crimes for a longer period of time than has the government. Whereas the FBI's first Hate Crime report covered the year 1991, the NGLTF conducted annual surveys of antihomosexual violence from 1985 to 1995.

Several decades later the disparity in hate crime statistics persists. The 2013 FBI annual hate crime report noted 1,402 offenses committed against gay men, lesbians, bisexuals, and transgender individuals. Yet the NCAVP posted the following statistics:

- 2001 incidents of anti-LGBT violence in 2013
- 18 homicides; 90 percent of victims were black or Hispanic and the rest were white
- Undocumented people, transgender women, people of color and gay men were at the most risk from violence
- Only 45 percent of survivors reported their incidents to the police.
- Of those reporting incidents to the police, 32 percent complained that they received hostile treatment from the law enforcement officers.

Transgender Victims

In the last few decades, there have been many references in the broadcast and print media to transgender individuals but many people might not understand the meaning of this term. The Gay and Lesbian Alliance against Defamation (GLAAD) offers the following useful explanation:

Transgender is an umbrella term for people whose gender identity differs from what is typically associated with the sex they were assigned at birth. Gender identity is someone's internal, personal sense of being a man or a woman (or as someone outside of that gender binary). For transgender people, the sex they were assigned at birth and their own internal gender identity do not match.

Trying to change a person's gender identity is no more successful than trying to change a person's sexual orientation—it doesn't work. Most transgender people seek to bring their bodies more into alignment with their gender identity. People under the transgender umbrella may describe themselves using one (or more) of a wide variety of terms, including (but not limited to) transgender, transsexual, and "genderqueer."

Transgender people may or may not alter their bodies hormonally and/or surgically, but it's important to know that being transgender is not dependent upon medical procedures. (GLAAD, 2015)

The murder of Brandon Teena on December 31, 1993, a girl who passed as a man, was probably the first anti-transgender homicide to receive wide media attention. The award-winning film *Boys Don't Cry* tells the story of Teena's life and tragic death.

Two decades later, Cecilia Chung, senior strategist at the Transgender Law Center, a national advocacy group, sadly notes that there has been an increase of violence and murders against transgender individuals.

Chung said that violence against transgender people occurs so frequently because they are marginalized by the systems and institutions in society. "If you look at some of the data, a high number of trans people of color make less than $15,000 a year and in order to survive they must be exposed to a lot of high-risk elements in their lives," she said. "Where they live, or the type of relationship they end up in—those all play a huge factor. The bottom line to that is, violence is an indicator of the marginalizing that our community faces" (Merevick, 2014).

Chung believes that several economic disparities, including lack of access to health care, housing, and education make transgender people more vulnerable to violence.

"We have a long way to go in addressing issues with housing, employment, and affordable healthcare," Fukui said. "This is about racism, control, and policing of our community in ways that are violent and actually increases violence. Our communities have the solutions and know what we need in order to survive. I think once we break this really intense spider web of oppression at work in the United States, we'll be able to really break this down."

Mara Keisling, executive director at the National Center for Transgender Equality, also said that the violence stems from cultural and economic problems. Because of these factors, "you're going to have more violence," she said. "You'd like to think that it's improving, but we've just had our worst recorded month of murder in the history of the transgender movement and we're not hearing about all of them, too."

In 2014, the NCAVP issued a comprehensive report in May that found 344 transgender people—more than 10 times the FBI's figure—were the victims of hate-motivated violence in 2013. That was up from 305 the year before. The group found 13 transgender people in the United States were killed last year in bias attacks.

Among the reasons federal statistics underrepresent attacks on transgender people is because many state and local hate crime laws don't include protections for LGBT people. Ohio has no statewide law to prosecute hate crimes against LGBT victims so can't report these incidents as hate crimes. Aaron Eckhardt, a leader of Buckeye Region Anti-Violence Organization (BRAVO), pointed out in an interview recently with BuzzFeed News, "According to Ohio, there have been zero hate crimes committed against people in those categories." But in Ohio alone, three transgender women were killed in 2013 in what the organization found were hate-driven crimes. In addition, BRAVO, which contributes to the NCAVP reports, found 14 incidents of nonfatal hate-motivated attacks in their state that year. Still, the FBI report issued today shows zero gender-identity hate crimes in Ohio. Many law enforcement agencies also don't have congenial or understanding relationships with transgender communities. Police frequently note the wrong gender in their reports and sometimes subject transgender victims to taunting and further violence. The result is that many transgender people do not report violence to police at all (Holden, 2014).

Major Violence against the LGBT Community since 1988

In recent years, the most widely reported hate crime against gays occurred in Wyoming. On October 6, 1998, Matthew Shepard, a 22-year-old gay student at the University of Wyoming, was lured from a local bar by two men, kidnapped, beaten with a .357 Magnum, and tied to a wooden fence. He hung there for almost 18 hours until a passing bicyclist noticed his bloodied body. He lay in a coma in a hospital in Fort Collins, Colorado, until he died on October 12. Sadly, there have been many other grotesquely violent incidents directed against gays and lesbians—or those thought to be gay—both before and after Shepard's murder:

- In May 1988, a lesbian couple, Rebecca Wright and Claudia Brenner, were victims of a gruesome murder in Pine Grove State Park in Pennsylvania. Stephen Ray Carr was convicted of first-degree murder and sentenced to life imprisonment.

- Also in May 1988, a college freshman committed a grisly murder of two gay men, Tommy Trible and Lloyd Griffin, in a Dallas, Texas, neighborhood. Although the prosecutor requested life imprisonment for the murderer, Richard Lee Bednarski, the trial judge imposed a 30-year sentence and callously declared, "I put prostitutes and gays at about the same level and I'd be hard put to give somebody life for killing a prostitute" (Belkin 1988).

- Vietnam War veteran James Zappalorti was brutally beaten in Staten Island, New York, on January 21, 1990. The murderers, Phillip Sarlo and Michael Taylor, later defiantly declared that they had "only killed a gay" (*Newsday*, November 4, 1990, p. 8).

- On October 27, 1992, Seaman Allen Schindler, while serving on a U.S. Navy ship stationed in Japan, was murdered outside his base. The assailant, Navy Airman Terry Helvey, who had recently learned of Schindler's homosexuality, stomped on his face and chest with his feet. Schindler's body was so disfigured by the brutal attack that seasoned Navy medics were sickened at the sight of the body.

- On July 1, 1999, Gary Matson and Winfield Scott Mowder, a gay couple, were shot to death in their home outside Redding, California. James Tyler Williams, the killer of the gay couple, was sentenced to 29 years to life in prison for the murders, plus a 19-year sentence for the firebombing of three Sacramento area synagogues. His brother, Benjamin Williams, who was an accomplice in the crimes, committed suicide in his Shasta County jail cell on November 17, 2002. Benjamin Williams reportedly said that the murder of the gay couple was "God's will."

- In Atlanta, Georgia, Gregory Love was attacked with a baseball bat by a fellow Morehouse College student because he believed Love was making a sexual pass at him in a dormitory shower. A jury found Aaron Price, a 19-year-old sophomore at Morehouse, guilty of aggravated assault and aggravated battery in the November 3, 2002, beating. Price received 10 years on each count, to be served concurrently. Price, who was subsequently expelled from Morehouse, was acquitted of a hate crime after prosecutors failed to convince jurors that Price's action was motivated by antigay feelings. Love also testified that he was not gay. This violent incident aroused great fears among gay students at Morehouse, a historically black men's college. As a result, many black gays and lesbians spoke out for the first time about antigay prejudice in the African American community. This trial was the first case involving Georgia's recently passed hate crimes enhancement penalty statute.

- On February 2, 2006, Jacob D. Robida, 18, of New Bedford, Massachusetts entered a gay bar and then attacked patrons with an axe and also shot at them. Three patrons were wounded by the gunfire and one of them also received head lacerations from the axe attack. Robida fled the state and was later killed as a result of the shootout with police.

- On January 16, 2009, in Sacramento, California, a transgendered woman, Brenda Torres, 20, was attacked inside the tunnel between Old Sacramento and the K Street Mall by two African American men who shouted transgendered slurs at her. She was assaulted with a beer bottle and robbed. There were eyewitnesses, but apparently none of them called the police or intervened. Police investigated the attack/robbery as a hate crime.

- On October 30, 2011, Burke Burnett, 26-year-old gay man, was the victim of a brutal hate crime in Reno, Texas, a small town just east of Paris and about 100 miles northeast of Dallas. He was at a private party when four men suddenly attacked him, stabbing him at least twice with a broken beer bottle before throwing him onto a fire. His attackers yelled vicious antigay epithets against him. Burnett said it took 30 stitches to close stab wounds to his back and forearm, as well as a cut above his left eye. He also sustained second-degree burns and severe bruises. "They knew I was gay," Burnett said Monday. "I'm convinced they were trying to kill me."

- On June 19, 2014, David Malcolm Strickland, 27, was apprehended in Helotes, Texas, a San Antonio suburb and charged with capital murder, aggravated assault with a weapon and aggravated sexual assault for the June 23, 2012 murder of a 19-year-old lesbian, Mollie Olgin, because of her sexual orientation. Her girlfriend, Kristene Chapa, then 18, survived the South Texas hillside attack but suffered serious head injuries.

- On November 17, 2014, the Justice Department's Civil Rights Division, the U.S. Attorney's Office for the Northern District of Texas, and the FBI's Dallas Division Office announced that Brice Johnson, 19, of Springtown, Texas, was sentenced to 183 months imprisonment for kidnapping a young gay man after luring the victim to his home and brutally assaulting him because of his sexual orientation. After the beating, Johnson locked the victim in the trunk of his own car and drove the car to a family friend's house. The victim suffered multiple skull and facial fractures from the beating, which required him to be hospitalized for 10 days.

Despite this very gloomy news, Valerie Jenness, a sociologist who has written extensively about hate crimes, was heartened when U.S. attorney general John Ashcroft held a nationally televised news conference on April 10, 2002, to announce that Darrell David Rice was to be charged with a federal hate crime for the murder of Laura Winans and Julianne Marie Williams, two lesbians who were found dead on June 1, 1996, in Shenandoah National Park in Virginia. (Later evidence required the U.S. government to dismiss the federal case against Rice.) Rice was then indicted by a grand jury in Prince William County, Virginia, on June 7, 2004, on charges of abduction, robbery, and malicious wounding of a 37-year-old woman in Manassas, Virginia, on February 24, 1996. In a plea bargain agreement he pleaded No Contest on August 24, 2005, to unlawful wounding in that case. The Federal Bureau of Prisons reported that on July 17, 2007, Rice, 39, was released from federal prison.

Nevertheless, this was reportedly the first case in which the federal government tried to use the Hate Crimes Sentencing Enhancement Act (1994) to prosecute a hate crime based on gender and sexual orientation. In his news conference, Ashcroft noted that he had met with the parents of the victims and learned about their lives. He declared that the Department of Justice would "pursue, prosecute, and punish those who attack law-abiding Americans out of hatred for who they are."

The 2014 FBI annual report on U.S. hate crimes—which covers the previous year—placed the number of antigay incidents at 1,454 for 2013. According to the report, the number of sexual orientation bias victims constituted 16.6 percent of all hate crime victims. This publication contained newly required data to be collected under the *Matthew Shepard and James Byrd Jr. Hate Crime Prevention Act of 2009* for hate crime victims. First, biases against gender (male or female) and gender identity (transgender and gender nonconformity) have been added to the list of bias categories. As a result, federal hate crimes law now addresses violent crimes based on a victim's race, color, religion, national origin, gender, disability, sexual orientation, and/or gender identity. Nevertheless, gay rights groups believe the FBI figures are gross underestimates.

The Human Rights Campaign (HRC), the nation's largest LGBT civil rights organization, responded to the 2014 report by urging all law enforcement to report hate crimes in their jurisdiction in order to ensure that the state of hate violence in the United States is accurately reported.

> "Hate crimes are different from other crimes because they affect not only the victims and their families, but generate fear and insecurity for the entire community they target," said David Stacy, HRC's Government Affairs Director. "While reporting statistics on hate crimes based on sexual orientation—and now on gender identity—are important first steps, so much more work is needed to prevent bias-motivated violence. For example, too many states still do not have an LGBT-inclusive state-level hate crimes law, and we are committed to working with our partners and allies to change that. All people should have the opportunity to live openly, honestly, and safely in their community without fear of harassment or violence."

In 2014, law enforcement agencies reported 5,928 hate crime incidents involving 6,933 offenses to the FBI. Of those, 20.2 percent of all hate crimes were motivated by sexual orientation, second to crimes motivated by racial bias, and 0.5 percent of hate crimes were based on gender identity. According to the FBI, more law enforcement agencies in the United States participated in the 2013 data collection effort than ever before. That year, 15,016 law enforcement agencies voluntarily reported their statistics to the FBI compared to 14,511 participating agencies in 2012.

There was a slight decrease in crimes against LGBT individuals in 2013, after increases each year since 2009. That year, 1,233 incidents based on sexual orientation were reported, down slightly from the past three years, when law enforcement agencies reported 1,299, 1,293, and 1,277 hate crimes in 2012, 2011, and 2010, respectively.

HRC believes that the low number of responses for hate crimes based on gender identity and gender nonconformity—31 incidents—suggests that law enforcement are mischaracterizing hate based crimes as ones based on either sexual orientation or gender. As in past years, the vast majority of the participating agencies (88%) reported zero hate crimes. In addition, thousands of police agencies across the nation did not submit data to the FBI, including at least one agency with a population of more than 250,000 people, and at least seven agencies in cities with a population between 100,000 and 250,000 (HRC Blog, 2014).

On October 28 2014, HRC and advocates across the country commemorated the fifth anniversary of the signing of the federal HCPA. The passage of the HCPA was a significant victory in the fight for equality because it was the first major piece of civil rights legislation protecting LGBT individuals.

Arab and Muslim Americans

Following the Arab terrorist attacks on the United States on September 11, 2001, there appeared to be a significant increase in anti-Arab and anti-Muslim prejudice throughout the country, resulting in a few widely reported incidents of harassment, vandalism, and occasionally violence. According to the annual FBI Hate Crimes Statistics, in the last several years anti-Muslim incidents have generally accounted for the second or third highest number of religious-motivated hate crimes, but anti-Catholic and anti-Protestant crimes were almost statistically similar. (Anti-Jewish crimes accounted for a significantly higher number of such incidents.)

Most of the deadliest hate crimes ostensibly aimed against Muslims were, in fact, committed against Sikhs, who wear turbans, and others who look Middle Eastern but are not Arab or Muslim. (See "Asian-American" subsection discussed earlier.)

The following list includes some of the most violent incidents directed against American Arabs or Muslims since the 9/11 terrorist attacks:

- On March 25, 2002, Charles D. Franklin crashed his pickup truck into the Islamic Center of Tallahassee, Florida, after evening prayers. No one was inside the mosque when the truck smashed into the doorway, causing about $1,000 in damage to the building.

- On September 12, 2001, 300 angry protestors tried to storm a mosque in Bridgeview, Illinois, a Chicago suburb. More than 100 police controlled the demonstrators and arrested three people.

- On September 11, 2001, the Islamic Center of Irving, Texas, which serves as a school and a mosque, was fired upon, leaving 13 to 14 bullet holes in the building. No one was injured. In the following week, there were also gunshots and vandalism directed at mosques in Toledo, Ohio; Bridgeport, Connecticut; Claremont, California; Lexington, Kentucky; and Sterling, Virginia, among other places.

- On September 29, 2001, Abdo Ali Ahmed, a Yemenite, was shot behind the counter of his store in Reedley, California. Recent incidents in the area indicated it was a bias-motivated crime against Arabs.

- In October 2002, hundreds of leaflets containing anti-Islamic obscenities and threats were distributed at the Muslim Association of Honolulu mosque. The FBI investigated the incident as a hate crime.

- In Salt Lake City, Utah, James Herrick, 32, was sentenced to more than four years in prison after pleading guilty to setting fire to the "Curry in a Hurry," a Pakistani American–owned restaurant, on September 13, 2001.

- On December 17, 2002, in what federal officials described as the most stringent penalty for a post–September 11, 2001, hate crime, Patrick Cunningham, 54, was sentenced to six-and-a half years for an assault on the Islamic Idriss mosque in Seattle two days after the terrorist attacks. He admitted to trying to set fire to parked vehicles and to threatening two worshipers with a loaded .22-caliber pistol. In an emotional plea before U.S. district judge Barbara Rothstein, Cunningham said that on the night of the assault he was drunk and distraught over the terrorist attacks. He apologized to his victims and thanked God "for intervening" before things got worse. Although Cunningham maintained he had fired his pistol only once, the prosecutors said that he had fired three additional times but that the weapon had misfired. No one at the mosque was injured. Judge Rothstein acknowledged the defendant's apologies and his crime-free record, but she also denounced his crime. She remarked that the ability to practice religion without fear of violence "is a foundation of our country. It's a reason why people come here" (*Seattlepi*, 2002, p. B1).

- Vandals hit all three floors of the Islamic Foundation of Central Ohio in Columbus on the evening of December 29, 2001, shredding copies of the Koran and breaking water pipes to cause damage to the building. According to a November 2002 Human Rights Watch report, the damage was estimated at $379,000.

- On August 24, 2002, federal authorities arrested Dr. Robert Goldstein, a 37-year-old Tampa, Florida, podiatrist, for plotting to bomb local mosques and an Islamic cultural center in south Florida. He pleaded guilty and was later sentenced to 12-and-a-half years in prison. The defendant wanted to get revenge for the September 11 terrorist attacks.

- During the last week of August 2003, a fire at the Islamic Center in Savannah, Georgia, destroyed a building that had been used as a mosque by approximately 100 of the estimated 400–500 Muslims in the area. Early evidence indicated that the arson was motivated by hate. During the first Gulf War, from 1990 to 1991, there were several recorded incidents of harassment and vandalism directed against Arab and Muslim Americans in cities throughout the country. On September 24, 1990, President George H. W. Bush declared that "death threats, physical attacks, vandalism, religious violence and discrimination against Arab-Americans must end."

- June 1, 2009: A Cape Girardeau man is charged with a hate crime for vandalizing the Islamic Center and a car parked near it. Nicholas T. Proffit, 31, was charged with two counts of felony property damage under Missouri's hate crime law, along with misdemeanor offenses for driving while intoxicated, speeding and failing to wear a seat belt. The large glass window on the south side of the mosque was broken out and the windshield of a Mercedes-Benz parked in the lot was also cracked. He is later sentenced to three years in prison.

- In October 2010, four Staten Island teens faced hate-crime charges for taunting a Muslim classmate because of his faith, calling him a "terrorist" and repeatedly punching him in the genitals. "They took advantage of me because I was quiet," the 16-year-old-victim, whose first name is Kristian, told the Staten Island Advance, which first reported the story of the abuse. Police said the four Staten Island boys—three 14-year-olds who are Latino and a 15-year-old who is black—were arrested October 10 on charges of assault and aggravated harassment, both as hate crimes. They are being charged as minors, and police did not release their names.

- On February 4, 2011, Bradley Kent Strott, 52, stabbed a 57-year-old Muslim man during a conversation at a bar. The defendant then became upset after the man told Strott he was a Muslim. He grabbed the victim by his shirt, and stabbed him in the neck with his pocket knife. The defendant stated that "Muslims are the root of the problem," Strott was charged with hate crime and aggravated battery.

- On October 5, 2012, the FBI announced hate crimes charges were filed in U.S. District Court in Toledo against an Indiana man stemming from the arson this week of the Islamic Center of Greater Toledo, Randolph Linn, 52, of St. Joe, Indiana, was charged with intentionally defacing, damaging, and destroying religious real property because of the religious character of that property and with using fire and explosives to commit a felony.

- In June 2013, Michael Enright, a college student was sentenced to nine-and-half years behind bars after pleading guilty to charges he attacked a New York City taxi driver from Bangladesh during an anti-Muslim tirade inside a cab on August 10, 2010. "I used a knife. I cut him in the throat," Michael Enright said in a low, voice when asked by a Manhattan judge to describe his crimes. Prosecutor James Zaleta argued that Enright deserved an 18-year prison term for a "vicious, cold-blooded attack" that came as the September 11 anniversary neared, which occurred at the same time as a contentious debate over a planned Islamic center and mosque near ground zero. "After insulting the tenets of Islam and mocking the restrictions of Ramadan, the defendant, unprovoked, reached through the cab partition and sliced the victim across his neck."

Sympathetic Reactions to Muslims and Arabs

Despite these disturbing hate crime incidents, there was much heartening news with the wide range of expressions of concern and support throughout the country from politicians and average citizens who understood that no single group should be scapegoated for the murder of some 3,000 Americans in the

September 11 terrorist attacks. The support ranged from the president of the United States to elementary-school children:

- Only a day after the terrorist attack, President George W. Bush wrote, in published remarks to Mayor Rudolph Giuliani: "Our nation should be mindful that there are thousands of Arab-Americans who live in New York City, who love their flag just as much as we do . . . we treat Arab-Americans and Muslims with the respect they deserve." The president also visited the Islamic Center of Washington, D.C., and issued similar supportive remarks.

- In 2003, both the U.S. Senate and House of Representatives passed a resolution "condemning bigotry against Arab-Americans, Muslim-Americans, South Asian-Americans, and Sikh-Americans."

- Governors, mayors, and town officials appeared publicly with Arab Americans and Muslims to condemn hate crimes and ensure the prosecution of perpetrators, according to a Human Rights Watch report, "We are Not the Enemy: Hate Crimes Against Arabs, Muslims, and Those Perceived to be Arab or Muslim After September 11," issued in November 2002. The authors of the report noted that this type of solidarity was uniformly expressed in every area of the country.

- The Anti-Defamation League (ADL), the largest Jewish civil rights organization in the United States, publicized anti-Arab and anti-Muslim hate crimes on its Web site and worked with law enforcement officers to prosecute these crimes. They actively cooperate with law enforcement agencies to ensure that Arabs and Muslims receive full legal protections.

- Dearborn, Michigan, which has a large Arab American population, experienced only two September 11–related assaults. Some officials credit an ongoing community police cooperative relationship with stemming any potential violence.

The following incidents also were indicative of the attitudes of most Americans after the September 11 attacks:

- According to the October 18, 2001, issue of the *Seattle Post-Intelligencer*, a bus driver in Seattle posted a sign on his bus exhorting riders to beware of Muslims. When a passenger filed a complaint, the driver was suspended from work and the sign was removed.
- Elementary school students at the Park Day School in Montclair, California, organized a "Walk of Acceptance" to raise money for a hate crimes information hotline.
- In Cambridge, Massachusetts, members of a local synagogue joined other religious groups in a march against hate. "I'm inundated with calls from rabbis," said Tahir H. Chaudhry, president of the Islamic Center of Boston, a Wayland, Massachusetts, mosque (*Boston Globe*, 2001).
- Harvard University president Larry Summers addressed a regular Friday prayer meeting for the school's Muslim community, emphasizing the university's commitment to its Islamic students. "We cannot tolerate any failure to respect individuals as individuals," he said. His expression of concern was typical of other college and university officials throughout the United States.
- In early 2014, Jews and Muslims in the Detroit area attended a conference "A Shared Future: Jews and Muslims in Metro Detroit," cosponsored by the Michigan Muslim Community Council and the American Jewish Committee—Detroit region. A survey conducted before the conference found high levels of interest among members of each group to learn about the other community's practices and customs and also demonstrated an eagerness to engage in joint activities (Building a shared future, 2014).

In addition, local synagogues, churches, and community groups around the country demonstrated their concern in a variety of interreligious activities, congregational visits, and local programs.

Although the press seemed to publicize—and, some would argue, exaggerate—the extent of anti-Muslim hate crimes, some Muslim Americans criticized their coreligionists for wrapping themselves in the "mantle of victimhood." In an open letter to his fellow Muslims, M.A. Muqtedar Khan criticized the attitudes of many of his coreligionists. Writing in the electronic journal Salon.com, the Adrian College (Michigan) professor wrote: "Muslims love to live in the U.S. but also love to hate it. As an Indian Muslim, I know for sure that nowhere on earth, including India, will I get the same sense of dignity and respect that I have received in the U.S. . . . In many places hundreds of Americans have gathered around Islamic centers in symbolic gestures of protection and embrace of American Muslims. In patience and in tolerance ordinary Americans have demonstrated their extraordinary virtues" (Khan 2001).

Similar sentiments have been expressed by a growing number of Muslim and Arab Americans on the Internet and in newspaper and magazine articles. The founding of the American Islamic Congress (AIC) raises hopes for better mutual understanding among Muslims and other Americans. The AIC explicitly notes its dual concerns: "We must work to guarantee our equal rights and prevent hate crimes. At the same time, we must condemn hate speech and calls for violence by Muslims. Hateful statements and actions by fellow Muslims threaten the reputation of our entire community. We must censure intolerance, whatever its source."

Islamophobia and Muslim Self-criticism

Like many minority groups, Arabs and Muslim Americans have been the victims of hate crimes.

But David J. Rusin, a fellow at the Middle East Forum, believes that despite Islamist attacks against the U.S. Muslims are not disproportionately victimized. He notes that the past decade (2002–2011), the FBI recorded hate 1,388 incidents against Muslims during this span, compared with 25,130 against blacks, 12,030 against homosexuals and bisexuals, 9,198 against Jews, and 5,057 against Hispanics. Even majority whites endured 7,185 incidents, while Christians (Protestants and Catholics combined) were targeted in 1,126 incidents. Adherents of "other religions" faced 1,335, very close to the anti-Muslim tally.

His analysis asserts that, despite several major terrorist attacks committed by American-based jihadis—from 9/11 to Fort Hood to the Boston bombing—"the statistics show that 'Islamophobia' has not become a part of American culture" (Rusin, 2013).

Abdur-Rahman Muhammad, a former member of the International Institute of Islamic Thought (IIIT), a U.S. Muslim Brotherhood front, recalls being at a group meeting in the early 1990s where the idea was proposed to use "Islamophobia" as a political weapon. Of the use of the word, Muhammad later said, "This loathsome term is nothing more than a thought-terminating cliche conceived in the bowels of Muslim think tanks for the purpose of beating down critics" (Clarion Project, 2015).

Nevertheless, many American Muslims claim that in their daily life, they are subject to suspicion, social ostracism and fear.

Native Americans

According to hate crimes expert Barbara Perry, there is an "absence of concrete data on hate crimes against Native Americans. There is no Native American equivalent to the annual audits of anti-Semitic violence or anti-gay violence published by the Anti-Defamation League and the National Gay and Lesbian Task Force." She notes that even though there is an extensive literature on the contemporary "victimization of American Indians as nations," there is little narrative material on racially motivated violence against individual Native Americans (Perry, 2008, 2).

According to the latest FBI hate crime statistics for 2013, only 4.5 percent of racially biased crime incidents that year were committed against American Indians or Alaskan natives; the statistical charts indicate there were 129 incidents with 159 victims. But some critics claim that the relatively small number of reported incidents minimize the problem. As earlier noted, underreporting of hate crimes occurs for a variety of reasons. Some sociologists and Native American scholars claim that "aboriginal peoples" are reluctant to report these crimes because of a hesitancy to engage in confrontation. These analysts also note that police are not often privy to information in a culture that "values informal community control" and "conciliation over retribution" (Perry, 2008, 3). But the much larger issue, according to Barbara Perry, are the lingering effects of the colonization of Native Americans since the arrival of Europeans in their land several centuries ago, resulting in their segregation in tribal areas. Sadly, the centuries-old discrimination and violence committed against them still has current resonance. In her book, she discusses the research and interviews conducted by her staff in tribal communities in Arizona, Montana, and Wisconsin and broadens the discussion about hate crimes by providing an historical and contemporary analysis on the plight of Native Americans (and also aboriginal peoples in Canada), not easily quantified by official U.S. government crime statistics.

Conclusion

The enactment of hate crime legislation in the 1990s and in the subsequent decades can be viewed as a continuation of the laws Congress mandated during the civil rights era. While that legislation was primarily enacted to protect the civil and legal rights of African Americans, hate crime laws have greatly expanded some protections to many other minorities: Jews, gays and lesbians, Asian Americans, Sikhs, Arabs, Muslims, among other groups. Minority groups have applauded these laws, which expand their sense of security in a pluralistic society and uphold the ideals of an open and tolerant society so many Americans cherish.

The passage of hate crime laws has provoked a long and vigorous debate, both philosophical and constitutional among proponents and opponents. The critics of these laws—who have expressed these unpopular opinions—merit our respect for raising important legal and social issues about the complex nature of a democracy and the need to ensure legal safeguards for all citizens, even those with reprehensible views. While some may not understand how these critics can oppose such laws, their commitment to a just and tolerant society should never be questioned—they passionately feel that a different approach is needed to deal with the festering problem of hate crimes.

By and large, though, the supporters of hate crime laws have decisively won the debate: more than two decades of legislative action and judicial decisions have established these laws as part of the American legal corpus. Although a few states still haven't passed hate crime statutes, the prevailing trend throughout the nation indicates that every state will offer these protections in the coming years.

While the debate about the constitutionality of these laws may have been settled, a few practical problems still remain: questions about the accuracy of hate crime statistics and the methodology of their collection. The Hate Crime Statistics Act authorized the FBI to collect statistics and publish an annual publication tallying their findings. This federal government document is now widely considered the preeminent source for assessing the extent of hate crime incidents throughout the country. Yet a few civil rights and ethnic groups have pointed out in detail serious problems with these statistics, claiming they are inadequately collected and thus underreport incidents on this disturbing topic that demands much greater national concern. Some groups—especially the ADL and the

NCAVP—compile their own reports, which frequently tally many more hate crime incidents than found in the FBI annual publication. Some analysts hope that these discrepancies might be bridged in coming years by increased cooperation with the FBI since these and other groups have expended much time and expense to gather, in their view, the most accurate statistics.

Hate crime expert Phyllis Gerstenfeld once raised a critical question about the meaning of the term to the American public: "hate crimes seem to be a topic of some interest to nearly everybody, and yet few people really know much about them" (Gerstenfeld, 2004, xv). She notes that many Americans adopt a "more literal interpretation of the term" based on widely publicized violent and extreme incidents. But some social scientists see hate crime as a social construct and engage in theoretical discussions about the nature of these incidents in a complex society. These different approaches don't necessarily converge, sometimes confusing the public and possibly exasperating academics who see no easy long-term solutions to dealing with these troubling crimes.

Since the terrorist attack on the United States on September 11, 2001, many Americans have become understandably fearful for their personal safety and security. But some minority groups in the country are worried because they feel unjustly blamed for these horrifying terrorist actions. Indeed, these attacks have provoked an increase in hate crimes, directed against Arabs and Muslims but especially among Sikhs, who are often erroneously perceived as Muslims because of their clothing.

The literature on the backlash against these minority groups, especially some of the published analyses, is very extensive. But sometimes the extent and breadth of these incidents have been exaggerated by some academics and journalists, inadvertently diminishing the disturbing nature of these crimes by using alarmist rhetoric and hyperbole. Indeed some of this literature that has appeared in respectable journals and books may make future readers—who were born after the September 11 attack—think that these backlash crimes were as bad—if not worse—than the terrorist attack which claimed the lives of almost 3,000 people. Nevertheless, serious crimes were committed against some Arab and Muslim Americans in the wake of the 9/11 terrorist attacks and it is important that these crimes be placed in a soberly discussed historical context.

The perpetrators of hate crimes are often perceived as being young white tattooed males—who look like or are skinheads—and commit violent crimes against African Americans, Jews, Hispanics, gays and lesbians, or other vulnerable minority groups. While this description has been accurate, it is only partially true. A perusal of the "Chronology" chapter demonstrates that many perpetrators of hate crimes are not always white: African Americans have assaulted gays and lesbians; Hispanics have committed hate crimes against Asian Americans; Muslim Americans have assaulted Jews and vandalized synagogues. The FBI aggregate statistics on hate crimes provide ample documentation of the diverse background of the offenders. As America becomes an increasingly multicultural society, hate crime perpetrators will invariably reflect the demographic diversity of the country. While one would hope that minority group members would be more sensitive given their historical vulnerability, it is important to note that they also perpetrate hate crimes. Nevertheless, we should be pleased that few women commit these crimes so full gender representation, is not at least in this case, always a desirable goal.

The festering problem of racism, anti-Semitism, and other forms of bigotry offers no easy legal solution. However, hate crime laws and severe criminal sentencing have certainly helped many victims and have presumably aided the safety and welfare of many communities. When a youth involved in an anti-Jewish crime is sentenced to serve time in prison, or the inciters of skinhead violence against African Americans are forced to pay restitution to the families of victims, or antigay felons are fully prosecuted for their crimes, violent bigots and their ilk are made aware that their hate-motivated criminal actions will have punitive consequences. This type of legislation is only about two decades old, so it is still too soon to assess its ultimate impact or success on U.S. society. Nevertheless, many human rights professionals agree with law enforcement officials that these federal and state laws are a useful and important measures in the long-term battle against hate crimes. Nevertheless, few proponents of hate crime legislation believe that these statutes will eradicate the growing problem of hate-motivated violence in the United States.

References

ADL Web site. 2015. http://www.adl.org.

ADL Audit. 2014. Anti-Semitic Incidents Declined 19 Percent across the United States in 2013. http://www.adl .org/press-center/press-releases/anti-semitism-usa/adl-audit-anti-semitic-incidents-2013.html.

ADL Blog. 2014. Some Anti-Semitism in U.S. in Reaction to Israeli Operations in Gaza. July 29. http://blog.adl.org/ international/some-anti-semitism-in-u-s-in-reaction-to-israeli-operations-in-gaza.

American Turban. 2011. California Senate President Darrell Steinberg. http://americanturban.com/2011/04/11/picture-of-the-day-california-senate-president-darrell-steinberg/

Asian Americans Advancing Justice. 2014. AAJC Testimony: U.S. Senate Judiciary Committee Hearing on "The State of Civil and Human Rights in the United States." http://www .advancingequality.org/news-media/publications/advancing-justice-aajc-testimony-us-senate-judiciary-committee-hearing-state.

Asian Week. 2001. "Hate Crime Charged in Death of Thung Phetakoune." August 17–23. http://www.asianweek.com/ 2001_08_17/news_deathhate.html.

Bekiempis, Victoria. 2014. "FBI Hate Crime Statistics: Are Bias Offenses Really on the Decline?" Newsweek online, December 9. http://www.newsweek.com/fbi-hate-crime-statistics-are-bias-offenses-really-decline-290023.

Belkin, Lisa. 1988. "Texas Judge Eases Sentence for Killer of 2 Homosexuals." *New York Times*, December 17, 8.

Boston Globe. 2001. "Jews, Muslims Finding Healing of Rifts." September 20.

"Building a Shared Future." 2014. http://www.umdilabs.com/sites/default/files/Final%20AJC%20Report.pdf.

Burton, Summer Anne. 2012. A Tragic History of Hate Crimes against Sikhs in the U.S. http://www.buzzfeed.com/summeranne/a-tragic-history-of-hate-crimes-against-sikhs-in-t#.jqDbkqPan.

California Attorney General. 2001. Reporting Hate Crimes. http://oag.ca.gov/sites/all/files/agweb/pdfs/publications/civilrights/reportingHC.pdf.

Clarion Project. 2015. http://www.clarionproject.org/content/abdur-rahman-muhammad.

Dinnerstein, Leonard. 1971. *Anti-Semitism in the United States*. New York: Holt, Rinehart and Winston.

FBI. 2014. Uniform Crime Report: *Hate Crime Statistics 2013*.

Fumento, Michael. 1996. "A Church Arson Epidemic? It's Smoke and Mirrors." *Wall Street Journal*, July 8.

Gellman, Susan. 1991. "Sticks and Stones Can Put You in Jail, but Can Words Increase Your Sentence? Constitutional and Policy Dilemmas of Ethnic Intimidation Laws." *UCLA Law Review* (December): 333–396.

Gellman, Susan B. and Lawrence, Frederick M. 2004. "Agreeing to Agree: A Proponent and Opponent of Hate Crime Laws Reach for Common Ground." *Harvard Journal on Legislation*, 41, No. 2 (Summer): 421–448.

Gerstenfeld, Phyllis. 2011. *Hate Crimes: Causes, Controls and Controversies*. Thousand Oaks, CA: Sage Publications.

GLAAD. 2015. "Transgender 101." http://www.glaad.org/transgender/trans101.

Greenawalt, Kent. 1992–1993. "Reflections on Justifications for Defining Crimes by the Category of Victim," pp. 617–628. In *Annual Survey of American Law*. New York: New York University School of Law.

Haas, S.M., Nolan, J.J., Turley, E., and Stump, J. 2011. *Assessing the Validity of Hate Crime Reporting: An Analysis of NIBRS Data*, July. Charleston, WV: Criminal Justice Statistical Analysis Center, Office of Research and Strategic Planning, Division of Justice and Community Services. www.djcs.wv.gov/SAC.

Herek, Gregory M., and Berrill, Kevin, eds. 1992. *Hate Crimes: Confronting Violence against Lesbians and Gay Men*. Newbury Park, CA: Sage Publications.

Holden, Dominic. 2014. "FBI Understates Hate-Motivated Attacks on Transgender People." http://www.buzzfeed.com/dominicholden/new-fbi-report-vastly-underrepresents-anti-transgender-hate#.yuwAXW1Nj.

HRC Blog. 2014. "For the First Time, FBI Reports on Hate Crimes Based on Gender Identity." http://www.hrc.org/blog/entry/for-the-first-time-fbi-reports-on-hate-crimes-based-on-gender-identity.

Human Rights Watch. November 2002. "We Are Not the Enemy: Hate Crimes against Arabs and Muslims and Those Perceived to Be Arabs and Muslims." http://www.hrw.org.

Jacobs, James B., and Potter, Kimberly A. 1997. "Hate Crimes: A Critical Perspective," pp. 1–50. In *Crime and Justice: A Review of Research 22*, edited by Michael Tonry. Chicago: University of Chicago Press.

Jenness, Valerie, and Broad, Kendal. 1997. *Hate Crimes: New Social Movements and the Politics of Violence*. New York: Aldine de Gruyter.

Jewish Exponent. 2014. "Jewish Student Assaulted at Temple University," August 21.

Khan, M.A. Muqtedar. 2001. "A Memo to American Muslims," October 18. http://www.philosophy-religion.org/world/a-memo.htm.

Kibelstis, Teresa Eileen. 1995. "Preventing Violence against Gay Men and Lesbians: Should Enhanced Penalties at Sentencing Extend to Bias Crimes Based on Victims' Sexual Orientation?" *Notre Dame Journal of Law, Politics and Public Policy*, 9, no. 1: 309–343.

Lawrence, Frederick M. 1999. *Punishing Hate: Bias Crimes under American Law*. Cambridge, MA: Harvard University Press.

Lawrence, Frederick. 2002. "Hate Crimes," pp. 774–778. In *Encyclopedia of Crime and Justice*, 2nd ed., edited by Joshua Dressler. New York: Macmillan Reference USA.

Louis D. Brandeis Center. 2014. Worst Campus Anti-Semitic Incidents of 2013–2014. http://brandeiscenter.com/blog/the-worst-campus-anti-semitic-incidents-of-2013–2014.

Leadership Conference. 2002. http://www.civilrights.org/hatecrimes/united-states/new-report-documents-increased-hate-crimes-and-intolerance.html.

Leadership Conference. 2009. "Hate Crimes against Asian Pacific Americans." http://www.civilrights.org/publications/hatecrimes/asian-pacific.html.

Leadership Conference. 2014. "FBI Report Indicates Decrease in Hate Crimes." December 11. http://www.civilrights.org/archives/2014/1482-hate-crimes-report.html.

Los Angeles Times. 2013. "Feds Charge 5 with Hate Crimes for Allegedly Imprisoning Disabled." http://articles.latimes.com/2013/jan/23/nation/la-na-nn-feds-charge-5-with-hate-crimes-for-imprisoning-disabled—20130123.

McMahon, B. T., West, S. L., Lewis, A. N., Armstrong, A. J., and Conway, J. P. 2004. "Hate Crimes and Disability in America." *Rehabilitation Counseling Bulletin*, 47: 66–75.

Merevick, Tony. 2014. "A Year Later, 'Nothing' Has Changed Since Transgender Woman Islan Nettles Was Killed." *BuzzFeed LGBT*. http://www.buzzfeed.com/tonymerevick/a-timeline-of-violence-agianst-transgender-people-in-the-us#.neMPo31DD.

NCAVP. 2014. Media Release: National Report on Hate Violence against Lesbian, Gay, Bisexual, Transgender, Queer and HIV-Affected Communities. http://www.avp.org/storage/documents/2013_mr_ncavp_hvreport.pdf.

New York Times. 1994. "Hasidic Gunshot Victim Crosses a Personal Bridge: City Gunshot Victim Crosses a Personal Bridge." October 20.

Perry, Barbara. 2008. *Silent Victims: Hate Crimes against Native Americans* Tucson: University of Arizona Press.

Perry, Barbara. 2009. "Hate Crimes Committed against Persons with Disabilities," pp. 173–197. In *Hate Crimes: The Victims of Hate Crimes*, vol. 3. Westport, CT: Praeger.

Potok, Mark. 2013. "DOJ Study: More Than 250,000 Hate Crimes a Year, Most Unreported." *HateWatch.* http://www.splcenter.org/blog/2013/03/26/doj-study-more-than-250000-hate-crimes-a-year-a-third-never-reported/

Rusin, David. J. 2013. "Hate-Crime Stats Deflate 'Islamophobia' Myth." http://www.nationalreview.com/articles/337417/hate-crime-stats-deflate-islamophobia-myth-david-j-rusin.

SALDEF. 2013. Turban Myths: The Opportunities and Challenges for Reframing Sikh American Identity in Post-9/11 America. http://saldef.org/policy-research/turban-myths/#.VLQqEKNWYSF.

Seattlepi. 2002. "Man Sentenced to 6 Years for Attack on Mosque." http://www.seattlepi.com/news/article/Man-sentenced-to-6-years-for-attack-at-mosque-1103400.php.

Sherry, Mark. 2010. *Disability Hate Crimes: Does Anyone Really Hate Disabled People?* Burlington, VT: Ashgate Publishing.

Trends in Hate. http://www.trendsinhate.com/dateinhate.html

United States Department of Justice. December 2014. Federal Bureau of Investigation. Hate Crime Statistics, 2013. http://www.fbi.gov/about-us/cjis/ucr/hate-crime/2013/resource-pages/about-hate-crime.

United States Department of Justice. 1998. National Church Arson Task Force. Second Year Report for the President. http://www.justice.gov/crt/church_arson/arson98.php.

United States Department of Justice. 2014. Former Klansman Pleads Guilty to Federal Hate Crime for Cross Burning. September 30. http://www.justice.gov/opa/pr/former-klansman-pleads-guilty-federal-hate-crime-cross-burning.

United States Department of Justice. 2014. Four Mississippi Men and Women Indicted for Racially Motivated Hate Crimes Spree in Jackson, Mississippi, July 16. http://www.justice.gov/opa/pr/four-mississippi-men-and-women-indicted-racially-motivated-hate-crimes-spree-jackson.

U.S. Department of Transportation. 2001. Carrying Out Transportation Inspection and Safety Responsibilities in a Nondiscriminatory Manner. http://airconsumer.ost.dot.gov/rules/20011012.htm.

USA Today. 1996. "Why Are Churches Burning?" June 28–30. (See other articles on church burning in these three issues.)

Winer, Anthony S. 1994. "Hate Crimes, Homosexuals and the Constitution." *Harvard Civil Rights Civil Liberties Review* (Summer): 387–438.

Like many current issues, the topic of hate crimes draws a wide range of opinions ranging from the philosophical, legal, and ideological, to name only a few. This section includes essays offering a variety of viewpoints: some essays cover material in the text but offer a specific viewpoint; other pieces discuss topics not directly addressed in the book.

The first essay, written by *Boston Globe* columnist Jeff Jacoby, questions the need for hate crime legislation. He believes that current laws already address these types of crime and that the "best hate-crimes law is none at all." In stark contrast, Michael Lieberman, the Washington counsel of the Anti-Defamation League, explains the legal and criminological justification for hate crime legislation.

The next essays explain the impact of hate crimes on particular communities. Ken Marcus, the president of the Louis D. Brandeis Center for Human Rights Under Law, discusses some incidents on college campuses where Jewish students were subjected to hatred, hostility, and, in a few instances, violence. When Mr. Marcus served as the assistant director of education for civil rights, he helped expand the mandate to protect the rights of Jews and other religious minorities. But other agency administrators were

---

On August 6, 2012, the day after a racist gunman killed six Sikh worshipers at the Sikh temple (gurdwara), the local Sikh community gathered for a candle light vigil in Brookfield, Wisconsin. Religious groups throughout the country and government leaders including President Obama condemned this terrible massacre. (AP Photo/M. Spencer Green)

either "unsteady" in their enforcement or else misunderstood the nature of these crimes. Although Sikhs constitute a tiny religious minority in the United States, they have suffered a disproportionate amount of hate crime violence. Simran Jeet Singh, assistant professor in the Department of Religion at Trinity University and the senior religion fellow for the Sikh Coalition, explains that it is a popular misconception that every attack against a Sikh American was committed because of their "apparent Muslim" appearance. He argues that the "deep history of xenophobia in the U.S. overlooks the fact that Sikhs are attacked precisely of who they are." Although the news media often covers the discrimination against undocumented individuals from mostly Spanish-speaking countries, three professors (Michele Stacey, Kristin Carbone-Lopez, and Richard Rosenthal) raise a seldom-asked question: "To what extent is ant-Hispanic hate crime related to patterns of Hispanic immigration to the United States?" The FBI annual hate crime statistics publication invariably lists lesbian, gay, bisexual, lesbian (LGBT) individuals as one of the most vulnerable groups in the United States, which is why gay rights groups are usually in the forefront of supporting hate crime legislation. But Harvard professor and longtime gay rights historian Michael Bronski raises some doubts about the efficacy of these laws. He notes that Matthew Shepard's murderers are serving two consecutive life sentences without the possibility of parole in Wyoming, which doesn't even have any hate crime statutes; Bronski also believes that hate crime laws are "based on emotion, not logic."

Finally, Ashley Thorne, the executive director of the National Association of Scholars, has written a provocative essay detailing hate crime hoaxes on college campuses in recent years. She believes that these documented incidents of crying wolf "erode the credibility of real wrongdoing."

Punish Crime, Not Thought Crime

Jeff Jacoby

When President Barack Obama signed the Matthew Shepard and James Byrd Jr. Hate Crimes Prevention Act in October

2009, he hailed it as "another step forward" on America's "journey towards a more perfect union" (Obama, 2009). In reality, it was just the opposite. For like all such laws, the measure signed by the president prevents not hatred, but fairness. Every criminal code punishes bad deeds; hate-crime statutes punish bad *opinions*. However well-intentioned, that is something no liberal democracy should tolerate.

The law was named for the victims in two of the most notorious murders of the 1990s. Matthew Shepard was a gay student at the University of Wyoming who was lured from a bar in Laramie by two acquaintances on the night of October 6, 1998 (Gumbel, 2013). They drove him to a remote spot out of town, pistol-whipped him to a bloody pulp, then tied him to a fence, and left him to die.

Four months earlier, three white supremacists in Jasper, Texas, had lynched James Byrd Jr., a middle-aged black man. It was a ghastly killing: The victim was stripped, chained by his ankles to the back of a pickup truck, and dragged along an asphalt road until he was decapitated. Byrd's shredded body parts stretched along a grisly, miles-long trail ("3 whites . . .", 1998).

The atrocities in Jasper and Laramie set off a vehement national outcry for the passage of stronger legislation to deter "hate crimes"—acts of violence motivated by bigotry, racism, or intolerance. Hate-crime laws, which increase the punishment for offenses fueled by bias, were already on the books in 41 states by 1998. But because Texas and Wyoming were among the few holdouts, Democrats (and a few Republicans) in Congress and the White House insisted it was imperative to enact a federal law.

"Crimes that are motivated by hate really are fundamentally different and I believe should be treated differently under the law," contended the then president Bill Clinton after meeting with members of Byrd's family ("Senate passes . . . ", 2000). Massachusetts Senator Ted Kennedy, the chief sponsor of a measure that would add new categories of hate crimes to the federal code, declared that if the bill were passed, "we'd have fewer hate crimes in all the days that follow" ("Mother of . . .," 1999).

The punishment meted out to Shepard's and Byrd's murderers could hardly have been stronger: Two received the death penalty, and the others were sentenced to life imprisonment with no possibility of parole. In any event, hate-crime laws were being widely enforced by the late 1990s. Not only had the great majority of states adopted such measures, but the federal government had as well. In 1988, Congress had passed the Hate Crimes Statistics Act. That was followed in 1994 by the Hate Crimes Sentencing Enhancement Act and the Violence Against Women Act, then by the Church Arson Prevention Act in 1996. The measure named for Shepard and Byrd, eventually passed during the Obama administration, broadened the federal government's reach still further, enlarging the power of U.S. attorneys to prosecute attacks based on race, religion, national origin, gender, sexual orientation, or disability.

For all their popularity, though, hate-crime statutes advance no legitimate criminal justice end. The laws serve a symbolic function, not a practical one—they proclaim that crimes inspired by certain types of bigotry are particularly wicked, and deserve to be punished with particular harshness. But that is tantamount to proclaiming that the exact same crimes, if spurred by bigotry against *other* groups, or by motives having nothing to do with bias at all, wouldn't be so terrible. Is that a message any decent society should wish to promote?

Bias crimes are said to be uniquely toxic because they target and terrorize both individuals and groups. "Hate violence is very personal," writes Wade Henderson, the president of the Leadership Conference on Civil and Human Rights, "with an especially emotional and psychological impact on the victim—and the victim's community" (Henderson, 2012). The Anti-Defamation League argues that a "priority response" is justified for hate crimes because they "may effectively intimidate other members of the victim's community, leaving them feeling isolated, vulnerable, and unprotected by the law. . . . These incidents can damage the fabric of our society and fragment communities" (Anti-Defamation League, 2012).

But isn't that true of all violent crime? Doesn't every murder, every rape, every armed robbery, every bombing intimidate or frighten more people than just the immediate victim?

When a child is abducted and killed, or a jogger is gang raped by "wilding" predators, or elderly bank customers are mugged outside an automated teller machine (ATM), entire neighborhoods or groups are apt to be rocked by panic and dread. It is hard to see the logic of demanding harsher penalties for crimes that inflict "an especially emotional and psychological impact" on, say, African Americans, gays, or Muslims, while refusing to demand the same penalties for attacks that have the same effect on senior citizens, or joggers, or young parents.

There is no evading the double standard: By definition, a law that cracks down harder on offenses that hurt members of certain groups signals simultaneously that hurting members of other groups isn't as bad. That is immoral and indefensible.

The lynching of James Byrd by three white bigots was unspeakable. Wouldn't it have been just as unspeakable had the killers been black? It should have made no difference to the law—or to the media, or to the political class—whether the monsters who murdered Byrd were motivated by racism, by a personal grudge, or by greed for his money. The blood of a man assaulted by bigots is no redder than that of a man attacked by ruthless thieves or thrill-seeking sadists. The grief of his loved ones is the same either way. So is the threat to society. A legal system that upholds the principle of "equal justice under law"—the very words are engraved over the door to the U.S. Supreme Court—must not have rules that make some victims of hatred more equal than others.

In fact, the law has no business intensifying the punishment for violent crimes motivated by bigotry at all. Murderers or arsonists or terrorists should be prosecuted and punished with equal vehemence regardless of their agenda. It is not a criminal's evil thoughts that society has a right to avenge, only his evil acts. Advocates of hate-crime laws maintain that what is being punished isn't the ugly state of mind, but the crime it led to. But that argument doesn't wash. When the judge has you thrown in prison for an extra 10 years because the crime you committed was influenced by your opinion of the victim, the inescapable conclusion is that your opinion has been criminalized.

That is "thought crime," in George Orwell's chilling phrase. And if big brother can penalize you today for your inappropriate thoughts about Jews, Asians, or lesbians, it is only matter of time until you can be penalized for having impermissible thoughts about anything else.

The best hate-crimes law is none at all. But if we are going to have such laws, let's not restrict them to only six or eight categories of victims. Lawmakers should expand their scope to cover every crime of violence—regardless of the attacker's motive, or of the group to which the victim(s) belong. Let us learn to treat every murder, rape, and brutal assault as a crime of "hate"—not the criminal's hate for his victim, but society's hate for the crime.

References

"3 Whites Indicted in Dragging Death of Black Man in Texas," CNN.com, July 6, 1998. Available at http://edition.cnn.com/US/9807/06/dragging.death.02/.

Anti-Defamation League. "Hate Crimes Law: the ADL Approach," 2012. Available at http://www.adl.org/combating-hate/hate-crimes-law/c/adl-approach-hate-crimes-laws.html.

Gumbel, Andrew. Matthew Shepard's Murder: "What It Came Down to Is Drugs and Money," *The Guardian*, October 14, 2013. Available at http://www.theguardian.com/world/2013/oct/14/matthew-shepard-murder-wyoming-book.

Henderson, Wade. "Bias Laws Ensure Action against Hate," *New York Times*, March 7, 2012. Available at

http://www.nytimes.com/roomfordebate/2012/03/07/
are-hate-crime-laws-necessary/bias-laws-ensure-actio
n-against-hate.

"Mother of Slain Student Pleads for Hate Crime Bill," CNN.
com, May 11, 1999. Available at http://www.cnn.com/
US/9905/11/hate.crimes/.

Obama, Barack. Remarks by the President at Reception
Commemorating the Enactment of the Matthew
Shephard and James Byrd Hate Crimes Prevention Act.
October 28, 2009. Available at http://www.whitehouse.
gov/the-press-office/remarks-president-reception-comm
emorating-enactment-matthew-shepard-and-james-byrd-.

"Senate Passes Hate Crimes Legislation; Prosecutors
Revisiting Murders of Chaney, Goodman, and Schwerner,"
CNN.com, June 20, 2000. Available at http://transcripts.
cnn.com/TRANSCRIPTS/0006/20/wt.07.html.

Jeff Jacoby is a columnist for The Boston Globe.

The Law vs. Violent Bigotry: The Case for Strong Hate Crime Laws in the United States

Michael Lieberman

All Americans have a stake in effective response to violent bigotry. Bias crimes have special impact; they are designed to intimidate the victim and members of the victim's community, leaving them feeling fearful, isolated, vulnerable, and unprotected by the law. Failure to address this unique type of crime often causes an isolated incident to explode into widespread community tension. The damage done by hate crimes, therefore, cannot be measured solely in terms of physical injury or dollars and cents. By making members of minority communities fearful, angry, and suspicious of other groups—and of the power structure that is supposed to protect them—these incidents can damage the fabric of our society and fragment communities.

Punishing Bias-Motivated Violence: The Policy Frame for Hate-Crime Laws

Criminal activity motivated by bias is distinct and different from other criminal conduct.

First, these crimes occur because of the perpetrator's bias or animus against the victim—the victim's race, religion, national origin, gender, gender identity, sexual orientation, or disability is the reason for the crime. One dramatic example of this phenomenon is the murder of Marcelo Lucero, a 37-year-old Ecuadoran immigrant who was killed in November 2008 in Patchogue, New York. According to the testimony of one of the Long Island teenagers who pleaded guilty to second-degree attempted assault as a hate crime, and other charges, several bored teenagers decided to go "beaner hopping"—a periodic practice in which they hunted Hispanics to beat up for sport. They had allegedly already shot at a Hispanic man on his porch with a BB gun and harassed another Hispanic man on a bike when they came across two Hispanic men near the Patchogue train station. The teenagers taunted the two with racist names and picked a fight. During the fight, Lucero was knifed. He subsequently died. His murderers were successfully prosecuted under federal hate crime laws.

Second, hate crimes have a very special emotional and psychological impact on the victim—and the victim's community. Few individual crimes can spark riots, but bias-motivated crimes can. Civic leaders and police officials have come to recognize that strong enforcement of these laws can have a deterrent impact and can limit the potential for a hate crime incident to explode into a cycle of violence and widespread community disturbances.

The FBI and law enforcement officials recognize the special impact of hate crimes. The FBI has been the nation's repository for crime statistics since 1930. It publishes an annual encyclopedic report called *Crime in the United States*. Every year, the FBI disaggregates that data and publishes just two other reports on crime issues that it believes have a dramatic impact on Americans. One report is focused on law enforcement officers killed and assaulted in the line of duty—and the other is about hate crimes in America. The FBI has been collecting this data, under the Hate Crime Statistics Act (HCSA), from state and local police since 1990. The most recent data, for 2013, documented that 1,826 police agencies reported about 5,900 hate crimes, which is almost one hate crime every ninety minutes of every day. Race-based hate crimes were most frequent, second were crimes based on sexual orientation, and third most frequent were crimes based on religious biases. This year, as in the past, more than 60 percent of the religious based-crimes were directed against Jews and Jewish institutions.

Third, hate crimes are message crimes. Gay men beaten outside of a gay bar are rarely robbed. Vandals do not often spray-paint messages like "Jane Loves Bobby" on the side of synagogues; it is much more frequently defacement featuring anti-Jewish threats or a swastika. And bigots do not burn parallelograms on the front lawns of African American families who have just moved into a previously all-white neighborhood. The message of a burning parallelogram might be misunderstood. But not the remains of a burned cross.

As Supreme Court Justice Sandra Day O'Connor wrote in a 2003 case involving a First Amendment challenge to the Commonwealth of Virginia's cross-burning statute:

> the burning cross often serves as a message of intimidation, designed to inspire in the victim a fear of bodily harm. Moreover, the history of violence associated with the Klan shows that the possibility of injury or death is not just hypothetical . . . when a cross burning is used to intimidate, few if any messages are more powerful. (*Virginia v. Black*, 538U.S.343, 357 [2003])

Finally, these laws demonstrate our society's commitment to fight discrimination. Hate-crime laws are a criminal justice system parallel to antidiscrimination civil rights laws. Under our nation's workplace civil rights laws, for example, an employer can refuse to hire, fire, or fail to promote employees for virtually any reason. It is only when that decision is made "by reason of" race, religion, national origin, gender, or disability (and in too-few state and local jurisdictions, sexual orientation and gender identity) that the conduct becomes unlawful.

The Constitutional Frame for Hate-Crime Laws: First Amendment Protections

Hate-crime statutes—federal criminal civil rights statutes and laws now on the books in 45 states and the District of Columbia—do not punish speech or thoughts. The First Amendment does not protect violence, nor does it prevent the government from imposing criminal penalties for violent discriminatory conduct. Americans are free to think, preach, and believe whatever they want. It is only when an individual commits a crime based on those biased beliefs and intentionally targets another for violence or vandalism that a hate crime statute can be triggered.

Over the years, federal and state hate crime laws have been upheld against a variety of challenges under the Fourteenth Amendment's Equal Protection Clause and Due Process Clause, and under the First Amendment. The most important case, *Wisconsin v. Mitchell* (508 U.S. 476 (1993)), involved a challenge to Wisconsin's penalty-enhancement hate crime statute, under which Mitchell had received an enhanced sentence for having instigated a vicious racial assault by a group of young black men against a white youth in Kenosha, Wisconsin. The United State Supreme Court unanimously upheld the Wisconsin hate crime law, stating that it was intended to address conduct that the Wisconsin legislature thought would "inflict greater individual and societal harm."

Expanding Federal Hate-Crime Protection: The Matthew Shepard and James Byrd Jr. Hate Crimes Prevention Act (HCPA)

Enacted in October, 2009, the HCPA (Public Law 111-84) provides new tools to combat violent hate crimes and encourages federal–state partnerships to investigate and prosecute them. In the five years since the HCPA passed, the Department of Justice has brought over two dozen hate-crime cases and has successfully defended the constitutionality of the Act against several challenges. Thousands of law enforcement officials have undergone training, and new hate-crime prevention resources have been developed. In addition, following the August, 2012 murder of six Sikh worshippers at their *gurdwara* in Oak Creek, Wisconsin, civil rights groups successfully lobbied for expanded categories of hate crimes to be collected by the FBI, including hate crimes against Sikhs, Arabs, and Hindus.

Yet there is still much work to be done. Five states have no hate crimes law, and too many states do not protect all victims of hate violence. We should have no delusions about hate-crime laws. Bigotry, racism, homophobia, and anti-Semitism cannot be legislated out of existence. The law is, in fact, a blunt instrument; it is much better to prevent these crimes from happening in the first place.

But when these crimes do occur, we must send an unmistakable message that our society takes them very seriously. Hate-crime laws demonstrate an important commitment to confront and deter criminal activity motivated by prejudice. Hate violence merits priority attention—and hate crime laws help ensure they receive it.

Michael Lieberman has been the Washington Counsel for the Anti-Defamation League (ADL) since January, 1989 and also serves as director of the League's Civil Rights Policy Planning Center. He led the broad coalition of civil rights, religious, law enforcement, educational, and professional organizations in Washington that worked for 13 years to secure passage of the Matthew

Shepard and James Byrd Jr. Hate Crimes Prevention Act—and is now working closely with Justice Department and FBI officials to educate about the Act and implement it.

Since 1913, the mission of ADL has been to "stop the defamation of the Jewish people and to secure justice and fair treatment to all." Over the past three decades, the League has been recognized as a leading resource on effective responses to violent bigotry, conducting an annual Audit of Anti-Semitic Incidents, *and drafting model hate crime statutes for state legislatures. ADL led the broad coalition of civil rights, religious, educational, professional, law enforcement, and civic organizations that worked in support of the Matthew Shepard and James Byrd Jr. Hate Crimes Prevention Act (HCPA) for more than a decade.*

Contemporary Anti-Semitism in American Higher Education

Kenneth L. Marcus

Although Jewish Americans today enjoy unprecedented tolerance, some American universities have maintained atmospheres that are hostile toward Jewish students. Research suggests that faculty and student attitudes toward Jewish students are generally favorable. Nevertheless, anti-Semitic incidents have worsened on several campuses since roughly the turn of this century, including assault, battery, vandalism, and hate speech. In 2006, the U.S. Commission on Civil Rights concluded that "[m]any college campuses throughout the United States continue to experience incidents of antisemitism" and that "[t]his is a serious problem which warrants further attention" (U.S. Commission on Civil Rights, 2006).

Prior to 2004, the U.S. Department of Education's Office for Civil Rights had refused to investigate anti-Semitism cases because it lacks jurisdiction over religion. Ten years ago, the U.S. Department of Education's Office for Civil Rights (OCR), under my direction, issued policy guidance to protect the rights of students who are members of groups that exhibit ethnic as well as religious characteristics. The 2004 policy, which clarified provisions of Title VI of the Civil Rights Act of 1964, applied to Jewish and Sikh students, among others. Over the ensuing years, OCR's enforcement of this policy has been unsteady, as agency leaders initially resisted it, then officially embraced it, while often appearing to misunderstand it. In some cases, they balked at the idea of extending Title VI to Jewish students; in others, they have had difficulty distinguishing between anti-Semitism and hostility to Israel; and in still others, they have interpreted challenged conduct as being protected by the First Amendment to the U.S. Constitution.

In 2004, the Zionist Organization of America (ZOA) filed an OCR complaint alleging a hostile environment for Jewish students at the University of California at Irvine. ZOA described rock-throwing, epithets, threats, among others. At my direction, OCR investigated. After my departure, regional officials proposed finding that a hostile environment had existed for Jewish students but that Irvine had responded adequately. OCR headquarters reversed this proposed determination. OCR then issued a decision closing the case. Specifically, OCR dismissed some allegations as untimely filed, including claims that anti-Israel activists destroyed a Holocaust memorial and called Jewish students "dirty Jew," telling at least one to "go back to Russia," and proposing to "slaughter the Jews." OCR conceded that other allegations were timely filed, including intimidation of Jewish students; defacement of an Israel flag on a student's dormitory room door; and allegations of anti-Semitic activities at anti-Israel protests. OCR found that some of these statements were offensive to Jewish students but nevertheless dismissed them on the questionable grounds that they were based on the Jewish students' political views rather than their ethnic identity.

While OCR was investigating *Irvine I*, ZOA provided investigators evidence of more recent incidents. OCR investigated these allegations in a separate case, *Irvine II*. *Irvine II* involved claims that Jewish students were targeted for adverse treatment, or otherwise subjected to a hostile environment, based on their Jewish identity, in nine separate incidents of varying severity. For example, Jewish students argued that a campus event comparing Israel with apartheid South Africa worsened the campus' anti-Jewish atmosphere. OCR countered that such matters are constitutionally protected free speech. A rabbi who attended the event was loudly taunted, "Don't you have somebody's money to steal?" OCR found this statement to be "offensive" but found that it was not, standing on its own, sufficiently serious to constitute a legal violation. This finding was odd, since the allegation was not "standing on its own." Rather, it was included with a myriad of other troubling allegations not only in *Irvine II* but also in the *Irvine I* complaint from which it had been separated. On August 19, 2013, OCR dismissed this case as well.

In 2009, University of California at Santa Cruz (UCSC) lecturer Tammi Rossman-Benjamin complained to OCR that UCSC had created a hostile environment for Jewish students at university-sponsored public events featuring strongly anti-Israel rhetoric. OCR dismissed this case on August 19, 2013, finding that the facts did not warrant finding a violation. OCR held that all of the events amounted to "expression on matters of public concern directed to the University community." He added that "exposure to such rough and discordant expressions, even when personally offensive and hurtful, is a circumstance that a reasonable student in higher education may experience" (UC Berkeley News Center, 2013).

In March 2010, during the so-called Israel Apartheid Week, Jewish undergraduate student Jessica Felber stood in Sproul Plaza at the University of California at Berkeley holding a sign that read, "Israel wants peace." In response, another student allegedly rammed a shopping cart into Felber, causing her physical injuries that required medical attention. Activists conducting a mock checkpoint protest during the so-called Israel Apartheid Week blocked Brian Maissy, a disabled Jewish student, from passage through the Berkeley campus. Felber and Maissy sued in federal court, arguing that Berkeley had tolerated a hostile environment for Jewish students. The court partially dismissed Felber and Maissey's complaint with leave to amend, holding that much of the protesters' activity was protected under the First Amendment. The students later settled their case with Berkeley. The students' lawyers then filed a similar complaint before OCR, repeating their hostile environment allegations. OCR dismissed this case.

In the wake of these cases, it is fair to ask whether OCR remains committed to its 2004 Title VI policy. Meanwhile, incidents are frequently reported at other campuses, such as the recent assault on a Jewish student at Temple University and the taunting of University of Michigan students as "kike" and "dirty Jew." These cases point to three problems. First, OCR needs further guidelines clarifying what constitutes anti-Semitism under its 2004 policy and what does not. Second, OCR should better clarify the relationship between First Amendment freedom of speech protections and its antiharassment regulations. Third, Congress should prohibit religious harassment at federally funded institutions, in order to close a glaring loophole that continues to exist in American civil rights law. Until these changes are made, Jewish students will face legal uncertainty amidst worsening campus climates.

References

UC Berkeley News Center. "Department of Education Dismisses Complaint Alleging Anti-Semitism at Berkeley," August 27, 2013. Available at http://newscenter.berkeley.edu/2013/08/27/doe-dismisses-anti-semitism-complaint/.

U.S. Commission on Civil Rights. "Findings and Recommendations of the United States Commission on Civil Rights Regarding Campus Anti-Semitism," April 3, 2006. Available at http://www.usccr.gov/pubs/050306FRUSCCRRCAS.pdf.

Kenneth L. Marcus is president and general counsel of the Louis D. Brandeis Center for Human Rights Under Law and author of

Jewish Identity and Civil Rights in America *(New York: Cambridge University Press: 2010)*. *Marcus founded the Brandeis Center in 2011 to combat the resurgence of anti-Semitism in American higher education.*

Anti-Hispanic Immigrant Hate Crimes

Michele Stacey, Kristin Carbone-Lopez, and Richard Rosenfeld

Over the course of the past century immigration patterns in the United States have changed. Prior to the 1970s the majority of immigrants came from Western European countries; by 2007, 80 percent of the foreign-born population in the United States originated in Latin American and Asian countries (Grieco, 2009). Along with these changing immigration patterns, there has been an increased concern both in public and political spheres over U.S. immigration policy, and a number of recent changes to those policies have been enacted (for example, SB 1070 in Arizona in 2010). Many of these policies are born out of and act to perpetuate an immigrant-as-threat narrative (Ibrahim, 2005), which portrays immigrants as threatening national security, economic security, and cultural security. To what extent these concerns have filtered down to the individual level remains uncertain. It is possible that the anti-immigrant sentiment that follows increased immigration may contribute to increased intolerance and subsequent violence against immigrant groups, including in the form of hate crime.

In this paper we examine the question of whether recent population changes in immigration patterns are associated with hate crimes against Hispanics. Specifically, we ask: To what extent is anti-Hispanic hate crime related to patterns of Hispanic immigration to the United States? While research on hate crimes has been increasing over the past decade, most studies focus on hate crimes against racial and sexual minorities. Less attention is paid to the role of ethnicity, specifically with regard to Hispanics, many of whom are immigrants. Immigrants, however, are not a protected category in hate crimes, and as such crimes against them are not considered "hate crimes." Therefore, we focus on bias crimes against Hispanics, who are often assumed to be immigrants, and hypothesize that Hispanics may be targeted in response to fear over changing patterns of immigration.

Blalock (1967) proposed a thesis on minority threat, which argues that minority groups pose a threat to the majority group when resources are limited. As the minority population grows in numbers, they compete with the majority for scarce economic and political capital. Group conflict increases as a result, and the majority group will seek to discriminate against the minority in both formal and informal ways. Research examining minority group threat has found evidence of these processes in studies of formal social control (Eitle, D'Alessio, and Stolzenberg, 2002), and recently research on hate crime (a form of informal social control) has shown evidence of similar processes (King, Messner, & Baller, 2009; Perry, 2001). Most of this research has focused on racially motivated hate crime, however, and where ethnic hate crime is considered, prior research does not address the role that immigration patterns and anti-immigrant sentiment may play.

To address this limitation in prior research, we use data from the Uniform Crime Reports (2000–2004), Department of Homeland Security (DHS), and the Census to examine Hispanic hate crimes. We hypothesize that an increase in Hispanic immigration will result in an increase in anti-Hispanic hate crime. We also expect, consistent with the traditional minority threat theory, that the relative size of the Hispanic population in the state will be positively related to anti-Hispanic hate crime. The threat framework also suggests that there may be a nonlinear effect of minority group size on social control, such that when the minority group grows large enough to exert political power, it may be able to limit the majority group's social control efforts. The minority threat framework also predicts that economic competition will result in increased social control from the majority group. To test this hypothesis we examine the effect of the ratio of white-to-Hispanic unemployment on anti-Hispanic hate crime, as well as the effect of general economic conditions on hate crime.

The results of the study reveal a positive relationship between state-level variation in anti-Hispanic hate crime and recent Hispanic immigration, consistent with our expectations and the minority threat framework. The relative size of the Hispanic population is negatively related to anti-Hispanic hate crime, however, suggesting that where Hispanics are more numerous, hate crimes against them are less frequent. Taken together, these results suggest that anti-Hispanic hate crime is a consequence of Hispanic immigration, and arguably the fear and anger it produces in segments of the majority population, rather than the relative size or economic position of the Hispanic minority, which if anything may serve as protective factors.

Our analysis is limited to the relationship between hate crime and legal immigration, despite the fact that the primary concerns of policymakers and public sentiment focus on the control of undocumented immigrants. The validity of our analysis rests heavily on two assumptions about the connection between legal and illegal immigration. The first is that the settlement patterns of both legal and illegal immigrants are largely the same. The second is that, as a practical matter, potential hate crime offenders are unable to distinguish readily between legal and illegal immigrants or, for that matter, between immigrants and the longstanding residents who resemble them. Although we believe both assumptions appear reasonable, more research is needed to validate them. The current estimates of illegal immigration are imperfect and vary considerably depending on the source (Bialik, 2010).

Likewise, while the measurement of hate crime has improved since the FBI first started collecting data, many agencies consistently fail to report any hate crime in their jurisdiction. Research shows that many police officers do not take victim reports of hate crime seriously or do not understand how to identify a hate crime (McDevitt, Balboni, Bennett, et al., 2003;

Nolan & Akiyama, 2003). The abundance of zeroes in the hate crime data indicates a need to improve hate crime reporting by both victims and law enforcement. Immigrant victims may be especially likely to forgo reporting an incident because they fear deportation. Although Congress has attempted to encourage and facilitate reporting of particular crimes by undocumented immigrants by creating special visa categories (the S, T, and U visas), it is unclear whether these alleviate the underreporting problem (Kittrie, 2006). There are limits on the number of such visas that can be extended, and only victims of certain crimes are eligible. An alternative approach may be the implementation of "sanctuary policies" with law enforcement agencies to ensure undocumented immigrant crime victims are not reported to federal immigration authorities (Kittrie, 2006). Additionally, specialized training of police officers is needed regarding hate-crime identification. Formal policies on how to handle hate crime within police agencies could also improve the accuracy and integrity of hate crime statistics. In addition, greater attention to crimes experienced by immigrants that go unreported to police is needed to assess victimization risk more accurately and strengthen policies to reduce the risk of hate crime.

References

Adapted from: Stacey, M., Carbone-Lopez, K., & Rosenfeld, R. 2011. "Demographic Change and Ethnically Motivated Crime: The Impact of Immigration on Anti-Hispanic Hate Crime in the United States." *Journal of Contemporary Criminal Justice*, 27: 278–398.

Bialik, C. 2010. "The Pitfalls of Counting Illegal Immigrants." *Wall Street Journal*, May 7. http://blogs.wsj.com/numbersguy/the-pitfalls-of-counting-illegal-immigrants-937/.

Blalock, H. M. 1967. *Toward a Theory of Minority-group Relations*. New York: John Wiley and Sons.

Eitle, D., D'Alessio, S. J., and Stolzenberg, L. 2002. "Racial Threat and Social Control: A Test of the Political, Economic, and Threat of Black Crime Hypotheses." *Social Forces*, 81: 557–576.

Grieco, E. M. 2009. Race and Hispanic Origin of the Foreign-Born Population in the United States: 2007, American Community Survey Reports, ACS-11. U.S. Census Bureau, Washington, DC.

Ibrahim, M. 2005. "The Securitization of Migration: A Racial Discourse." *International Migration*, 43: 163–187.

King, R. D., Messner, S. F., and Baller, R. D. 2009. "Contemporary Hate Crimes, Law Enforcement, and the Legacy of Racial Violence." *American Sociological Review*, 74: 291–315.

Kittrie, O. F. 2006. "Federalism, Deportation, and Crime Victims Afraid to Call the Police." *Iowa Law Review*, 91: 1449–1508.

McDevitt, J., Balboni, J. M., Bennett, S., Weiss, J. C., Orchowsky, S., and Walbolt, L. 2003. "Improving the Quality and Accuracy of Bias Crime Statistics Nationally: An Assessment of the First Ten Years of Bias Crime Data Collection." In B. Perry (Ed.), *Hate and Bias Crime: A Reader*. New York: Routledge.

Nolan, J. J. and Akiyama, Y. 2003. "Assessing the Factors that Affect Law Enforcement Participation, in Hate Crime Reporting." In P.B. Gerstenfeld and Diana Grant (Eds.), *Crimes of Hate: Selected Readings* (reprint). New York: Sage Publications.

Perry, B. 2001. *In the Name of Hate: Understanding Hate Crimes*. New York: Routledge.

Stacey, M., Carbone-Lopez, K., & Rosenfeld, R. 2011. "Demographic Change and Ethnically Motivated Crime: The Impact of Immigration on Anti-Hispanic Hate Crime in the United States." *Journal of Contemporary Criminal Justice*, 27: 278–398.

Michele Stacey is assistant professor of Criminal Justice at East Carolina University. Her current research focuses on the social control of minority groups, both formally and informally, with a particular interest in hate crimes.

Kristin Carbone-Lopez is associate professor in the Department of Criminology and Criminal Justice at the University of Missouri—St. Louis. Her research focuses on gender and the connections between crime and victimization across the life course with a particular emphasis on violence against women.

Richard Rosenfeld is Founder Professor of Criminology and Criminal Justice at the University of Missouri—St. Louis. His current research encompasses the economic correlates of crime trends and policing effects on crime. He is a fellow and past president of the American Society of Criminology and currently serves on the Science Advisory Board of the Office of Justice Programs, U.S. Department of Justice.

Hate Crimes against Sikh Americans

Simran Jeet Singh

Their distinct religious identity, including turbans and beards, has marked Sikhs as "other" since their arrival in North America in the late 1800s. In the first major incident of anti-Sikh violence in America—the Bellingham Riots of 1907—violent mobs targeted and physically assaulted hundreds of Sikh civilians on the streets of Bellingham, Washington.

Early Sikh settlers contributed to American society through various means, such as farming, building railroads, and serving in the military. Bhagat Singh Thind served with the U.S. Army during World War I, and he famously fought for the right of non-Caucasians to receive U.S. citizenship. The 1923 Supreme Court decision in *United States vs. Bhagat Singh Thind* ruled in favor of the United States and specifically denied the right of South Asians to become U.S. citizens. After more than a decade, Thind applied for U.S. citizenship through the state of New York and finally received it in 1936.

As the 20th century progressed, Sikhs have been increasingly subsumed into a new de facto racial category—the apparent Muslim. This category includes all those with physical features similar to those associated with terrorism (e.g., brown skin, facial hair, turbans). The distinctive visible identity of Sikh Americans, coupled with the practice of associating this identity with terrorism, has led to a disproportionate amount of hate crimes targeting Sikh Americans.

After the terrorist attacks of September 11, 2001, xenophobia and hate crimes against the "apparent Muslim" surged dramatically. The violent backlash that swept around the country primarily targeted those who resembled the perpetrators. Four days after the attacks, a Sikh American became the first casualty of a hate crime in post-9/11 America. Balbir Singh Sodhi was gardening outside his gas station in Mesa, Arizona when Frank Roque drove up and shot him. According to doctors, Sodhi was dead within seconds.

Witnesses reported hearing Roque express hate speech prior to the murder, including his desire to "shoot some rag heads," "slit some Iranian throats," and "kill Middle Eastern People." Roque's words and actions evidence a sense of racialized religious identity that conflate the distinctive religious articles of Sikhism with features that have commonly been associated with terrorism.

Roque's hateful murder of Sodhi is representative of the Sikh experience in post-9/11 America. The Sikh Coalition has documented more than 700 bias-related instances against Sikhs since September 11, 2001, and its studies have shown that more than 60 percent of Sikh children are bullied in school. Sikhs also continue to endure discriminatory policies enacted by the U.S. government, such as racial profiling and workplace discrimination. These policies perpetuate negative stereotypes and implicitly condone treating Sikh Americans as second-class citizens.

On August 5, 2012, white supremacist Wade Michael Page wreaked havoc on a *gurdwara* (Sikh place of worship) in Oak

Creek, Wisconsin, carrying out the largest hate crime at a place of worship in recent American history. Page opened fire on the congregation, killing six and wounding four others, before taking his own life. Page was a member of the Hammerskins, one of the largest and most violent groups in the United States. U.S. attorney general Eric Holder characterized this attack as domestic terrorism, and First Lady Michelle Obama marked the significance of this moment in American history by visiting the Sikh community in Wisconsin. The Oak Creek Massacre also led the FBI to begin tracking hate crimes against Sikh Americans as well as other minority communities in 2013.

The media has typically described hate crimes against Sikh Americans as instances of "mistaken identity," a moniker that was also widely applied to the Oak Creek Massacre. However, scholars have rejected the framework of mistaken identity for a number of reasons. First, the descriptor "mistaken" implies that there is a correct identity that should have been targeted (i.e., Muslim). This framework also takes away from the agency of the perpetrator by characterizing their actions as unintentional. Perhaps most significantly, it wrongly assumes that every attack against a Sikh American was actually intended for a Muslim American. This naïve outlook ignores the deep history of xenophobia in the United States and overlooks the fact that sometimes Sikhs are attacked precisely because of who they are. The broad application of the "mistaken identity" framework has led to a general misdiagnosis of the problem, and therefore the resolution still remains at large.

The question of intention continues to loom over the Oak Creek Massacre. Page did not reveal what motivated his attack, and the media framed his motivation as a case of "mistaken identity" (i.e., that he actually intended to harm Muslims). However, a quick perusal of neo-Nazi discussion boards that Page was known to frequent complicates this assumption. Users regularly direct xenophobic hate speech toward Sikh Americans while clearly demonstrating knowledge that Sikhism is an independent religion.

The Sikh experience in modern America is closely tied to the experiences of all those who fall within the racial category of the "apparently Muslim." Yet hate violence against Sikh Americans does not only come in this form. Sikhs have long been targets of xenophobia—both in the homeland and in the diaspora—and if history holds true, their distinctive identity and commitment to standing up for justice will make them targets of xenophobia in the years to come.

Simran Jeet Singh is an assistant professor in the Department of Religion at Trinity University and the senior religion fellow for the Sikh Coalition. He earned his PhD from the Department of Religion at Columbia University, a master's degree from Harvard University, and his bachelor of arts from Trinity University. Simran currently serves as a Truman National Security Fellow and speaks and writes frequently on a wide range of issues relating to religion and culture.

Hate Crimes and the LGBT Community

Michael Bronski

Many members of the LGBT community, and most of its national and local state advocacy groups, fervently believe that hate crime legalization is good for LGBT people. They believe that it deters crime, and that hate crime laws make LGBT people are safer. They are not alone. Progressive groups such as The National Association for the Advancement of Colored People (NAACP) and the Jewish Anti-Defamation League (ADL) agree. The correctness of this position seems confirmed when you consider that conservative, often overtly homophobic organizations, such as Focus on the Family and Concerned Women of America, are vehemently against hate crime legislation that they fear may impede conservative religious people from voicing beliefs and upholding what they understand to be "traditional values."

But political disagreements are not rational conclusions and basic questions remain: Do hate crime laws work? Do they deter violence? Do they make LGBT people safer? And, most important, are they just and fair?

The LGBT community's or liberals' support for hate crime laws is not universal. Progressive LGBT groups, such as Queers for Economic Justice and the Sylvia Rivera Law Project, do not support them for two primary reasons. The first is that these laws are disproportionately used against poor people and people of color. The second is that they address bias crime by putting people in prison for longer periods of time. This often produces more hardened criminals. The American Civil Liberties Union (ACLU) has long objected to many (not all) hate-crime laws because they are predicated on punishing not only action—such as assault—but also constitutionally protected speech. They argue that hate-crime laws criminalize thoughts, and that it is not a crime to think or articulate hurtful statements about people. Hurting someone's feelings may be offensive, even emotionally painful; it should not be a crime.

Many religious and conservative groups argue against hate crime laws—particularly the inclusion of LGBT people as a protected class—fearing that they will criminalize the articulation of deeply held moral or religious beliefs. Mike Pence, governor of Indiana, lobbied against the Matthew Shepard and James Byrd Jr. Hate Crime Prevention Act legislation when he was a Congressman stating:

> The issue of hate crimes legislation that continues to be advanced on Capitol Hill is part of a larger effort that we already see working in state statutes. And however well intentioned, hate crimes statutes around the country have been used to quell religious expression. Individual pastors who may wish to preach out of Romans Chapter 1 about what the bible teaches about homosexual behavior, but they could be charged or subject to intimidation for simply expressing a biblical moral view on the issue of homosexual behavior. (Bronski, Pellegrini, and Amico, 2013)

Pence's misstates how hate-crime legislation works. His argument is a scare tactic aimed at demonizing LGBT activists as dictators who punish people who for not agreeing with them. In reality, these religious organizations are simply upset that any protections are being put in place for minority groups. Proponents of hate crime laws make two primary arguments. The first is that enhanced penalties deter attacks on minorities. The second is that they are just in dealing with criminal activity. Both are, on the face of it, appealing arguments.

Do hate crime laws deter crime? Hundreds and hundreds of studies have argued that the death penalty deters murder—all of them have been debunked for statistical and methodological reasons. Far fewer studies have been done on hate crime laws as a deterrent; none have demonstrated this is the case. They certainly don't change hateful opinions.

Hate crime law proponents often argue that we don't need scientific proof, only common sense. They argue that laws shape public attitudes, and hence behavior." Laws do shape attitudes, but we don't write laws to shape attitudes; we write them to justly and fairly punish behaviors. People who commit crimes and are caught almost always get punished. Getting rid of hate crime laws would not let convicted criminals go free.

Most groups who oppose hate crime legislation don't have a problem with the official recording of crime statistics that give a snapshot of social attitudes. They do, however, oppose the enhanced penalty provisions. Prisons are not the place to change social attitudes; it is in schools, around the dinner table, at houses of worship, and places where people can talk, and learn that disagreement may be a productive means of growth.

There is no evidence that hate crime laws deter crime, and people who commit these crimes—which may range from intimidation to vandalism—are, if caught, given harsh punishments under existing law. Why do LGBT people, and others, feel so deeply that we need them? The Matthew Shepard case provides some insight. In 1998 21-year-old college student Matthew Shepard was found brutally beaten in a desolate field in Laramie, Wyoming. He died six days later. Russell Henderson and Aaron McKinney, both 21, were arrested, confessed, and were convicted—but not under a hate crime law since Wyoming did not have one—in two separate trials. They are each serving two consecutive life terms in Wyoming State Penitentiary. In 2009, federal legislation titled the Matthew Shepard and James Byrd Jr. Hate Crimes Prevention Act was passed—after a decade of obstruction by a Republican Congress—and signed into law by Barack Obama. The legislation expanded the 1969 federal hate crime law to include religion, national origin, gender, sexual orientation, gender identity, and disability.

Was Shepard's murder a hate crime? Was he killed simply for being gay? Or was it a robbery gone horribly wrong with no clearly articulated animus? No one knows for sure, but his murder is a case study in how multiple causes can affect people's actions. In "A Boys Life: For Matthew Shepard's Killers What Does It Take to Be a Man?" journalist JoAnn Wypijewski persuasively argues Matthew Shepard's murder perhaps had more to do with poverty, economic conditions, a deadly methamphetamine drug culture, and American ideas about masculinity than antigay bias. We will never know for certain if Matthew Shepard was murdered because he was gay. But we do know that his killers are serving two consecutive life sentences without possibility of parole without a "hate crime" law (Jiminez, 2013).

The public outcry over the Matthew Shepard case, which led to the demand to include LGBT people as protected categories in existing hate crime laws, was based on emotion, not logic. There is no evidence that hate crime laws prevent crimes, but they do make people feel safe, and that the legal system cares about them. But it is vital to realize that "feeling safe" and "being safe" are very different.

There is another, very understandable, reason why people support hate-crime laws. That is the very basic human emotion of vengeance. LGBT people are well aware of the injustices committed against them. They are acutely aware of the long history of these injustices. The impulse to vengeance is completely understandable. But the law exists precisely to make sure that justice and fairness take the place of vengeance. Just as basing laws on "feeling safe" makes bad legal policy, laws that do not promote justice and fairness have no place in our legal codes.

Violent actions are already punishable under the law. Does more punishment equal more justice? Where do we draw that line? And whose hateful behavior rises to the threshold of a hate crime? Whose is cast as a private affair? In America hate crime laws are enforced very selectively. Do parents of LGBT youth who intimidate and physically abuse their children because they are queer get charged with hate crimes? How often are police convicted of hate crimes when they routinely intimidate or physically abuse LGBT people or people of color? Unless laws can be written and enforced equally and with complete fairness, they are not just.

If hate crime laws are not an answer to discriminatory violence, what is? Kay Whitlock, in "Reconsidering Hate: Policy and Politics at the Intersection," argues that the simplistic framework of "hate" to describe and punish violence is inadequate to address the deeper cultural divisions that are the root of the problem. Arresting people and placing them, for long periods of time, in prisons that make no attempt at rehabilitation and place many of them in the way of more violence, are part of the problem: not a solution (Wypijewski, 1999).

Whitlock (2001, 2012) suggests that as a country and a political system we can move beyond a culture of violence is to work from the bottom-up, not the top-down. We need to address violence and hatred on the most basic interpersonal levels and at the level of small communities. Working within communities, schools, and neighborhoods to examine the racial, economic, and psychological reasons that are often underpinning these crimes will move us beyond the simple rhetoric of an ambiguously defined "hate." Hate-crime laws do none of this. Nor do they prevent violence against LGBT people.

References

Bronski, Michael, Pellegrini, Ann, and Amico, Michael. 2013. "Hate Crimes Laws Don't Prevent Violence Against LGBT People," *The Nation*, October 2. Available at http://www.thenation.com/article/176437/hate-crime-laws-dont-prevent-violence-against-lgbt-people#

Jimenez, Stephen. 2013. *The Book of Matt: Hidden Truths about the Murder of Matthew Shepard*. Hanover, NH: Steerforth Press.

Whitlock, Katherine. 2001. *In a Time of Broken Bones: A Call to Dialogue on Hate Violence and the Limitations of Hate Crimes Legislation*. Philadelphia, PA: American Friends Service Committee.

Whitlock, Kay. 2012. "Reconsidering Hate: Policy and Politics at the Intersection." Cambridge, MA: A Political Research Associates Discussion Paper.

Wypijewski, JoAnn. 1999. "A Boy's Life: For Matthew Shepard's Killers, What Does It Take to Pass as a Man," *Harpers*, September.

Michael Bronski is professor of the Practice in Activism and Media in the Studies of Women, Gender and Sexuality at Harvard University. He is the author of several books, including A Queer History of the United States, *and most recently coauthored* "You Can Tell Just by Looking": And 20 Other Myths about LGBT Life and People.

Hate Crime Hoaxes on College and University Campuses

Ashley Thorne

Two labels said "whites only," and two said "colored."

Created with a label-maker, they were found the morning of August 28, 2014, on doors and the water cooler on the fourth floor of a first-year residence hall at all-female Sweet Briar College in Virginia. It was the first day of class.

The night before, new student orientation had included a performance of a play on Sweet Briar's history of slavery from when it was a plantation in the 19th century. Sweet Briar president James F. Jones wrote to the campus community on the afternoon of the day the labels were found, calling the act an "assault on human dignity" and saying that either "We have among us someone who is essentially bigoted and mean-spirited who would recall the Jim Crow days of separation," or, "Someone, moved by the play, sought to use the old, abusive words to remind us that while such terms were part of the historical past, some of the emotions lurking behind the words might still linger in a few" (Sweet Briar College, August 29, 2014).

The latter turned out to be the case; a few days later, the student who was responsible for the labels confessed to the administration and apologized anonymously to the college community. President Jones announced, "I can tell you that she is African-American and that I believe her apology was sincere" (Sweet Briar College, September 3, 2014).

The student wrote that she had placed the labels because she "was trying to make a point" that "While moving forward, we can never really shake the past" (Sweet Briar College, September 2, 2014).

The next day an unidentified man—who apparently was unaware of the student's confession—called the college demanding, "who is the white girl that did this?" and threatened to come to Sweet Briar to exact "justice." The campus went on lockdown; sirens blared; police investigated; students huddled in their rooms behind bolted doors (WSET-TV, 2014).

This episode at Sweet Briar is one of numerous similar stories in which American college campuses have been thrown into panic over hate crimes that turned out to be hoaxes. The hatred isn't real in these cases, but the resulting fear and disruption is.

Sadly, real bias-motivated insults and slurs, as well as physical harassment and violence, also happen on campus, though it remains unclear how often (Jaschik, 2013). At the same time, false hate is on the rise.

Examples are plentiful. In the last 25 years, nearly 200 hoax hate crimes have been documented (Fake Hate Crimes, 2015), more than 30 of which were perpetrated by college students or teachers (Wilcox, 1994; Freddoso, 2013; Grasgreen, 2012; Travis, 2015; MacDonald, 2013). (In addition to these, numerous incidents where culprits were never found leave open the possibility of hoaxes (Chan, 2008).) Here are a few:

In the fall of 2013, two Vassar College students, including transgendered student Genesis Hernandez, the sole member of the Bias Incident Response Team, scrawled a series of racist and anti-transgender messages in graffiti in residence halls, and then filed reports (Soave, 2013). In April 2013, University of Wyoming student Meghan Lanker-Simons received an anonymous Facebook rape threat against her because she "runs her liberal mouth all the time," but police determined that Lanker-Simons wrote the message herself and then lied about it (Owens, 2013). In spring 2013, Oberlin College students Dylan Bleier and Matt Alden, who considered themselves "white allies against racism," drew swastikas and wrote "No N*****s," "Whites Only," and "N*****faggot" on walls and posters around campus. They were caught in the act and admitted that they had written the slurs as "a joke to see the college overreact to it as they have with the other racial postings that have been posted on campus" (Ross, 2013). In 2012, Central Connecticut State University student Alexandra Pennell received hate letters for being a lesbian. Authorities investigated the case and caught her on camera slipping new notes under her own door (Owens and Munoz, 2012). In April 2011, University of North Carolina-Chapel Hill student Quinn Matney filed a police report saying he was branded with hot metal for being gay; officials found he had made up the story ("Quinn Matney . . . ," 2011). Later that month, third-year UVA law student Johnathan Perkins, who is part African American, wrote a 900-word letter to the editor of the law school's student newspaper claiming to have been racially profiled and harassed by the university police. None of his story was true (Lat, 2011).

In December 2007, a conservative Princeton student, Francisco Nava, said he had received hate e-mails with death threats and had been assaulted by cloaked attackers after he published a controversial article in the *Princetonian* warning against the campus hookup culture. Three days later Nava confessed to police that he had sent the e-mails himself, and that his injuries were self-inflicted ("Princeton Attack . . ., " 2007).

Thankfully these were not real instances of targeted hate. But what can we make of this troubling trend? How did students at campuses all over the country, both liberal and conservative, get into their heads that faking hate crimes was a good idea? One answer is that their colleges are teaching them to do it. Students are constantly told that bias is everywhere. This doctrine needs examples to keep it alive; if there are no examples, then they have to be invented. Hoax hate crimes are the answer. They enable students to substantiate what they've been taught.

Faculty have also internalized this idea—the most notorious hoax crime by a faculty member was in 2004, when Claremont McKenna visiting professor of psychology Kerri Dunn vandalized her own car, announced she'd been the victim of a hate crime, lied to federal investigators, and tried to collect insurance money (Harden, 2010).

Colleges, for their part, employ a feint of their own. In many cases, before all the details are known in an apparent bias incident, the college enacts a full-on response, usually involving a day of diversity rallies and canceled classes (e.g., Oberlin College canceled classes and held a "Day of Solidarity"; see Office of Communications, 2013). Hate crimes provide instances of both the victimized and the victimizers in their purest forms, and so while colleges affect sorrow when they hear of a hate crime, they in fact leap at the chance to show that bias exists. Their large-scale reactions to reported bias incidents, in turn, incentivize more hoaxes.

And though some institutions punish hoax-perpetrators (Sweet Briar, for instance, expelled the responsible student), others let culprits off the hook and allow the idea to remain that the campus is infected with hatred. UVA's law school allowed Johnathan Perkins to receive his degree, and he went on to become an attorney representing universities and corporations (Lat, 2012).

Ultimately those who perpetuate hoaxes are hurting both themselves and the larger community. As individuals, they show that they lack the work ethic and character to face obstacles in their lives, and that they have to play the victim to get ahead. As members of society, they are taking themselves out of the game—they are resolved not to be responsible adults accountable for their actions.

All Americans should strive toward good citizenship and against public displays of ill will against others. Name-calling, ad hominem attacks, and threats of violence weaken a community. Ceasing such attacks begins with individuals practicing temperance and generosity of mind toward people around them.

Frequent hoaxes tend to cause people to assume on first hearing that a reported bias incident is a fraud. For example, Michelle Malkin, who has documented decades of hoax hate crimes, said that as soon as she heard about the racist graffiti at Oberlin, "the fake hate crime alarm bells went off" (Malkin, 2013). But crying wolf erodes the credibility of real wrongdoing. We will be better equipped to respond to true instances of hate crimes when false ones fall away.

Finally, hoax crime culprits often say they were motivated by a desire to "raise awareness" of the presence of prejudice. They seek to establish that hate is still with us. "The race problem in America persists," wrote Perkins. "We can never really shake the past," wrote the Sweet Briar label-maker. But what we really need to be aware of is plain reality. Awareness of something perpetuated by a lie is worthless. We can shake the past. The way to move forward is to live in the real world today and live by the truth.

References

Chan, Sewell. "Professor in Noose Case Is Cited for Plagiarism," *New York Times* City Room, February 20, 2008. http://cityroom.blogs.nytimes.com/2008/02/20/victim-of-noose-crime-is-cited-for-plagiarism/?_php=true&_type=blogs&_r=0

Fake Hate Crimes: A Database of Hate Crime Hoaxes in the USA. http://www.fakehatecrimes.org/.

Freddoso, David. "A Recent History of Hate-Crime Hoaxes," August 23, 2013. Conservative Intelligence Briefing. http://www.conservativeintel.com/2013/08/23/a-recent-history-of-hate-crime-hoaxes/

Grasgreen, Allie. "Hate Crime Hoaxes," *Inside Higher Ed*, July 31, 2012. https://www.insidehighered.com/news/2012/07/31/hate-crime-hoaxes-present-burdens-lessons-college-campuses

Harden, Nathan. "The Godmother of Fake Hate Crimes," *National Review*, March 15, 2010. http://www.nationalreview.com/phi-beta-cons/39720/godmother-fake-hate-crimes

Lat, David. "A Law Student Plays the Race Card—and Gets Busted, Big Time," *Above the Law*, May 7, 2011. http://abovethelaw.com/2011/05/a-law-student-plays-the-race-card-and-gets-busted-big-time/

Lat, David. "An Update on Johnathan Perkins: Did He Get His Law Degree?" *Above the Law*, January 10, 2012. http://abovethelaw.com/2012/01/an-update-on-johnathan-perkins-did-he-get-his-law-degree/

MacDonald, Steve. "A Collection of Recent Hate-Crime Hoaxes," Granite Grok, August 26, 2013. http://granitegrok.com/blog/2013/08/a-collection-of-recent-hate-crime-hoaxes

Malkin, Michelle. "Oberlin College: Still Manufacturing Hate Crimes Hoaxes after All These Years," *Michelle Malkin*,

March 5, 2013. http://michellemalkin.com/2013/03/05/
oberlin-college-still-manufacturing-hate-
crimes-hoaxes-after-all-these-years/

Office of Communications. "Classes Canceled: Monday,
March 14, 2013," Oberlin OnCampus, March 4, 2013,
https://oncampus.oberlin.edu/source/articles/2013/03/04/
classes-canceled-monday-march-4–2013.

Owens, David, and Muñoz, Hilda. "CCSU Police Say
Student Faked Anti-Gay Notes," *Hartford Courant*, July 2,
2012. http://articles.courant.com/2012–07–02/news/
hc-new-britain-ccsu-bias-made-it-up-0703–20120702_
1_ccsu-police-anti-hate-rally-notes

Owens, Eric. "Police Say 28-Year-Old Undergrad Threatened
Herself with Rape in Facebook Hoax," *The Daily Caller*,
May 1, 2013. http://dailycaller.com/2013/05/01/
police-say-28-year-old-undergrad-threatened-hers
elf-with-rape-in-facebook-hoax/#disqus_thread

"Princeton Attack Was Hoax," *Newsmax*. December 18, 2007.
http://www.newsmax.com/InsideCover/Princeton-Attac
k-Was-Hoax/2007/12/18/id/322449/

"Quinn Matney, UNC Student, Allegedly Faked Hate Crime
Report," *Huffington Post*, June 12, 2011. http://www.huff
ingtonpost.com/2011/04/12/quinn-matney-unc-student-_
n_848372.html

Ross, Chuck. "Meet the Privileged Obama-Supporting White
Kids Who Perpetrated Cruel Oberlin Race Hoax," *The
Daily Caller*, August 22, 2013. http://dailycaller
.com/2013/08/22/meet-the-privileged-obama-suppo
rting-white-kids-who-perpetrated-cruel-oberlin-race-hoax/

Soave, Robby. "EXCLUSIVE: Shocking Discovery in
Hoax Bias Incident at Vassar College," *The Daily Caller*,
November 27, 2013. http://dailycaller.com/2013/11/27/
exclusive-shocking-discovery-in-hoax-bias-incident-
at-vassar-college/

Sweet Briar College. "Important Message from President Jones," August 29, 2014. http://sbc.edu/news/uncategorized/important-message-president-jones/

Sweet Briar College. "Important Update from President Jones," September 3, 2014. http://sbc.edu/news/uncategorized/important-update-president-jones-2/

Sweet Briar College. "Important Update from President Jones," September 2, 2014. http://sbc.edu/news/uncategorized/important-update-president-jones/

Travis, J.P. Bogus Hate Crimes. http://www.bogushatecrimes.com/ByDate.php.

Wilcox, Laird. *Crying Wolf: Hate Crime Hoaxes in America,* 1994. http://www.fakehatecrimes.org/Crying-Wolf-by-Laird-Wilcox.pdf

WSET-TV. "Update: Student Who Put Up Labels at Sweet Briar Leaves School," September 8, 2014. http://www.wset.com/story/26437771/update-threat-to-sweet-briar-college-in-reaction-to-racial-incident

Ashley Thorne is the executive director of the National Association of Scholars.

People

Much information on hate crimes and violent extremist groups comes from the research and publications of human rights activists and organizations, college and university professors, investigative journalists and authors. Because their work often involves exposing the activities of violent individuals and organizations, some of these human rights activists prefer to remain out of the public eye. Their legitimate concerns have been respected, and they have not been included in this chapter. The following are brief biographies of some notable experts on hate crimes, racial and religious bigotry, and political extremists.

Zainab Al-Suwaij (1971–)

Zainab Al-Suwaij is the executive director of the American Islamic Congress (AIC). This organization represents the diverse political and cultural interests of Muslim Americans and aims to combat both hate crimes committed against Muslims and those crimes perpetrated by their coreligionists. Born in Basra, Iraq, Al-Suwaij comes from a religious Muslim family. She was on a visit to Kuwait in 1990 when Iraq invaded that country. In 1991 she returned to Iraq, participated in the failed uprising against Saddam Hussein's regime, and fled to Jordan. According

---

Jim Mohr, a Washington state college official, is on the board of the Gonzaga University Institute for Hate Studies in Spokane, a unique center dedicated to the academic study of hate. (AP Photo/Rajah Bose)

to a *Boston Globe* story on April 7, 2003, she bears a thin scar from an Iraqi army attack during the rebellion. After the first Gulf War, she fled to the United States to complete her studies. She has worked as a refugee case manager and a teaching fellow in Arabic at Yale. On April 4, 2003, Al-Suwaij and other prominent Iraqi Americans met with President George W. Bush at the White House. Al-Suwaij has written articles in support of the coalition war against Hussein's tyranny and has also published essays against Muslim intolerance for the *New York Times, Boston Globe*, and *Wall Street Journal*. She helped organize a Boston memorial service for slain Jewish *Wall Street Journal* reporter Daniel Pearl—which were also held in London, New York, and Los Angeles—and observed that "to remember Daniel Pearl is to remind ourselves of the human side of terror and intolerance." In addition to her work with the American Islamic Congress, she is involved in developing education programs in Iraq.

Chip Berlet (1949–)

Chip Berlet has spent several decades studying prejudice, hate groups, reactionary backlash movements, theocratic fundamentalism, civil liberties violations, police misconduct, government and private surveillance abuse, and other antidemocratic phenomena. He worked for many years at Political Research Associates, an independent, nonprofit research center that publishes extensive reports on hate group activities aimed against blacks, Jews, gays, lesbians, and other minority groups. Berlet has written chapters in several scholarly books, reviewed articles for sociology journals, and prepared entries in encyclopedias on fundamentalism, millennialism, and criminal justice. He was coauthor with Matthew N. Lyons of *Right-Wing Populism in America: Too Close for Comfort* (Guilford Press, 2000) and also has written op-ed pieces for the *Boston Globe*, the *New York Times* and other major newspapers and magazines. Following the terrorist bombing in Oklahoma City, Berlet frequently appeared in the media to discuss the nature and overlap of right-wing populism, the patriot movement, and armed militias. He has personally attended meetings held by right-wing patriots, armed militia activists, white supremacists, Holocaust deniers, the Ku Klux Klan (KKK), and neo-Nazis. He also was among the first researchers to warn of the attempt by anti-Jewish and other white supremacist hate groups to recruit financially failing Midwest farmers in the late 1970s and early 1980s. A longtime critic of the extremist ideologue Lyndon LaRouche, Berlet has been sued twice by the LaRouche movement for his characterization of it as a conspiracist neo-Nazi movement engaged in illegal fund-raising activities. LaRouche's organization lost both cases. In 1985 Berlet cofounded the Public Eye BBS, the first computer bulletin board system designed to challenge the information circulated by the KKK and neo-Nazis on racist and anti-Jewish bulletin boards. He has worked on joint projects with many groups, including Facing History and Ourselves, Planned Parenthood, the National Gay and Lesbian Task Force, the Massachusetts chapter of the American Jewish Congress, and the Chicago chapter of the American Jewish Committee.

Heidi Beirich (1967–)

Heidi Beirich leads the Southern Poverty Law Center's (SPLC) Intelligence Project, "one of the most respected anti-terror organizations in the world," according to the *National Review*. She is an expert on various forms of extremism, including the white supremacist, nativist and neo-Confederate movements as well as racism in academia. She oversees the SPLC's yearly count of the nation's hate and hard-line antigovernment groups and is a frequent contributor to the SPLC investigative reports. Heidi Beirich has appeared on numerous television news programs and is quoted regularly by journalists and scholars in both the United States and abroad. Prior to joining the SPLC staff in 1999, Heidi earned a doctorate in political science from Purdue University. She has published widely in academia and is the coeditor and author of several chapters of *Neo-Confederacy: A Critical Introduction*, published by the University of Texas Press in 2008.

Kathleen M. Blee (1953–)

Professor Blee has written pioneering studies on women involved in racist and extremist movements. She received her BA in sociology from Indiana University in 1974. She carried out her graduate studies at the University of Wisconsin, Madison, earning the MS and PhD in sociology in 1976 and 1982, respectively. Professor Blee began her faculty career in 1981 at the University of Kentucky where she eventually held the rank of professor. While at Kentucky, she served as associate dean for the College of Arts and Sciences (1989–1991; 1992) and as director for the Women's Studies Program (1987–1989). Blee joined the University of Pittsburgh's Department of Sociology at the rank of professor in 1996, and her recruitment to Pitt included appointment as the director of the Women's Studies Program. She served in that capacity from 1996 to 2001. Blee was appointed distinguished professor of sociology in 2007, and she has served as chair of the Department of Sociology since 2008. She has affiliated appointments in Departments of History and Psychology, as well as the Women's Studies Program. She is also associated with the Cultural Studies Program and the Center for Race and Social Problems. A highly productive scholar who communicates her research through both scholarly articles and books, Blee has published 76 journal articles, encyclopedia entries, and book chapters. She has published three edited or coedited books and has four scholarly monographs (one coauthored) published or in press. Her first monograph, *Women in the Klan: Racism and Gender in the 1920s*, was published by the University of California Press in 1991. Her coauthored book with Dwight Billings, *The Road to Poverty: The Making of Wealth and Hardship in Appalachia*, was published by Cambridge University Press in 2000. *Inside Organized Racism: Women in the Hate Movement* was published by the University of California Press in 2002. Blee's monograph, *Making Democracy: How Activist Groups Form*, was published in 2012.

Floyd Cochran (1956–)

Floyd Cochran was the founder and director of Education & Vigilance, a Pennsylvania-based grassroots group that monitored and exposed white supremacist activity. Born in rural Cortland, New York, Cochran, like many individuals involved in racist hate movements, came from a troubled background. His mother was jailed for armed robbery and his father physically abused him. He was eventually placed in a foster home. Early on, Cochran developed an interest in Nazism and Adolph Hitler. After high school, he became a member of the Ku Klux Klan. He married and soon divorced his wife after they had two sons. In 1990 he moved to the Pacific Northwest and became active in the largest neo-Nazi group in the United States, Aryan Nations, whose headquarters were in northern Idaho. He soon became a major spokesman for the group, recruiting skinheads and other disaffected individuals. "In six months," he once boasted, "I went from milking cows in upstate New York to being in *Newsweek*. There are very few racists who could smile and make hatred sound as palatable as I could." At a 1992 youth festival, however, he was shocked when he heard someone talking about killing disabled people. His son, then four years old, had been born with a cleft palate. He became disillusioned, left the movement, and eventually met with two individuals who had formerly been his most bitter adversaries: Lenny Zeskind and Loretta Ross, a Jewish man and an African American woman who worked with the Center for Democratic Renewal. After several meetings with Zeskind and Ross, Cochran eventually renounced his racist and anti-Jewish views. He soon emerged as a leading national speaker warning against the dangers of racist hate movements. He now tours the country, speaking to civic groups and on radio and television. He recounts his odyssey in the racist movement, especially aiming his message at susceptible young people. Cochran recalls indoctrinating one youth who was later convicted of firebombing the Tacoma, Washington, office of the National Association for the

Advancement of Colored People. Although his life has been repeatedly threatened by former comrades, Cochran continues to give public talks. He often ends his speeches with a heartfelt sentiment: "If my racism harmed you in any way, directly or indirectly, I am sorry."

Rabbi Abraham Cooper (1950–)

Rabbi Abraham Cooper is the associate dean of the Simon Wiesenthal Center, a leading Jewish human rights organization with a reported 400,000 family members or affiliates. Born in New York City, he has been a longtime activist for Jewish and human rights causes on five continents. His extensive involvement in Soviet Jewry included visiting refuseniks in the 1970s, helping to open the first Jewish Cultural Center in Moscow in the 1980s, and lecturing at the Soviet Academy of Sciences and the Sakharov Foundation in the 1990s. In 1977, he came to Los Angeles to help Rabbi Marvin Hier found the Simon Wiesenthal Center. Rabbi Cooper worked with Simon Wiesenthal for nearly 30 years. Together with Rabbi Hier, Rabbi Cooper regularly meets with world leaders, including the former Pope Benedict XVI, presidents and foreign ministers to defend the rights of the Jewish people, combat terrorism and promote intergroup relations. For several decades, Rabbi Cooper has overseen the Wiesenthal Center's international social action agenda ranging from worldwide anti-Semitism and extremist groups, Nazi crimes, to interfaith relations and the struggle to thwart the anti-Israel divestment campaign, to worldwide promotion of tolerance education. He has been a pioneer and international authority on issues related to digital hate and the Internet. In 1992, and 2003 he helped coordinate international conferences in Paris on anti-Semitism cosponsored by UNESCO. In 1997, he coordinated the Center's international conference, Property and Restitution-The Moral Debt to History in Geneva, Switzerland. In 2000, he coordinated an International Conversation on Digital Hate in Berlin, which was cosponsored by the German government. He has testified before the United Nations (where the Wiesenthal Center is an official NGO) in New York and Geneva, presented testimony at the U.S. Senate, the Japanese Diet, the French Parliament, the Organization for Security and Co-operation in Europe (OSCE) and is a founding member of Israel's Global Forum on Antisemitism. Rabbi Cooper's work in Asia has reportedly countered negative stereotypes about Jews and has opened new venues in dialogue and intergroup relations in Japan, South Korea, The People's Republic of China, India, and Indonesia. He was a leader of the SWC mission to China that brought the first Jewish-sponsored exhibition to the world's most populous nation. Rabbi Cooper brought the Center's special Anne Frank and the Holocaust to tour Japan, which has been viewed by a reported two million Japanese in each of Japan's 47 prefectures. He brought the Center's Courage to Remember Holocaust Exhibit to the Gandhi Cultural Center in New Delhi. Rabbi Cooper is the editor-in-chief of the center's *Response* magazine. His editorials have appeared in major newspapers throughout the world. He supervises the center's Digital Terrorism and Hate Project, supervised the center's entry into the digital age through www.wiesenthal.com, and created the Center's innovative AskMusa.com, a multilingual Web site designed to familiarize Moslems around the world to the values of the Jewish people, its history and Faith. Rabbi Cooper earned his BA and MS from Yeshiva University and a PhD from the Jewish University of America. He is a recipient of Yeshiva University's Bernard Revel Community Service Leadership Memorial Award and of the Orthodox Union's National Leadership Award.

Morris S. Dees (1936–)

The son of an Alabama farmer, Morris Seligman Dees gave up a successful career running a mail order and book publishing business to pursue his commitment to civil rights. A graduate of the University of Alabama Law School, Dees filed a suit in

1967 to stop the construction of a white university in an Alabama city that already had a predominantly black state college. In 1969, he filed a suit to integrate the all-white Montgomery YMCA. Dees and his law partner Joseph Levin Jr. saw the need for a nonprofit organization dedicated to seeking justice and, with civil rights activist Julian Bond, founded the Southern Poverty Law Center (SPLC) in 1971. As chief trial counsel for the SPLC, he filed suit against white supremacist Tom Metzger and his White Aryan Resistance group for their responsibility in the beating death of a young Ethiopian student in Portland, Oregon. His second book, *Hate on Trial: The Case against America's Most Dangerous Neo-Nazi* (Villard Books, 1993) chronicles this case, which resulted in an unprecedented $12.5 million judgment against a U.S. hate group. His autobiography, *A Season for Justice* (Charles Scribner) was published in 1991, and the American Bar Association later released it in 2001 as *A Lawyer's Journey: The Morris Dees Story*. His third book, *Gathering Storm: America's Militia Threat*, exposes the danger posed by today's domestic terrorist groups (Harper-Collins, 1996).

Steven Emerson (1954–)

Steven Emerson is an expert on terrorism and national security and an author who also serves as the executive director of a consulting firm, The Investigative Project. He was one of the earliest researchers to warn about the dangers posed by Islamic extremists who were living in the United States and preaching violence against Americans here and abroad. Emerson started The Investigative Project in late 1995, following the broadcast on public television of his documentary film *Jihad in America*, which portrayed the clandestine operations by militant Islamic terrorist groups on U.S. soil. This film later received the George Polk Award in 1994 for best television documentary. Since the mid-1990s, Emerson has testified before Congress and has briefed the National Security Council at the White House as well. He has won three awards from the organization Investigative Reporters and Editors for magazine journalism. Emerson's latest book is *American Jihad: The Terrorists Living among Us* (Simon & Schuster, 2002). He has authored or coauthored four other books: *Terrorist: The Inside Story of the Highest- Ranking Iraqi Terrorist Ever to Defect to the West* (Villard/Random House, 1991); *The Fall of Pan Am 103: Inside the Lockerbie Investigation* (Putnam, 1990); *Secret Warriors: Inside the Covert Military Operations of the Reagan Era* (Putnam, 1988); and *The American House of Saud: The Secret Petrodollar Connection* (Franklin Watts, 1985). Between 1990 and 1993, Emerson served as a special investigative correspondent for CNN, where he was an international reporter. He has also served as a senior editor for *U.S. News & World Report*. He earned a BA and an MA from Brown University.

Phyllis B. Gerstenfeld (1967–)

Phyllis B. Gerstenfeld is professor and chair of criminal justice at California State University—Stanislaus, where she has taught a hate crimes class for over 20 years. She is the author of several works on hate crime, including *Hate Crimes: Causes, Controls, and Controversies*, which is currently in its third edition. She is also coauthor of one of the leading textbooks on criminal justice. Her recent work has focused on approaches to hate crimes outside the United States, especially in Croatia, where she twice received Fulbright grants. Her other areas of research include juvenile justice and psychology and law. She earned a BA in psychology from Reed College, and a PhD in psychology and a JD from the University of Nebraska-Lincoln.

Mark S. Hamm

A professor of criminology at Indiana State University, Hamm is a major scholar of prison radicalization in the United States. In the 1980s and 1990s he wrote widely about white right-wing extremists in this country, as well as subjects as diverse as apocalyptic violence, cop killer violence, ethnography and terror, and the USA Patriot Act. His books include *Terrorism as Crime: From Oklahoma City to Al-Qaeda and Beyond* (2007); *In Bad*

Company: America's Terrorist Underground (2002); *Apocalypse in Oklahoma: Waco and Ruby Ridge Revenged* (1997); and *American Skinheads: The Criminology and Control of Hate Crime* (1993). Professor Hamm received two major grants from the National Institute of Justice: one to study crimes committed by terrorist groups and the other to study terrorist recruitment in American correctional institutions. He is currently working on a study of terrorist recruitment in U.S. and British prisons and is compiling a database on the subject.

Gregory Herek (1954–)

Gregory M. Herek, a professor of psychology at the University of California at Davis (UCD), is an internationally recognized authority on prejudice against sexual minorities, antigay violence, and AIDS-related stigma. He received his PhD in social psychology from UCD in 1983, then was a postdoctoral fellow at Yale University. He subsequently served as a faculty member at Yale and the Graduate Center of the City University of New York before returning to UCD, first as a research psychologist and later as a tenured professor. He has been a pioneer in the scientific study of heterosexuals' prejudice against lesbian, gay, bisexual, and transgender people, as well as the effects of that prejudice on its targets. Professor Herek serves or has served on the editorial board of several academic journals, including *Basic and Applied Social Psychology*, *The Journal of Social Issues*, *The Journal of Sex Research*, *The Journal of LGBT Health*, and *The Journal of Homosexuality*. Professor Herek is a fellow of the American Psychological Association (APA) and the Association for Psychological Science (APS). He is the recipient of the 2006 Kurt Lewin Memorial Award for "outstanding contributions to the development and integration of psychological research and social action," presented by the Society for the Psychological Study of Social Issues. He is a past chairperson of the APA Committee on Lesbian and Gay Concerns and has also served on the APA Task Force on Avoiding Heterosexist Bias in Research and the APA Task Force on AIDS. He worked closely with the late Evelyn Hooker to organize the Wayne F. Placek Award, administered by the American Psychological Foundation from a bequest left to Dr. Hooker. Professor Herek was a member of the NAS Institute of Medicine's Committee on Lesbian, Gay, Bisexual and Transgender (LGBT) Health Issues and Research Gaps and Opportunities, and coauthored that panel's 2011 consensus report, *The Health of Lesbian, Gay, Bisexual, and Transgender People: Building a Foundation for Better Understanding*. He has also contributed his professional expertise to government policy work involving lesbian and gay concerns and AIDS issues. In 2011, he provided oral and written testimony for the U.S. Commission on Civil Rights hearings on Federal Enforcement of Civil Rights Laws to Protect Students Against Bullying, Violence and Harassment. In 1997, he was an invited participant at President Clinton's White House Conference on Hate Crimes. In 1993, he testified on behalf of the APA, the APS, and four other national professional associations for the House Armed Services Committee hearings on gays and the U.S. military. In 1986, he testified on behalf of the APA for the House Criminal Justice Subcommittee's hearings on antigay violence. He also has assisted the APA in preparing amicus briefs in more than 30 major court cases and served as a consultant or expert witness for numerous court cases and administrative proceedings involving the civil rights of lesbians and gay men and people with disabilities.

Paul Iganski

Paul Iganski is professor of criminology and criminal justice in the Lancaster University Law School in the United Kingdom. For almost two decades, he has specialized in research, writing, teaching, and public engagement about hate crime. His books include *Hate Crime and the City* (Policy Press, 2008), *Hate Crimes against London's Jews* (Institute for Jewish Policy Research, 2005) and the edited volumes *Hate Crime: The Consequences of Hate Crime*, and *The Hate Debate* (Profile Books, 2002). He mostly conducts his research in collaboration with, or commissioned by, nongovernmental organizations (NGOs) and the "equalities sector" in the UK and internationally. At Lancaster University he teaches courses on criminological perspectives on violence, hate crime, human rights and the state.

James B. Jacobs (1947–)

James Jacobs is the director of the Center for Research in Crime and Justice and the Chief Justice Warren E. Burger Professor of Constitutional Law and the Courts at the New York University School of Law. A leading critic of hate crimes legislation, he has written widely on the topic in many law and academic journals, including the *Journal of Criminal Law & Criminology, Annual Survey of American Law, Criminal Justice Ethics*, and *The Public Interest*. Jacobs is the coauthor, with Kimberly Potter, of *Hate Crimes: Criminal Law and Identity Politics* (Oxford University Press, 1998). He has a JD and a PhD in sociology from the University of Chicago. His first book, *Statesville: The Penitentiary in Mass Society* (University of Chicago Press, 1977), is a standard textbook in college and university classrooms.

Valerie Jenness (1963–)

Valerie Jenness, the chair of the Department of Criminology, Law and Society and an associate professor in the Department of Sociology at the University of California at Irvine, has written widely on sociological aspects of hate crimes and hate crime legislation. Her research focuses on the links between deviance and social control (especially law), gender, and social change. She is the coauthor of two recent books on hate crimes: *Making Hate a Crime: From Social Movement to Law Enforcement Practice* (Russell Sage Foundation, 2001) and *Hate Crimes: New Social Movements and the Politics of Violence* (Aldine de Gruyter, 1997). She has also written for academic journals on a variety of subjects, including the politics of prostitution, AIDS, and civil liberties, hate crimes and hate crime law, the gay/lesbian movement, and the women's movement in the United States.

She has served as an associate editor for the journal *Social Problems* and is active on several committees of the American Sociological Association.

Brian Levin (1963–)

A civil rights attorney, Brian Levin is an associate professor of criminal justice and the director of the Center for the Study of Hate and Extremism at California State University, San Bernardino, where he specializes in the analysis of hate crimes, and terrorism. Previously, Levin served as the associate director of legal affairs For the Southern Poverty Law Center's Klanwatch/ Militia Task Force in Montgomery, Alabama; legal director of the Center for the Study of Ethnic and Racial Violence in Newport Beach, California; and as a corporate litigator for a law firm. He was also a New York City policeman in the drug-plagued sections of Harlem and Washington Heights during the 1980s. Levin began his academic career in 1996 as an associate professor at Stockton College in New Jersey. A graduate of Stanford Law School, he was awarded the Block Civil Liberties Award for his work on hate crime. An author or coauthor of many publications on extremism and hate crime, he also wrote briefs in the U.S. Supreme Court case of *Wisconsin v. Mitchell* in 1992–1993, analyzing criminological data that established the prevalence and severity of hate crimes.

Jack Levin (1941–)

Jack Levin is the Irving and Betty Brudnick Professor of Sociology at Northeastern University, where he has taught since 1970. He has authored or coauthored more than two dozen books; his most recent include *Dead Lines: Essays in Murder and Mayhem* (Allyn & Bacon, 2001) and *The Violence of Hate: Confronting Racism, Anti-Semitism and other Forms of Bigotry* (Allyn & Bacon, 2002). A social psychologist and media personality, Levin's research interests focus on prejudice. As the codirector of the Brudnick Center on Conflict and Violence at

Northeastern, he has researched school violence, riots, celebrities in popular culture, and hate crimes. Levin is the coauthor of *Hate Crimes: The Rising Tide of Bigotry and Bloodshed* (Westview Press, 1993) and the revised and updated work, *Hate Crimes Revisited: America's War against Those Who Are Different* (Westview Press, 2002). Levin has written extensively on hate crimes for academic and popular journals and lectures widely on the topic. He received a BA from American International College and a PhD from Boston University.

Daniel Levitas (1960–)

Daniel Levitas has written on the subject of extreme right-wing racist, anti-Jewish, and neo-Nazi organizations. Starting in 1986 he has testified as an expert witness or provided pretrial consulting expertise on the Ku Klux Klan, anti-Semitism, Holocaust denial, the skinhead movement, Aryan Nations, and hate-motivated violence. From 1989 to 1992, Levitas served as the executive director of the Center for Democratic Renewal in Atlanta, a nonprofit organization that monitored hate groups. Levitas is the author of *The Terrorist Next Door: The Militia Movement and the Radical Right* (St. Martin's, 2002). He was also a contributing author to *Anti-Semitism in America Today* (Birch Lane Press, 1995). From 1991 to 1992 he edited *When Hate Groups Come to Town: A Handbook of Effective Community Responses*, a 192-page handbook about constructive responses to local hate group activity and violence. Levitas contributed articles to *Grolier's Multimedia Encyclopedia* on the history of American anti-Semitism, hate crimes, and the U.S. militia movement. He has written for the *Nation*, the *Los Angeles Times Book Review*, the *New York Times, Roll Call, Congress Monthly, Reform Judaism* magazine, and other publications.

Michael Lieberman

Michael Lieberman has been the Washington counsel for the Anti-Defamation League since January 1989 and also serves as director of the League's Civil Rights Policy Planning Center.

He helps coordinate the ADL's involvement in legislative initiatives before Congress and develops and implements ADL policy positions on a wide range of domestic and international affairs. He previously served as the ADL's Midwest civil rights director in Chicago. Before coming to work for ADL in September of 1982, Lieberman served as legislative assistant and counsel in Washington for two different members of Congress. He received his BA from the University of Michigan where he majored in Judaic studies and international relations. He received his law degree from Duke University where he served as a member of the *Duke Law Journal,* and editor-in-chief of the Duke International and Comparative Law Institute. Lieberman is the League's point person on federal and state response to bias-motivated crimes and chairs the coalition of religious, civil rights, law enforcement, education, and civic organizations in Washington promoting improved federal response to hate violence. He has testified on hate crime issues before Congress and before a number of state legislative bodies. He has participated in a number of academic and law enforcement training seminars on hate violence—including training at the FBI Academy at Quantico—and has written on this issue for a number of criminal justice and civil rights publications.

Kenneth L. Marcus (1966–)

Kenneth L. Marcus is president and general counsel of the Louis D. Brandeis Center for Human Rights Under Law and author of the award-winning *Jewish Identity and Civil Rights in America* (New York: Cambridge University Press, 2010). Marcus founded the Brandeis Center in 2011 to combat the resurgence of anti-Semitism in American higher education. In November 2012, Marcus was named to the Forward 50, the *Jewish Daily Forward's* listing of the "American Jews who made the most significant impact on the news in the past year." The *Forward* described its 50 honorees as "the new faces of Jewish power," predicting that "if Marcus has any say in it, we may witness a new era of Jewish advocacy." During his public service career, Marcus served as staff director at the United States Commission on Civil Rights and was delegated the authority of assistant secretary of education for civil rights and assistant secretary of housing and urban development for fair housing and equal opportunity. Shortly before his departure from the Civil Rights Commission, the *Wall Street Journal* observed that "the Commission has rarely been better managed," and that it "deserves a medal for good governance." For his work in government, Marcus was named the first recipient of the Justice and Ethics Award for Outstanding Work in the Field of Civil Rights. Marcus also serves as associate editor of the online *Journal for the Study of Antisemitism* and vice president of the International Association for the Study of Antisemitism. Marcus previously held the Lillie and Nathan Ackerman Chair in Equality and Justice in America at the City University of New York's Bernard M. Baruch College School of Public Affairs (2008–2011) and was chair of the Scholars for Peace in the Middle East Legal Task Force. Before entering public service, he was a litigation partner in two major law firms, where he conducted complex commercial and constitutional litigation. He publishes frequently in academic journals as well as in more popular venues such as *Commentary*, *The Weekly Standard*, and *The Christian Science Monitor*. Marcus is a graduate of Williams College, magna cum laude, and the University of California at Berkeley School of Law.

Karen K. Narasaki (1958–)

Karen Narasaki is an independent civil and human rights consultant. President Barack Obama appointed Narasaki to the U.S. Commission on Civil Rights in July 2014.

She is the immediate past president and executive director of the Asian Americans Advancing Justice, one of the nation's premier civil rights organizations. Prior to that position, she was the Washington Representative for the Japanese American Citizens League.

Ms. Narasaki began her career as a law clerk for Judge Harry Pregerson of the U.S. Court of Appeals for the Ninth Circuit from 1985 to 1986. Ms. Narasaki is currently chair of the Asian American Diversity Advisory Council for Comcast/NBCU and co-chair of the Asian American Advisory Council for Nielsen Media Research. She also manages the Shelby Response Fund for Neo Philanthropy.

She has served on many boards and commissions throughout her career, including vice chair of the Leadership Conference on Civil and Human Rights and chair of the Rights Working Group. She was a board member for Common Cause, the Lawyers Committee for Civil Rights Under Law, Independent Sector, the National Adult Literacy Commission, National Immigration Law Center and the National Asian Pacific American Bar Association. Narasaki received a BA from Yale College, magna cum Laude, and a JD from the University of California, Los Angeles School of Law.

Barbara Perry (1962–)

Barbara Perry is professor and associate dean in the Faculty of Social Science and Humanities at the University of Ontario Institute of Technology in Oshawa, Ontario, Canada. She has written extensively on hate crime, including several books on the topic, among them, *In the Name of Hate: Understanding Hate Crime* (Routledge, 2001) and *Hate and Bias Crime: A Reader* (Routledge, 2003). She has also published in the area of Native American victimization and social control, including one book entitled *The Silent Victims: Native American Victims of Hate Crime*, based on interviews with Native Americans (University of Arizona Press, 2008). She has also written a related book on policing Native American communities—*Policing Race and Place: Under- and Over-enforcement in Indian Country* (Lexington Press, 2009). She was the general editor of a five-volume set on *Hate Crime* (Praeger, 2009), and the editor of volume 3: *Victims of Hate Crime*. Perry continues to work in the area of hate crime, and has begun to make contributions to the limited scholarship on hate crime in Canada. Most recently, she has contributed to a scholarly understanding of anti-Muslim violence, hate crime against LGBTQ communities, and the community impacts of hate crime.

Mark Potok (1955–)

As director of publications and information for the Southern Poverty Law Center's Intelligence Project (formerly known as Klanwatch), Potok is frequently interviewed in the national media about right-wing extremist and violence-prone groups. Before joining the center, Potok was the southwest correspondent for *USA Today*, covering the siege in Waco, Texas; the bombing in Oklahoma City; and the trial of Timothy McVeigh. Potok has also worked at the *Dallas Times Herald* and the *Miami Herald*. In early 2000, he presented a paper at a United Nations conference in Geneva on hate on the Internet and also testified at a U.S. Senate hearing on that topic. Potok is the editor of the journal *Intelligence Report*, a publication frequently consulted and quoted by journalists and law enforcement officials.

Kenneth Stern (1953–)

Attorney Kenneth S. Stern is a program specialist on anti-Semitism and extremism for the American Jewish Committee (AJC). Since joining the AJC in October 1989, Stern has written for a variety of publications on the militia movement, bigotry on campus, hate on talk radio, hate on the Internet, anti-Zionism, skinheads, David Duke, Louis Farrakhan, and the extremist Christian Identity movement. His AJC report *Militias: A Growing Danger*, issued two weeks before the Oklahoma City bombing, predicted such attacks on government buildings. He also wrote *Holocaust Denial*, one of the earliest works on the dissemination of lies by anti-Jewish propagandists about the Nazi Holocaust. His investigative study of the

PBS documentary *The Liberators: A Background Report* (American Jewish Committee, 1993) questioned the accuracy of the film; PBS later withdrew the documentary from distribution. Stern's book *Loud Hawk: The United States vs. The American Indian Movement* (University of Oklahoma Press, 1994) surveys prejudice against Native Americans and *A Force upon the Plain: The American Militia Movement and the Politics of Hate* (Simon & Schuster, 1996) details the growth in that extreme right-wing movement. As an attorney for the AJC, he has written a critique of the court of appeals decision in the matter of Nazi war criminal John Demjanjuk and was of counsel on AJC's brief in *Wisconsin v. Mitchell*, the landmark hate crimes case decided by the U.S. Supreme Court. Stern was an adviser to the defense in the historic London-based Holocaust denial trial of *Irving v Penguin*. He has helped create two major Web sites to combat bigotry. Stern has written and spoken about the upsurge of anti-Jewish activities on college campuses following the collapse of the Arab–Israeli peace process. In 1997 Stern served as an invited presenter at the White House Conference on Hate Crimes and was an official member of the U.S. delegation to the Stockholm International Forum on Combating Intolerance in 2001. He also serves as a board member of the Gonzaga University Institute for Action against Hate, which publishes the *Journal of Hate Studies*. Stern earned an AB at Bard College and a JD from Willamette University College of Law.

Lu-in Wang (1962–)

Lu-in Wang teaches and writes in the area of antidiscrimination law. She is currently on the faculty of the University of New Mexico Law School, after teaching for 19 years at the University of Pittsburgh School of Law, where she received the University of Pittsburgh Chancellor's Distinguished Teaching Award in 2001 and the Student Bar Association's Excellence in Teaching Award in 2000 and 2006. Wang's scholarship examines different types of discrimination and also explores the relationship between social and economic stereotypes and how the law reinforces their connection. Her latest project examines tipped service transactions as a vehicle for discrimination on both the customer and server sides, as well as the employer's role in promoting that discrimination. Her book, *Discrimination by Default: How Racism Becomes Routine* (New York University Press 2006), draws on social psychology to detail three commonplace but generally unrecognized ways in which unconscious assumptions lead to discrimination in a wide range of everyday settings and how these dynamics interact to produce an invisible, self-fulfilling, and self-perpetuating prophecy of racial disparity. Wang's earlier work examined more extreme forms of discrimination. In addition to being the author of *Hate Crimes Law* (West, 1994), the first legal treatise on that subject, Wang has published several articles that apply insights from historical, sociological, and social psychological literature to illuminate the legal issues related to bias-related violence. Wang's articles have appeared in many journals including the *Southern California Law Review*, the *Ohio State Law Journal*, the *Boston University Law Review*, the *Lewis & Clark Law Review*, and the *Michigan Journal of Race and Law*. Before she began teaching, Wang was an attorney at law firms in Chicago, Illinois, and Ann Arbor, Michigan, and also served as a staff attorney for The Center for Social Gerontology, a national support center on law and aging. She also served as a law clerk for the late Justice Ralph J. Cappy of the Supreme Court of Pennsylvania. Wang is an elected member of the American Law Institute and The Fellows of the American Bar Foundation. She has a BS and a BA degree from Pennsylvania State University and a JD from the University of Michigan.

Bill Wassmuth (1941–2001)

A leading activist against neo-Nazi and white supremacists in the Northwest region of the United States, Bill Wassmuth was praised by Idaho governor Dirk Kempthorne as an "early voice for human rights and human dignity in our state" (News

Release, Idaho Office of the Governor, August 28, 2002). Born in Green Creek, Idaho, a small farming community, Wassmuth later entered the Catholic priesthood and became a well-known activist. He was appointed chairman of the Kootenai County Task Force on Human Relations, a civil rights group formed in 1981 in response to the harassment of a multiracial family. In September 1986, a pipe bomb exploded at Wassmuth's Coeur d'Alene home, causing extensive damage but no injuries. Local authorities determined that the bombing was carried out by neo-Nazi members of the Aryan Nations in retaliation for Wassmuth's human rights work. They were later convicted of the crime. After leaving the priesthood in June 1988, Wassmuth moved to Seattle and later became the first executive director of the Northwest Coalition against Malicious Harassment. This nonprofit Seattle-based human rights organization formed under his guidance, served Washington, Idaho, Oregon, Montana, Wyoming, and Colorado and was composed of approximately 100 smaller organizations and 2,500 individual members. In his book *Hate Is My Neighbor* (Stand Together Publishers, 1999), written with Tom Alibrandi, Wassmuth said, "To ignore hate groups, even though they usually include relatively small numbers of people, is to miscalculate the impact that they can have on a community." Wassmuth retired from the Northwest Coalition in December 1999 but remained active in human rights circles. He died of amyotrophic lateral sclerosis, commonly known as Lou Gehrig's disease, in 2001.

Organizations

This section includes descriptions of selected human and civil rights organizations and also government agencies that monitor hate crimes and extremist and violent hate groups and/or try to foster interethnic and interreligious harmony.

American Islamic Congress (AIC)

Organized by concerned Muslims in New Haven, Connecticut, following the September 11, 2001 terrorist attacks, the

AIC is dedicated to building interfaith and interethnic under-standing. In order to counteract the charge that many Ameri-can Muslims were silent in the face of Muslim extremism, this nonprofit, nonreligious organization aims to foster respect and tolerance between Muslims and non-Muslims by promoting civil and human rights through advocacy, engagement, and education.

According to the AIC statement of principles: American Muslims have been profoundly influenced by their encounter with the United States and the organization works to guaran-tee equal rights within American society for Muslims while at the same time condemning Muslim hate speech and calls to violence against non-Muslims. AIC believes that hateful state-ments and actions by their fellow Muslims threaten the integ-rity and reputation of the entire community.

The AIC strongly advocates for the rights of minorities in the Muslim world and strives for equality for Muslim women. The organization advocates for an end to "honor killings" and strongly believes that knowledge about past episodes of intoler-ance in the Muslim world will help combat disturbing current trends.

AIC members live throughout the United States and also in largely Muslim countries throughout the world, including Egypt, Malaysia, Nigeria, Tunisia Kuwait, and Morocco. The organization has been featured on major television and radio programs, and articles by and about the group have been pub-lished in the *Toronto Globe and Mail*, the *Boston Globe*, and the *Wall Street Journal*. AIC has organized many programs includ-ing Cairo Human Rights Film Festival and established advo-cacy groups for the Persecution of Marginalized Individuals (to combat the persecution of Iraqi gays and lesbians in Iraq), inter-faith councils, among other projects. Project Nur, a student-led group, actively tries to build mutual respect between Muslims and all other communities.

One of the first events sponsored by AIC after its founding was a memorial vigil conducted by a rabbi, imam, and minister for Daniel Pearl, the Jewish *Wall Street Journal* reporter who was murdered by Muslim terrorists in Pakistan in 2002.

American Jewish Committee (AJC)

Founded in 1906 in response to anti-Jewish pogroms in Russia and other parts of Europe, the AJC is a membership organization with chapters nationwide. Its programs are guided by the values of Jewish teachings and the principles of American democracy. Committed to working in partnership with the diverse racial, ethnic, and religious groups in the United States, the AJC promotes intergroup relations and combats anti-Jewish hatred and other forms of racism and bigotry. On Capitol Hill and in statehouses across the country, the AJC supports legislation mandating severe penalties for hate crimes and for the collection of reliable statistics about these incidents. In its earlier years, the AJC pioneered the "quarantine" or "dynamic silence" approach to counter notorious anti-Jewish and racist rabble-rousers. This tactic aimed to minimize the publicity for these speakers. Instead of confronting these bigots in counterdemonstrations, Jewish and civil rights advocates stayed away from these racist rallies and thus the news media had no story to cover so the event went unreported. Although this approach was successful for many years, one commentator pointed out that the Internet and talk show programs have now limited the effectiveness of this strategy. In recent years, the AJC has actively exposed extremist groups and publicized the violent activities of the militia movement even before the 1995 bombing in Oklahoma City. The AJC is actively involved in many current issues including energy security, human rights, immigration reform, and the Iran threat, among others. The organization is particularly interested in promoting intergroup understanding and cooperation, among many ethnic and religious groups, for example, Christian, Hindu, Muslim, and African American, and others. The organization has regional offices in major U.S. cities and overseas bureaus in Jerusalem, Berlin, Brussels, and Rome.

Anti-Defamation League (ADL)

In 1913, Sigmund Livingston, a Chicago attorney, persuaded B'nai B'rith, the oldest Jewish communal organization in the country whose Hebrew name means "Children of the Covenant," to establish a defense agency to combat growing anti-Jewish hatred in the United States. Only two years later, a mob in Georgia lynched Leo Frank, a Jewish factory supervisor in Atlanta who was falsely accused of murdering a thirteen-year-old female employee.

This notorious lynching was spurred on by much anti-Jewish agitation and sparked great fear among American Jews in the early 20th century.

The ADL is the preeminent U.S. organization that combats anti-Semitism, all forms of bigotry, and discrimination and helps promote harmonious relations among diverse religious, ethnic, and racial groups. The ADL's mission is to "stop the defamation of the Jewish people and to secure justice and fair treatment to all citizens alike." National headquarters are in New York City, along with many regional and local offices throughout the United States. The ADL also has offices outside the United States, including in Israel.

The League has led state and national efforts to deter and combat hate-motivated crimes. In 1981, it developed model hate crime statutes that have subsequently been adopted by most state governments and many municipalities throughout the United States. The League has also been at the forefront to develop sentencing options for youths who commit bias crimes. The ADL provides training on issues related to hate crimes to agents of the Federal Bureau of Investigation as well as to state and local law enforcement agencies. The organization publishes an extensive number of materials on human relations, diversity, and intergroup relations. *Audits of Anti-Semitic Incidents* is the most comprehensive nongovernmental annual report documenting anti-Jewish attacks on individuals and property in the United States. The Web site contains a survey of anti-Jewish and racist hate groups. LEARN (Law Enforcement Agency

Research Network) provides a wide variety of materials for police and other law enforcement officials.

Asian Americans Advancing Justice (AAJC)

Founded in 1991, Asian Americans Advancing Justice works to advance the human and civil rights of Asian Americans, and to build and promote a fair and equitable society for all.

AAJC is a leading advocate for the Asian American community covering a wide variety of issues: affirmative action, anti-Asian violence prevention/race relations, census, immigrant rights, immigration, fair and equal access to justice in the courts, language access, television diversity, and voting rights. The organization has affiliate groups in Los Angeles, San Francisco, and Chicago and is committed to building an inclusive society, combating hate crimes, and promoting social understanding between diverse racial and ethnic groups.

Brudnick Center on Violence and Conflict

The Brudnick Center for the Study of Violence and Conflict at Northeastern University "seeks solutions to problems of hostility and hatred arising from inter-group conflict and differences. In order to achieve this mission, the center initiates research projects and educational endeavors in the area of intergroup conflict and violence (e.g., intergroup tensions and violence in the schools, state-sponsored terrorism, hate crimes, international conflict and warfare, hate speech on campus, skinhead activity, religious persecution, organized hate groups). It also brings together faculty from different disciplines to foster collaborations between academicians and practitioners in order to share knowledge and develop solutions to the global challenges of security and sustainability."

The center serves as a repository of information about violence and conflict. The Northeastern faculty and students seek to generate and evaluate practical interventions for the purpose of reducing harmful forms of violence and conflict throughout society.

The center assists faculty and students in articulating individual and collective projects, applying for appropriate support through federal agencies and private foundations, carrying on research projects and disseminating research findings. Faculty members communicate their research findings to a broad audience by writing for major newspapers as well as academic journals and books. In addition, the center holds conferences and events on campus in order to bring together researchers and practitioners from around the country as well as relevant parts of the world.

Bureau of Justice Statistics (BJS)

The Bureau of Justice Statistics was first established on December 27, 1979, under the Justice Systems Improvement Act of 1979, Public Law 96–157 (the 1979 Amendment to the Omnibus Crime Control and Safe Streets Act of 1968, Public Law 90–351). The BJS mission is to collect, analyze, publish, and disseminate information on crime, criminal offenders, victims of crime, and the operation of justice systems at all levels of government. These data are critical to federal, state, and local policymakers in combating crime and ensuring that justice is both efficient and evenhanded.

The Bureau of Justice Statistics (BJS) is a component of the Office of Justice Programs in the U.S. Department of Justice.

The Hate Crime Statistics Act (28 U.S.C. § 534) defines hate crimes as "crimes that manifest evidence of prejudice based on race, gender or gender identity, religion, disability, sexual orientation, or ethnicity." The National Crime Victimization Survey (NCVS) measures crimes perceived by victims to be motivated by an offender's bias against them for belonging to or being associated with a group largely identified by these characteristics. For a crime to be classified as a hate crime in the NCVS, the victim must report at least one of three types of evidence that the act was motivated by hate: the offender used hate language, the offender left behind hate symbols, or police investigators confirmed that the incident was hate crime.

The BJS, the NCVS, and the FBI's Uniform Crime Reports (UCR) Hate Crime Statistics Program are the principal sources of annual information on hate crime in the United States and use the definition of hate crime provided in the Hate Crime Statistics Act.

Committee against Anti-Asian Violence (CAAAV)

Founded in 1986, this New York–based community organization is committed to building the capacity of poor and low-income Asian immigrant communities to join other struggles for racial, economic, women's, and environmental justice. The organization addresses issues of police brutality, housing, welfare, immigration, labor, public education, and especially, issues related to anti-Asian violence.

The organization arose out of concern about the growth in anti-Asian violence culminating in the murder of Vincent Chin in 1982 by auto workers who felt Asians were jeopardizing their jobs.

Among its accomplishments are the following:

- The CAAAV pressured the city to allocate $14 million to build parks and open green space accessible to Chinatown and Lower East Side residents along the East River waterfront, rather than the original plan of high-end stores and private developments.
- It organized the Southeast Asian community in the Bronx to challenge the failed Welfare to Workfare programs.
- It advocated for the rights of street vendors in Chinatown that were targeted during former NYC Mayor Giuliani's Quality of Life campaign.
- It worked in a city-wide coalition that pushed Mayor Bloomberg to sign an Executive Order providing language access for immigrant New Yorkers.
- It coordinated almost a thousand volunteers and members as first responders in Chinatown following Hurricane Sandy.

Disability Law Center

The Disability Law Center (DLC) is a private, nonprofit organization responsible for providing protection and advocacy for the rights of Massachusetts residents with disabilities. DLC receives federal, state, and private funding but is not part of the state or federal government. The organization provides information, referral, technical assistance, and representation regarding legal rights and services for people with disabilities.

Federal Bureau of Investigation (FBI)

As part of its responsibility to uphold the civil rights of the American people, the FBI takes a number of steps to combat the problem of hate crimes:

- The FBI is the sole investigative force for criminal violations of federal civil rights statutes.
- Cold Case Initiative: In 2007, the FBI announced renewed focus on racially motivated killings from the civil rights era, involving FBI agents from more than a dozen field offices who—with the assistance of our law enforcement partners, community leaders, and the media—identified cases and then began tracking down witnesses and locating family members, pursuing leads, reviewing law enforcement records and other documents, and seeking closure for family members. As reported in the October 2012 Attorney General's Fourth Annual Report to Congress Pursuant to the Emmett Till Unsolved Civil Rights Crime Act of 2007, investigations into 92 of the 112 cold cases identified have been concluded (in most of these 92 cases, the subjects are deceased). The initiative has, so far, resulted in one successful federal prosecution and one successful state prosecution.
- Law Enforcement Support: The FBI works closely with state/local authorities on investigations, even when federal charges are not brought. FBI resources, forensic expertise, and experience in identification and proof of hate-based

motivations often provide an invaluable complement to local law enforcement. Many cases are also prosecuted under state statutes such as murder, arson, or more recent local ethnic intimidation laws. Once the state prosecution begins, the Department of Justice monitors the proceedings in order to ensure that the federal interest is vindicated and the law is applied equally among the 95 U.S. Judicial Districts.

- The FBI forwards completed reports to U.S. attorneys and the Civil Rights Division at the Department of Justice, which decide whether a federal prosecution is warranted. They may move forward, for example, if local authorities are unwilling or unable to prosecute a crime of bias.

- Hate crimes directed at the U.S. government or the American population may be investigated as acts of domestic terrorism. Incidents involving hate groups are also investigated as domestic terrorism (the FBI's Civil Rights Program cannot investigate groups, only individuals).

Gonzaga University Institute for Hate Studies

Founded in 1997 in response to some racist incidents on the Gonzaga University campus, the institute is an academic organization devoted to combating hate through research, education, and advocacy.

"The Gonzaga Institute for Hate Studies advances the interdisciplinary field of Hate Studies and disseminates new theories, models, and discoveries about hate.

As a working definition, Hate Studies inquire into "the human capacity to define, and then dehumanize or demonize, an 'other,' and the processes that inform and give expression to, or can curtail, control, or combat, that capacity."

In furtherance of its mission, the Institute for Hate Studies

- publishes the *Journal of Hate Studies*;
- convenes the International Conference on Hate Studies;
- hosts the annual Take Action Against Hate Banquet;

- presents the annual Eva Lassman Take Action Against Hate Awards;
- coordinates educational events;
- fosters interdisciplinary courses and course materials on the study of hate;
- conducts interdisciplinary research on hate and directly related social problems;
- consults with and provides research findings, data, and curricular innovations to interested schools, organizations, and agencies;
- provides graduate and undergraduate level research awards in hate studies;
- maintains a Web site, listserv, and social networking sites on hate studies;
- advocates for the field of hate studies and encourages increased discussion about hate across disciplines;
- answers inquiries from the media, government, and governmental organizations; and
- serves as a central address for those interested in better understanding hatred.

As part of a Jesuit institution located in Spokane, Washington, the Institute for Hate Studies advances the social justice mission of the University as well as its commitments to academic excellence, diversity, global engagement, and peace-building.

Institute for the Study of Global Antisemitism and Policy (ISGAP)

Founded in 2004, ISGAP is the first interdisciplinary research center based in North America dedicated to the study of anti-Semitism, as well as other forms of prejudice, including racism, as it relates to policy, in the age of globalization. Through the examination of anti-Semitism and policy, ISGAP disseminates analytical and scholarly material to help combat hatred and promote understanding.

The Institute encourages, develops, and supports interdisciplinary research; promotes relations among scholars, the public at large, leaders, and government officials. A key goal of ISGAP is to promote excellence in research and to develop accessible social scientific understanding. Attention is placed on policy analysis and consultation in local, national, and international contexts.

ISGAP organizes research projects, seminars, public meetings, conferences, and events, and publishes periodicals, reports, and scholarly articles.

The institute is a nonpartisan organization that encourages dialogue among all peoples and worldviews and is dedicated to the promotion of justice, understanding, respect, and harmony in a rapidly globalizing world.

International Association of Jewish Lawyers and Jurists (IAJLJ)

Founded in 1969, IAJLJ was organized to combat terrorism, Holocaust denial and anti-Semitism. The organization contributes toward the establishment of an international legal order based on the rule of law, promoting the principles of equality, and the right of all states and people to live in peace. IAJLJ enhances the study of and research into the source of Jewish law with reference to the legal concepts of other nations and fosters the study of legal problems of special interest to Jewish communities within the framework of international and domestic law. The organization publishes a quarterly print and online journal which has a worldwide circulation.

Leadership Conference on Civil Rights (LCCHR)

The Leadership Conference on Civil and Human Rights is a coalition of more than 200 national organizations to promote and protect the civil and human rights of all persons in the United States. The Leadership Conference, a 501(c)(4) organization, engages in legislative advocacy. It was founded in 1950 and has coordinated national lobbying efforts on behalf of every major civil rights law since 1957.

The Leadership Conference Education Fund helps promote federal policies that protect the civil and human rights of all Americans. The Education Fund's campaigns empower and mobilize advocates around the country to push for progressive change. This special fund was founded in 1969 as the education and research arm of The Leadership Conference.

Confronting the New Faces of Hate: Hate Crimes in America published in 2009 is an update of the 2004 report, *Cause for Concern.* Sadly, five years later, the problem of hate crimes continues to be a significant national concern. The purpose of this report is to highlight the need for a coordinated response by every sector of society to eradicate this problem. The report is freely available online at http://www.protectcivilrights.org/pdf/reports/hatecrimes/lccref_hate_crimes_report.pdf

Matthew Shepard Foundation

The Matthew Shepard Foundation was founded by Dennis and Judy Shepard in memory of their 21-year old son, Matthew, who was murdered in an antigay hate crime in Wyoming in October 1998.

Created to honor Matthew in a manner that was appropriate to his dreams, beliefs, and aspirations, the foundation seeks to "Replace Hate with Understanding, Compassion, and Acceptance" through its varied educational, outreach, and advocacy programs and by continuing to tell Matthew's story.

The foundation supports schools and theatre companies producing "The Laramie Project," a spoken-word play that tells Matt's story and the community's reaction to his murder. The foundation provides educational and technical support for putting on the play, and where it can, provides on-the-ground assistance to augment the productions with community forums.

The Shepard Foundation provides online resources and a blogging platform for youth who are struggling to deal with coming out, family acceptance, bullying and harassment, or faith issues. Through a Web site called Matthew's Place, the foundation is particularly focused on helping youth who live in rural areas who have few in-person resources to which they can turn. The foundation frequently hears from teenagers and young adults who are grateful for their work.

The foundation advocates for full equality for all lesbian, gay, bisexual, and transgender Americans and actively supports legislation in support of this community.

National Archive of Criminal Justice Data (NACJD)

NACJD, a part of the Inter-University Consortium for Political and Social Research (ICPSR) at the University of Michigan, designed a *resource guide* for Web users to learn about the FBI's Uniform Crime Reporting Program and to connect to other related information sources.

With this guide, first time users or experienced analysts can

- find general information about the Uniform Crime Reporting Program;
- connect to other Uniform Crime Reporting Program and related sites;
- find hate-crime data about crimes that manifest evidence of prejudice based on race, religion, sexual orientation, ethnicity, and mental or physical disabilities. The FBI began to collect this data under the Hate Crime Statistics Act of 1990. Information contained in the data includes the number of victims and offenders involved in each hate crime incident, type of victims, bias motivation, offense type, and location type.

National Center for Victims of Crime (NCVC)

The National Center for Victims of Crime's vision emerged from one family's tragedy: in 1985, Ala Isham and Alexander Auersperg established the National Center for Victims of Crime, originally the Sunny Von Bulow National Victim Advocacy Center. Motivated by their mother's victimization and their family's traumatic experience with the criminal justice system, the founders believed it was fundamentally wrong that crime victims were often shut out of and "revictimized" by the very system that was supposed to help them. They wanted to redefine what justice for crime victims means by giving them a voice in the criminal justice system.

Since those early days, the NCVC has become the nation's leading resource and advocacy organization for victims of all types of crime and for the people who serve them.

NCVC is in contact with elected officials, policymakers, business leaders, law enforcement officers, judges, media representatives, educators, and health care providers to help them understand that justice for victims involves more than holding offenders accountable for their crimes. It involves providing victims full participation in the criminal justice process and the means to overcome the physical, emotional, and financial consequences of crime.

The NCVC offers hate crime information and Web links.

National Coalition of Anti-Violence Programs (NCAVP)

Founded in 1995, the National Coalition of Anti-Violence Programs (NCAVP) is the only national coalition dedicated to reducing violence and its impacts on lesbian, gay, bisexual, transgender, queer, and HIV-affected (LGBTQH) communities in the United States. NCAVP currently brings together LGBT antiviolence programs in cities and regions across the United States and in Montreal, Quebec and Toronto, Ontario.

NCAVP works to research and document bias and hate crimes, domestic violence in LGBT relationships, sexual assault and abuse, "pick-up" crimes, and other characteristic forms of violence affecting LGBT individuals, and is dedicated to helping local communities establish, promote, and expand antiviolence education, prevention, organizing, advocacy, and direct services.

NCAVP helps promote policies that assist victims of violence, addresses the perpetrators of violence, and tries to positively change the social atmosphere to reduce this violence.

Through its Violence Response Initiative, NCAVP also provides direct response to critical incidents of anti-LGBT violence around the country and assists local communities, survivors, and families in coping with incidents. In addition, the NCAVP provides support to local communities seeking to create long-term responses to violence through technical assistance, guidance, and information and materials-sharing with the goal of creating more local anti-violence programs across the country.

Since 1998, NCAVP has compiled the only national survey report analyzing thousands of same-gender domestic violence incidents documented by its members each year. This report has had an important impact in the domestic violence service community, where it has helped garner more attention to same-gender domestic violence issues and needs.

National Gay and Lesbian Task Force (NGLTF)

The NGLTF is the leading civil rights organization for lesbian, gay, bisexual, and transgender rights. Founded in New York in 1973, the organization combats antigay violence and job discrimination and lobbies for gay rights legislation. In 1984 the NGLTF published the first national study focusing exclusively on antigay violence. Two years earlier the task force created an antiviolence project to promote an official response to violence and harassment perpetrated against individuals because of their sexual orientation. The NGLTF's publications include *Hate Crimes Map*, a unique source indicating the extent of hate crime laws covering sexual orientation in all 50 states, press releases, and other materials concerning local and federal hate crimes legislation.

New York City Gay and Lesbian Anti-Violence Project (AVP)

Founded in New York City in 1980, this pioneering organization was organized in response to antigay neighborhood violence and the lack of response from the local police.

Currently, the AVP serves lesbian, gay, transgender, bisexual, and HIV-positive victims of violence, and others affected by violence, by providing free and confidential services. Although this organization primarily focuses on antigay violence in New York City, the AVP serves as a national clearinghouse for statistics and information on hate crimes motivated by sexual orientation throughout the United States. AVP remained an all-volunteer organization until 1984, when the first full-time executive director was hired. With a full-time staff, AVP was able to broaden its services to provide professional counseling to survivors of hate violence, intimate partner violence, sexual violence, and HIV-related violence. Currently, AVP provides free and confidential assistance to thousands of lesbian, gay, bisexual, transgender, queer, and HIV-affected (LGBTQH) people each year from all five boroughs of New York City. A member of the National Coalition of Anti-Violence Programs (see entry earlier) the AVP compiles and distributes an annual hate crimes report through its Web site.

Not in Our Town (NIOT)

Not in Our Town (NIOT) is a movement to stop hate, address bullying, and build safe, inclusive communities for all. NIOT Our Town films, new media, and organizing tools help local leaders build vibrant, diverse cities and towns, where everyone can participate. Their approach is based on the premise that real change takes place at the local level and focus on solutions to inspire and empower communities to create a world where:

NIOT.org offers films and tools to use in communities or schools.

* 100+ short films that can spark community dialogue
* 50+ school films with accompanying lesson plans and activity guides
* Sample materials from towns which have stood up—and worked to prevent hate and intolerance in their communities

* Special video collections include what to do when a hate group comes to town, how to address hate on your campus, and how to start an anti-bullying campaign.

Office of Juvenile Justice and Delinquency Prevention (OJJDP)

Charged by Congress to meet the challenge of juveniles in crisis, OJJDP collaborates with professionals from diverse disciplines to improve juvenile justice policies and practices.

OJJDP, a component of the Office of Justice Programs, U.S. Department of Justice, accomplishes its mission by supporting states, local communities, and tribal jurisdictions in their efforts to develop and implement effective programs for juveniles. The office strives to strengthen the juvenile justice system's efforts to protect public safety, hold offenders accountable, and provide services that address the needs of youth and their families.

Through its components, OJJDP sponsors research, program, and training initiatives; develops priorities and goals and sets policies to guide federal juvenile justice issues; disseminates information about juvenile justice issues; and awards funds to states to support local programming.

Healing the Hate: A National Hate Crime Prevention Curriculum for Middle Schools is designed for middle-school teachers and other professionals who work with youth. This curriculum addresses the extent of hate crime in America and instructs youth in strategies that are proving effective in reducing hate crimes, which are motivated by the offender's bias against race, religion, ethnic/national origin, or sexual orientation.

Police Executive Research Foundation (PERF)

The Police Executive Research Forum (PERF) is an independent research organization that focuses on critical issues in policing. Since its founding in 1976, PERF has identified best practices on fundamental issues such as reducing police use of force; developing community policing and problem-oriented policing, using technologies to deliver police services to the community, and evaluating crime reduction strategies.

PERF strives to advance professionalism in policing and to improve the delivery of police services through the exercise of strong national leadership, public debate of police and criminal justice issues, and research and policy development.

The organization has been advocating hate-crime data collection since 1987, when it became one of the first national police associations to endorse the Hate Crime Statistics Act.

Simon Wiesenthal Center

Founded in 1977, the Simon Wiesenthal Center is an international institute for Holocaust remembrance and the defense of human rights for Jewish people and other groups. Headquartered in Los Angeles, the center's mandate combines social action, public outreach, scholarship, education, and media projects. The organization also maintains offices in New York, Toronto, Miami, Jerusalem, Paris, and Buenos Aires. The Wiesenthal Center monitors the activities of hate groups, publicizes the existence of violent hate Web sites, assists in the prosecution of Nazi war criminals, and has offered monetary rewards for information leading to the prosecution of hate crime perpetrators. The Task Force against Hate and Terrorism, established in 1991, helps combat Holocaust denial and educates students and teachers about anti-Jewish and other forms of bigotry. Located in New York and Los Angeles, the Museum of Tolerance is a hands-on experiential museum that focuses on two themes in its exhibits: racism and prejudice in the United States and the history of the Holocaust. The Wiesenthal Center publishes *Response*, a quarterly newsletter sent to supporters.

Southern Poverty Law Center (SPLC)

Founded in 1971 by Morris Dees and Joe Levin, two southern lawyers, the SPLC monitors hate activity across the United States, promotes tolerance education, and litigates against violent racist groups. Located in Montgomery, Alabama, the center's Civil Rights Memorial commemorates 40 individuals who died during the civil rights era. Since 1979, the SPLC has helped victims of racist violence sue for monetary damages by bringing lawsuits against white supremacist organizations. As the result of a 1990 civil suit in response to the killing of Mulugeta Seraw, an Ethiopian student in Oregon, SPLC attorneys won $12.5 million in damages from Tom Metzger and his racist organization, White Aryan Resistance. In September 2000, an Idaho jury awarded a $6.3 million judgment against the racist group Aryan Nations for assaulting a Native American woman and her son near their compound. The SPLC staff and Alabama headquarters require highest level security because of constant death threats against the organization, including the attempted of murder of Morris Dees.

The SPLC sued the organization on the victims' behalf and effectively bankrupted the largest neo-Nazi organization in the United States. The SPLC's publications include *Intelligence Report*, an award-winning quarterly magazine providing extensive coverage of racist and violent hate groups and individuals, and *Teaching Tolerance*, a semiannual journal aimed at educators to promote positive intergroup relations. The Web site publishes a regularly updated list of hate crime incidents around the country, which they kindly allowed the editor to adapt for the Chronology chapter of this book.

Stephen Roth Institute for the Study of Contemporary Anti-Semitism and Racism

The Stephen Roth Institute for the Study of Contemporary Anti-Semitism and Racism undertakes academic research and provides a forum for discussion of issues related to anti-Semitism and racism, their history, and their social, institutional, and cultural settings. The focus of the institute is the social and political manifestations of these phenomena since the end of World War II.

To that end, the institute does the following:

- Undertakes research projects on aspects of anti-Semitism and racism, adopting an interdisciplinary approach that draws on the skills and resources of various departments at Tel Aviv University (TAU)

- Organizes international conferences and workshops, both independently and in cooperation with academic institutions within and outside Israel

- Hosts visiting scholars and distinguished academic lecturers from outside Israel for extended periods

- Publishes an annual survey of anti-Semitic trends throughout the world in cooperation with TAU's Kantor Center for the Study of European Jewry. The annual report is based on an authoritative database of anti-Semitic manifestations worldwide that is accessible through the Internet

- Provides support for graduate students from a variety of faculties and departments at TAU whose research projects focus on various aspects of anti-Semitism or racism

- Acts as a resource center for persons interested in this subject, both within Israel and outside

U.S. Commission on Civil Rights

The Civil Rights Act of 1957 created the U.S. Commission on Civil Rights. Since then, Congress has reauthorized or extended the legislation creating the Commission several times; the last reauthorization was in 1994 by the Civil Rights Commission Amendments Act of 1994.

Established as an independent, bipartisan, fact-finding federal agency, their mission is to inform the development of national civil rights policy and enhance enforcement of federal civil rights laws. They pursue this mission by studying alleged deprivations of voting rights and alleged discrimination based on race, color, religion, sex, age, disability, or national origin, or in the administration of justice. The commission plays a vital role in advancing civil rights through objective and comprehensive investigation, research, and analysis on issues of fundamental concern to the federal government and the public.

Vidal Sassoon International Center for the Study of Antisemitism

The Vidal Sassoon International Center (SICSA) was established in 1982 as an interdisciplinary research center dedicated to an independent, nonpolitical approach to the accumulation and dissemination of knowledge necessary for understanding the phenomenon of anti-Semitism. The center engages in research on anti-Semitism throughout the ages, focusing on relations between Jews and non-Jews, particularly in situations of tension and crisis. The Felix Posen Bibliographic Project on anti-Semitism comprises online databases containing about 50,000 items. New material is added on a regular basis. The full-texts of many reports are freely accessible from this site.

This chapter contains both documents and primary source material on hate crimes, important resources for students and others researching this topic. The FBI Web site provides an overview of this agency's mandate to investigate and prosecute hate crimes. The excerpted reports, *Hate on the Internet* and *Vulnerable to Hate*, document hate speech and violence affecting the most vulnerable segments of society—children and the homeless. The NCAVP annual report is the most comprehensive survey of hate violence inflicted on members of the LGBT community. The New York State model hate crimes policy suggests important guidelines for law enforcement officials. The other documents contain the text of federal statutes on hate crime violence and prevention. Finally, two speeches demonstrate the concern of major American political figures: Senator Kennedy's speech about the importance of hate crime legislation and President Barack Obama hailing the passage of the Matthew Shepard and James Byrd Jr. Hate Crime law, historic legislation expanding government actions over bias-motivated crime.

A protester displays a placard during a rally at the Philippine Department of Foreign Affairs to demand justice for the killing of Filipino transgender Jeffrey "Jennifer" Laude, with a U.S. marine as a possible suspect, on October 15, 2014, at suburban Pasay city, south of Manila, Philippines. The activists demanded that Washington hand over the marine implicated in Laude's murder, which the demonstrators labeled a hate crime. (AP Photo/Bullit Marquez)

Hate Crime Overview

Since the initial enactment of federal legislation on hate crimes, the FBI has been designated as the official U.S. government agency to collect and analyze hate crimes statistics. This overview, published on the FBI Web site, details the FBI's jurisdiction of nationwide hate crime incidents.

Investigating hate crime is the number one priority of our Civil Rights Program. Why? Not only because hate crime has a devastating impact on families and communities, but also because groups that preach hatred and intolerance plant the seeds of terrorism here in our country.

Defining a Hate Crime

A hate crime is a traditional offense like murder, arson, or vandalism with an added element of bias. For the purposes of collecting statistics, Congress has defined a hate crime as a "criminal offense against a person or property motivated in whole or in part by an offender's bias against a race, religion, disability, ethnic origin or sexual orientation." Hate itself is not a crime—and the FBI is mindful of protecting freedom of speech and other civil liberties.

History

The FBI investigated what are now called hate crimes as far back as World War I. Our role increased following the passage of the Civil Rights Act of 1964. Before then, the federal government took the position that protection of civil rights was a local function, not a federal one. However, the murders of civil rights workers Michael Schwerner, Andrew Goodman, and James Chaney, near Philadelphia, Mississippi, in June 1964 provided the impetus for a visible and sustained federal effort to protect and foster civil rights for African Americans. MIBURN, as the case was called (it stood for Mississippi Burning), became the largest federal investigation ever conducted in Mississippi. On October 20, 1967, seven men were convicted of conspiring to violate the constitutional rights of the slain civil rights workers. All seven were sentenced to prison terms ranging from three to ten years.

FBI Jurisdiction

A hate crime is not a distinct federal offense. However, the federal government can and does investigate and prosecute crimes of bias as civil rights violations, which do fall under its jurisdiction. These efforts serve as a backstop for state and local authorities, which handle the vast majority of hate crime cases. A 1994 federal law also increased penalties for offenses proven to be hate crimes.

In 2009, the passage of a new law—the first significant expansion of federal criminal civil rights law since the mid-1990s—gave the federal government the authority to prosecute violent hate crimes, including violence and attempted violence directed at the gay, lesbian, bisexual, and transgender community, to the fullest extent of its jurisdiction. The Matthew Shepard and James Byrd, Jr., Hate Crimes Prevention Act also provides funding and technical assistance to state, local, and tribal jurisdictions to help them to more effectively investigate, prosecute, and prevent hate crimes.

The FBI's Role

As part of its responsibility to uphold the civil rights of the American people, the FBI takes a number of steps to combat the problem of hate crimes:

- **Investigative Activities:** The FBI is the sole investigative force for criminal violations of federal civil rights statutes. In 2012, we initiated 200 hate crime investigations, many jointly with our state and local law enforcement partners.
- **Cold Case Initiative:** In 2007, we announced this renewed focus on racially-motivated killings from the civil rights era, involving FBI agents from more than a dozen field offices who—with the assistance of our law enforcement partners, community leaders, and the media—identified

cases and then began tracking down witnesses and locating family members, pursuing leads, reviewing law enforcement records and other documents, and seeking closure for family members. As reported in the October 2012 Attorney General's Fourth Annual Report to Congress Pursuant to the Emmett Till Unsolved Civil Rights Crime Act of 2007, investigations into 92 of the 112 cold cases identified have been concluded (in most of these 92 cases, the subjects are deceased). The initiative has, so far, resulted in one successful federal prosecution and one successful state prosecution.

- **Law Enforcement Support:** The FBI works closely with state/local authorities on investigations, even when federal charges are not brought. FBI resources, forensic expertise, and experience in identification and proof of hate-based motivations often provide an invaluable complement to local law enforcement. Many cases are also prosecuted under state statutes such as murder, arson, or more recent local ethnic intimidation laws. Once the state prosecution begins, the Department of Justice monitors the proceedings in order to ensure that the federal interest is vindicated and the law is applied equally among the 95 U.S. Judicial Districts.

- The FBI forwards completed reports to U.S. Attorneys and the Civil Rights Division at the Department of Justice, which decide whether a federal prosecution is warranted. They may move forward, for example, if local authorities are unwilling or unable to prosecute a crime of bias.

- Hate crimes directed at the U.S. government or the American population may be investigated as acts of domestic terrorism. Incidents involving hate groups are also investigated as domestic terrorism (the FBI's Civil Rights Program cannot investigate groups, only individuals).

- **Hate Crimes Working Groups (HCWGs):** The majority of the FBI's field offices participate in local Hate Crime Working Groups. These Working Groups combine community and law enforcement resources to develop strategies to address local hate crime problems.

- **Public Outreach:** The FBI has forged partnerships nationally and locally with many civil rights organizations to establish rapport, share information, address concerns, and cooperate in solving problems. These groups include such organizations as the NAACP, the Southern Poverty Law Center, the Anti-Defamation League, the National Asian Pacific American Legal Consortium, the National Organization for Women, the Human Rights Campaign, and the National Disability Rights Network.

- **Training:** The FBI conducts hundreds of operational seminars, workshops, and training sessions annually for local law enforcement, minority and religious organizations, and community groups to promote cooperation and reduce civil rights abuses. Each year, the FBI also provides hate crimes training for new agents, hundreds of current agents, and thousands of police officers worldwide.

How Hate Crimes Are Investigated and Prosecuted

- The FBI initiates a hate crime investigation when an allegation is received from a reliable source. Most complaints are received from the victim, a witness, or a third party. Many cases are also initiated by media reports, community group complaints, referrals from Department of Justice or U.S. Attorneys, and congressional inquiries.

- Under guidelines developed in conjunction with the Department of Justice, once a complaint is received, the FBI will determine if the matter warrants a preliminary or full investigation.

- Once a case is opened, a logical investigation is conducted within a reasonable period of time.

Source: Hate Crime Overview. Federal Bureau of Investigation. Available online at http://www.fbi.gov/about-us/investigate/civilrights/hate_crimes/overview.

Investigation of Hate Crimes Model Policy

This policy is aimed at New York State law enforcement officials to acquaint them with how to identify hate crimes and also how to assist victims and their communities.

I. Purpose

This policy is designed to assist employees in identifying and investigating hate crimes and assisting victimized individuals and communities. A swift and strong response by law enforcement can help stabilize and calm the community as well as aid in a victim's recovery.

II. Policy

Any acts or threats of violence, property damage, harassment, intimidation, or other crimes motivated by hate and bias and designed to infringe upon the rights of individuals are viewed very seriously by this agency and will be given high priority. This agency shall employ necessary resources and vigorous law enforcement action to identify and arrest hate crime perpetrators. Also, recognizing the particular fears and distress typically suffered by victims, the potential for reprisal and escalation of violence, and the far-reaching negative consequences of these crimes on the community, this agency shall be mindful of and responsive to the security concerns of victims and their families.

III. Definitions

A. New York State Penal Law §485.05 Hate crimes.

   1. A person commits a hate crime when he or she commits a specified offense and either:

      (a) intentionally selects the person against whom the offense is committed or intended to be committed in whole or in substantial part because of a belief or perception regarding the race, color, national origin, ancestry, gender, religion, religious practice, age, disability or sexual orientation of a person, regardless of whether the belief or perception is correct, or

(b) intentionally commits the act or acts constituting the offense in whole or in substantial part because of a belief or perception regarding the race, color, national origin, ancestry, gender, religion, religious practice, age, disability or sexual orientation of a person, regardless of whether the belief or perception is correct.

2. Proof of race, color, national origin, ancestry, gender, religion, religious practice, age, disability or sexual orientation of the defendant, the victim or of both the defendant and the victim does not, by itself, constitute legally sufficient evidence satisfying the people's burden under paragraph (a) or (b) of subdivision one of this section.

For purposes of this section:

(a) the term "age" means sixty years old or more;

(b) the term "disability" means a physical or mental impairment that substantially limits a major life activity.

The crimes that can be charged under the Hate Crime statute are listed in attachment A.

B. Penal Law § 240.31 Aggravated harassment in the first degree.

A person is guilty of aggravated harassment in the first degree when with intent to harass, annoy, threaten or alarm another person, because of a belief or perception regarding such person's race, color, national origin, ancestry, gender, religion, religious practice, age, disability or sexual orientation, regardless of whether the belief or perception is correct, he or she:

1. Damages premises primarily used for religious purposes, or acquired pursuant to section six of the religious corporation law and maintained for purposes of religious instruction, and the damage to the premises exceeds fifty dollars; or

2. Commits the crime of aggravated harassment in the second degree in the manner proscribed by the provisions of subdivision three of section 240.30 of this article and has been previously convicted of the crime of aggravated harassment in the second degree for the commission of conduct proscribed by the provisions of subdivision three of section 240.30 or he or she has been previously convicted of the crime of aggravated harassment in the first degree within the preceding ten years; or

3. Etches, paints, draws upon or otherwise places a swastika, commonly exhibited as the emblem of Nazi Germany, on any building or other real property, public or private, owned by any person, firm or corporation or any public agency or instrumentality, without express permission of the owner or operator of such building or real property;

4. Sets on fire a cross in public view; or

5. Etches, paints, draws upon or otherwise places or displays a noose, commonly exhibited as a symbol of racism and intimidation, on any building or other real property, public or private, owned by any person, firm or corporation or any public agency or instrumentality, without express permission of the owner or operator of such building or real property.

Aggravated harassment in the first degree is a class E felony.

C. Penal Law § 240.30(3) Aggravated harassment in the second degree.

A person is guilty of aggravated harassment in the first degree when with intent to harass, annoy, threaten or alarm another person, he or she:

(3) Strikes, shoves, kicks, or otherwise subjects another person to physical contact, or attempts or threatens to do the same because of a belief or perception regarding such person's race, color, national

origin, ancestry, gender, religion, religious practice, age, disability or sexual orientation, regardless of whether the belief or perception is correct.

Aggravated harassment in the second degree is a class A misdemeanor.

The additional crimes that can be charged under the Hate Crime statute are listed in Attachment A.

IV. Procedures

A. Goals

1. Officers shall conduct a thorough and complete investigation in all suspected and confirmed hate crime incidents and assist the local prosecutor.
2. Officers should make every effort to become familiar with organized hate groups operating in the community and police contacts should be documented.

B. Initial Response Procedures

Initial responding officers at the scene of a suspected hate crime shall take preliminary actions deemed necessary, including, but not limited to, the following:

1. Secure the scene. Steps should be taken so that the initial situation does not escalate. This includes but is not limited to:

    a. Stabilizing injured victims and requesting medical aid.

    b. Providing protection to victims and witnesses by increased police presence.

    c. Protect the crime scene and have technician collect and photograph physical evidence such as hate literature, spray paint cans, and symbolic objects used by hate groups, such as swastikas and crosses.

2. Identify criminal evidence on the victim if applicable.

3. Request the assistance of a translator or counselor when necessary.

4. Request the assistance of an investigator and supervisor.

5. Conduct a preliminary investigation and record information on;

   a. the identity of suspected perpetrators,

   b. the identity of witnesses, including those no longer at the scene,

   c. prior bias-motivated occurrences in the immediate area or against the same victim. (check with Crime Analyst, NYSIC (518) 786–2100 and/or Regional Crime Analysis Center if one exists),

   d. statements made by suspects; exact language is critical.

6. Arrest suspected perpetrators if probable cause exists.

   a. Conduct interview and attempt to establish motive

   b. Consult with prosecutor if there is a question as to proper criminal charges

7. Take measures to ensure that necessary preliminary actions have been taken and brief the responding supervisor as to those action

During your investigation, look for possible signs that the incident may be a hate crime:

- The motivation of the perpetrator or lack of motive.
- Statements made by the perpetrator.
- The presence of multiple perpetrators.
- The display of offensive symbols, words or acts.
- Was any hate literature found in the possession of the suspect?
- Is the victim the only person of a particular group at a park or facility?
- Is the victim from a different racial, ethnic, religious group than the perpetrator?
- The absence of any motive. The brutal nature of a particular incident could denote a hate crime,

particularly when the perpetrator and victim don't know each other.

- The perpetrator's perception of the victim, whether accurate or not.
- The date, time or circumstances of the occurrence, such as on a religious holiday, or an event occurring at a gathering of a group of people affiliated by ethnicity, religion, sexual orientation, etc.
- Multiple incidents occurring in a short time period and all the victims were of the same identifiable group.
- Were the real intentions of the perpetrator racial, color, religious or ethnic oriented, or were there other reasons such as pranks, unrelated vandalism, or a dispute arising out of a non-bias related disagreement?
- Incident occurred in proximity to an establishment that could be associated with one of the protected classes.
- The perpetrator targeted a particular portion of the victim's body; i.e. Sikh victims forcibly having his hair cut, or a victim targeted for his/her sexual orientation being attacked near or around his or her genitalia.
- The victim's perception that he/she was selected because they are a member of an identifiable group.

8. The mere mention of a bias remark does not make an incident bias motivated, just as the absence of a remark does not make an incident without bias. Even the mere perception that the incident may be motivated by bias shall necessitate a notification to a patrol supervisor.

9. Be cognizant of dual motivation by some suspects. Example: A suspect may be looking to commit robberies but specifically targets elderly victims.

    10. Note that an attack against a transgender victim could be covered under sexual orientation or gender.

C. Supervisory Responsibilities

The supervisor shall confer with the initial responding officer(s), take measures to ensure that necessary preliminary actions have been taken, and make appropriate departmental notifications as necessary. The supervisor shall request any appropriate additional personnel necessary to accomplish the following:

1. Provide immediate assistance to the crime victim.

    a. Express the law enforcement agency's official position on the importance of these cases, and describe the measures that will be taken to apprehend the perpetrators.

    b. Express the department's interest in protecting victims' anonymity whenever possible.

    c. Allow the victim a period in which to express his or her immediate concerns and express his or her feelings.

    d. Communicate with concerned community-based organizations, civic groups, and religious institutions regarding the suspected or confirmed bias incident.

    e. Identify individuals or agencies that may provide support and assistance. These may include family members or close acquaintances, a family clergyman or departmental chaplain, as well as community service agencies that provide victim assistance, shelter, food, clothing, child care, or other related services. Provide information regarding New York State Crime Victims Board (Attachment B).

    f. Tell the victim about the probable sequence of events in the investigation and prosecution.

    g. Explain security measures and precautions to the victim.

2. Ensure that officers and investigator conduct a thorough preliminary investigation.

3. Ensure that all relevant facts are documented on an incident or arrest report or both and make an initial determination as to whether the incident should be classified as a hate crime.

4. Notify other appropriate personnel in the chain of command, depending on the nature and seriousness of the offense and its potential inflammatory and related impact on the community.

5. Take preventive measures to ensure the safety of the victim.

D. Investigators' Responsibilities

In responding to the scene of an alleged hate crime, investigators shall assume control of the follow-up investigation to include the following:

1. Ensure that the scene is properly protected, preserved, and processed and that all physical evidence of the incident is removed as soon as possible after the offense is documented. If evidence of an inflammatory nature cannot be physically removed (e.g., painted words or signs on a wall), the owner of the property shall be contacted to do all that is possible to ensure that the graffiti is removed as soon as possible. The officer or investigator shall follow-up to ensure that this is accomplished in a timely manner.

2. Conduct a comprehensive interview with all victims and witnesses (and depose) at the scene, or as soon as possible thereafter, and canvass the neighborhood for additional sources of information.

3. Work closely with the prosecutor's office to ensure that a legally adequate case is developed for prosecution.

4. Coordinate the investigation with agency, state, and regional crime analysis centers. These sources shall provide the investigative officer with an analysis of any

patterns, organized hate groups, and suspects potentially involved in the offense.

5. Coordinate the investigation with other units of the agency and with outside agencies where appropriate.

6. Maintain contact with the initial responding officer and keep him or her apprised of the status of the case.

7. Recommend to Commanding Officer whether the incident should be classified as a hate crime.

8. Investigative officers shall take steps to ensure that appropriate assistance is being provided to hate crime victims, to include the following measures:

   a. Contact the victim periodically to determine whether he or she is receiving adequate and appropriate assistance.

   b. Provide ongoing information to the victim about the status of the criminal investigation.

   c. Attempt, whenever possible, to conduct all interviews with victims at their convenience and minimize, to the degree possible, interactions in which victims have to relate the incident.

E. Recommended Steps When Suspect is Not in Custody or Has Not Been Identified

   a. Coordinate investigation with other department units.

   b. Work with Analyst or Regional Crime Analysis Center to research leads and prepare bulletins.

   c. Conduct extensive canvass and distribute bulletins in area of the incident.

   d. Debrief individuals arrested in the area.

   e. Work with media to attempt to garner witnesses and investigative leads.

   f. Follow-up leads in timely manner.

F. Incident Report Preparation

Incident reports should clearly indicate the following information:

- Offense—Hate Crime designated Penal Law
- Victim age, gender, race, and ethnicity (when victim(s) is an individual(s))
- Offender age, gender, race, and ethnicity (when available)

The narrative portion of the Incident report should document that the victim(s) was intentionally selected or that the act was intentionally committed because of a belief or perception regarding such victim's race, color, national origin, ancestry, gender, religion, religious practice, age, disability, or sexual orientation. The specific bias motivation of the perpetrator should be documented (Ex: selected victim because he was Hispanic, Jewish, Muslim, etc. . .)

Source: New York Association of Chiefs of Police. Available online at http://www.nychiefs.org/ModelPolicies/MPTC_Hate_Crimes_Model_Policy.pdf Used by permission of New York Association of Chiefs of Police, Inc.

Hate on the Internet

Written by the Anti-Defamation League and funded by the U.S. Department of Justice and U.S. Department of Education, this excerpt from the Hate on the Internet *manual aims to "provide families and educators with useful information about hate on the internet and to provide strategies to help prepare children for the hate they may encounter as they navigate the World Wide Web."*

II. Defining the Problem: The Internet as a Tool for Hate
The Emergence of Hate Speech Online
By using any of the many search engines available through the World Wide Web, an Internet search of the words "Ku Klux Klan"

will produce an extensive list of Web sites promoting hate. These sites are readily accessible to the approximately 160 million Americans, including significant numbers of impressionable children and youth, who today use the Internet.

Even before the birth of the World Wide Web, media-savvy leaders of some organized hate groups recognized the potential of technology to disseminate their messages and further their goals. In the 1980s, Louis Beam, a leader of the Ku Klux Klan, and neo-Nazi publisher, George Dietz, collaborated to create a computerized bulletin board accessible to anyone with a computer, phone line, and modem. The bulletin board, "Aryan Nation Liberty Net," was subscription-based and designed to recruit young people, raise money, and incite hatred against the "enemies" of white supremacy.

In the early 1990s, many bigots united in organized online discussion groups called USENETs. USENET newsgroups were similar to the "Aryan Nation Liberty Net" but were more easily accessible to anyone with Internet access. USENETs were free and provided a venue for participants to write, read, and respond to messages of hate.

The evolution of the Internet into the World Wide Web, with its easily accessible and inviting graphic interface, has provided people, including extremists, with new ways to communicate with each other and with a vast new potential audience, using not only words, but also pictures, graphics, sound, and animation.

Don Black, a former Klan leader and convicted felon who learned to use computers while incarcerated, is attributed with creating one of the earliest hate sites, *Stormfront*, in 1995 (McKelvey, 2001). Since its creation, *Stormfront* has served as a veritable supermarket of online hate, stocking its shelves with materials that promote anti-Semitism and racism. *Stormfront* is among the most visited hate sites on the Internet, claiming upwards of five million visits to the site over the past decade. When first created, the site contained links to a scant handful of other Web sites with similar messages of hate. Today,

Stormfront provides links to hundreds of white supremacist sites, and hundreds of other sites are easily found online.

Who Is Spreading Hate Online?

A wide variety of people with bigoted ideologies, including Holocaust deniers, "Identity" adherents, Ku Klux Klan members, and virulent homophobes, use the Internet to spread their views.

Extremists Seeking Credibility

A common rationale among extremists is to use the Web to build increased respectability and mainstream acceptance of their ideas. Such groups typically characterize themselves as legitimate activists who have been unfairly denied mainstream attention. For example, David Duke, former leader of the Knights of the Ku Klux Klan, veils an ideology of white supremacy behind misleading rhetoric of "white rights." By couching bigotry in pseudo-scientific and sociological terms, Duke articulates a subtle but virulent brand of racism that exploits race-related issues such as illegal immigration and affirmative action. Other examples of Web sites designed to increase the respectability of extremist groups include the Council of Conservative Citizens and American Renaissance, which sponsor both a monthly print publication by the same name and a Web site.

Holocaust Deniers

Holocaust denial is a propaganda movement that seeks to deny the reality of the Holocaust, the systematic mass murder of six million Jews and millions of others deemed "inferior" by the Nazi regime in Europe during World War II. Misrepresenting their propaganda as "historical revisionism," Holocaust deniers attempt to disseminate their extremist ideas by offering unsupported arguments against the established historical facts of the Holocaust. Their beliefs include accusations that Jews have falsified and exaggerated the tragic events of the Holocaust in order to exploit non-Jewish guilt. Holocaust denial groups have posted thousands of Web pages, filled with distortions and fabrications, designed to reinforce negative stereotypes such as the contention that Jews maintain control of academia and the media. Among the most visited sites promoting Holocaust denial are the Institute for Historical Review, Bradley Smith and his Committee for Open Debate of the Holocaust (whose efforts focus largely on U.S. college campuses), and sites sponsored by Ahmed Rami, Ernst Zundel, and David Irving.

Identity Adherents

The Identity Church, a pseudo-theological movement that promotes racism and anti-Semitism, emerged in the U.S. during the late 1970s and early 1980s. Proponents of this movement use inflammatory and degrading language to promote hate against many groups of people, including Jews, African Americans, and other people of color. Identity organizations that have a notable presence on the Internet include Aryan Nations, the Posse Comitatus, the Church of New Israel, America's Promise Ministries, Scriptures for America, and the 11th Hour Remnant Messenger.

Ku Klux Klan Members

Although the Ku Klux Klan has undergone many permutations throughout its violent 130-year existence, the group is currently fragmented. The Internet is providing a means for the group's various factions to gain strength. Web sites of these factions share many commonalities, including information on upcoming rallies, explanations of customs (such as cross burning), and spurious accounts of Klan history. The American Knights and the Imperial Klans of America are two factions with a significant online presence.

Neo-Nazis

Numerous groups and individuals have created and maintain Web sites promoting the anti-Semitic, racist ideas of Adolf

Hitler's Nazi party. The National Alliance, one of the largest and most active neo-Nazi organizations in the United States today, was founded by William Pierce, author of *The Turner Diaries*. The stated mission of this group is "to build a better world and a better race" and to create "a new government . . . answerable to White people only" (*Extremism in America*, 2001). When Pierce died in July 2002, leadership for this group was transferred to Erich Gliebe, who recently expressed his admiration for both domestic and international terrorist groups. Though Gliebe does not necessarily agree with their political views, he praised the Islamic terrorists who attacked the United States on September 11, 2001, describing them as "serious, patient, and organized, and they had the discipline to keep their mouths shut so as not to leak any information about what they were planning" (*Extremism in America*, 2001).

The National Alliance Web site features transcripts from a weekly anti-Semitic radio broadcast, online access to many articles from the group's National Vanguard magazine, and a catalog of books with over six hundred titles. The National Alliance has recently focused most of its attention on recruiting young racists through the online marketing of white power music. In recent years, dozens of violent crimes, including murders, bombings, and robberies, have been either traced to National Alliance members or appear to have been inspired by neo-Nazi propaganda. Other neo-Nazis groups and individuals with a significant online presence include the National Socialist Movement, Matt Koehl, and Gerhard Lauck. In Germany, where distribution of hate literature is now illegal, Lauck has successfully used the Internet to sidestep national laws and widely distribute his literature and ideas throughout the country.

Racist Skinheads

Racist skinhead groups share common hateful beliefs and promote these beliefs with others. Skinheads typically align themselves with the perception of strength, group belonging and superiority promoted by the white power movement. A major aspect of racist skinhead life is devotion to musical groups who record rock music with hateful lyrics. Skinheads have effectively combined bigotry-laced hard rock and the Internet as a main propaganda weapon and means of attracting young recruits. Resistance Records, owned by the National Alliance, is a multi-million dollar enterprise that uses its Web site to market white power rock CDs by groups such as Angry Aryans, and subscriptions to *Resistance* magazine—the *Rolling Stone* of the hate movement. Other notable racist skinhead Web sites include those of the Hammerskin Nation, Plunder & Pillage, and Panzerfaust Records.

Westboro Baptist Church

Incorporated in 1967 as a not-for-profit organization, the Westboro Baptist Church (WBC) describes itself as an "Old School (or Primitive)" Baptist Church. Promoting virulent homophobia, the WBC claims responsibility for staging tens of thousands of protest rallies across the U.S. and abroad. The WBC Web site is devoted to spreading hate against people who are gay through homophobic language and ideas, photos and other graphics, and a variety of documents that support their position that the United States is "doomed" because of support and tolerance for gay Americans.

World Church of the Creator (WCOTC)

The World Church of the Creator is one of the fastest-growing hate groups in the U.S. today. The group's primary goals, articulated in their motto, "RaHoWa" (Racial Holy War) and their belief system, Creativity, is the "survival, expansion, and advancement of [the] White Race exclusively" (*Extremism in America*, 2001). Creators, as group members call themselves, do not align themselves with any religious beliefs, instead placing race as the ultimate issue influencing all realms of life. The hatred of WCOTC members is directed toward many groups, including mainstream Christians, African Americans and other people of color, and Jews, who are particularly vilified. The WCOTC Web site is extensive, frequently updated, and designed to make membership easy. Visitors to the site are provided with a membership form, a list of local "churches," and a detailed manual that explains the group's beliefs and practices, including such topics as planning WCOTC wedding ceremonies and dealing with law enforcement. The group also sponsors more than thirty other affiliated Web sites and distributes propaganda through extensive online mailing lists, bulletin boards, and chat rooms. A "Comedy" section of the WCOTC Web site includes pictures, jokes, and free downloadable racist video games targeted toward teens.

How Do Children Encounter Hate Online?

Today, children and youth regularly use the Internet for schoolwork, entertainment, and socializing. A report based on a 1999 national survey on parents and their children and the Internet (*Children, Families and the Internet*, 2000) conducted by Grunwald Associates, in collaboration with the National School Board s Foundation, reported that 25.4 million children ages 2–17 access the Internet in the U.S. on a regular basis, as illustrated in the chart to the right. This number is an approximate 40-percent increase since the previous year. These children may encounter hate on the Internet in a variety of ways, including online bulletin boards, chat rooms, Web sites, and USENET newsgroups.

The USENET, an Internet communication system that contains thousands of public discussion groups, attracts hundreds of thousands of participants each day, both active (those who write) and passive (those who simply read postings). Newsgroups have been compared to community bulletin boards, providing another forum for extremists to debate and discuss their ideas and to insult, harass, and threaten the targets of their hatred.

It should be noted that while some USENET newsgroups are devoted specifically to white supremacy, most are concerned with mainstream, legitimate topics. A common tactic of online bigots is to post messages promoting their beliefs on multiple mainstream newsgroups with the hope of attracting new supporters. Some groups, including the National Alliance, have engaged in this strategy for many years, often tailoring their messages to the particular interests of the newsgroup where they are posting. For example, for a newsgroup focusing on food, extremists have posted messages promoting the "kosher tax," a falsehood which suggests that standards required of vendors to maintain compliance with kosher food standards result in increased food prices for all consumers.

The strategies employed by hate groups have been expanded to Web-based bulletin board systems, particularly those hosted by legitimate companies such as CNN, America Online, and Yahoo! People who visit such bulletin boards, expecting to find rational, informative conversations on topics of mutual interest, instead can encounter disturbing messages posted by extremists.

Chat Rooms

"Chat" rooms provide opportunities for multiple computer users from diverse geographic locations to engage in simultaneous real-time online communication. Once a chat has been initiated, participants can join the conversation by typing text on their home computers and sending it via their modem. Entered text appears almost instantaneously on the monitors of all other participants in the chat room. In many respects, chat rooms are similar to conference calls. Many hate group extremists, including white supremacists such as WCOTC leader Matt Hale, regularly host chat sessions in order to interact with their supporters. As with USENET newsgroups, extremists also try to enter mainstream chat rooms in search of new recruits.

Instant Messaging

Instant messaging allows an Internet user to engage in a private chat room with another person or persons with access to the same instant messaging system. Typically, the instant messaging system alerts the user when someone on the user's private list is online. The user can then initiate a chat session with that particular individual. Instant messaging resembles a traditional telephone conversation between two people.

Computer users with online access can add anyone on the same instant messaging system to their private list. Unsuspecting users, including children, can easily be added to the instant messaging lists of white supremacists or other hate groups. The following is an account of the experience of one 11-year-old Jewish boy (Lieberman, 1999):

> Out of the blue, someone asked if my grandparents were one of the Six Million. I responded, 'No, they survived.' The next statement that appeared on my computer screen was, 'Oh—that's too bad.' The remark puzzled me. I then asked what was meant by that statement. The person wrote, 'Any Jew that survived was a mistake—and now—you're here.' I got very scared and shut down my computer.

E-mail

E-mail can easily and inexpensively be used to spread hate propaganda. Extensive mailing lists may be purchased for an established fee, or can be readily created using one of a number of free online directories. Large-scale e-mail mailings are free of the typical postal fees and materials costs associated with traditional mass postal mailings. Without ever revealing their identities, enterprising groups and individuals are now able to mass-mail unsolicited hate materials to tens of thousands of people.

Hateful e-mail can also be directed at a single, specific target. When the 11-year-old described earlier turned his computer back on, he found hundreds of anti-Semitic e-mail messages in his mailbox from "Adolph Jr." with the subject "Jewish extermination part two."

The World Wide Web

Though purveyors of hate make use of all the communication tools the Internet provides, Web site development is their forum of choice. Bigots, promoting their messages of hate on bulletin boards, in chat rooms, via instant messages, or with e-mail, often encourage their readers to gain additional information by visiting their Web site.

In addition to the World Wide Web's multimedia capabilities and popularity with Internet users, the Web also allows bigots to present their messages of hate without mediation. Although civil rights activists may critique a group's manifestoes in USENET newsgroups and other interactive forums, hate groups are under no obligation to publish these differing perspectives on their Web sites. When children visit a hate site, they see only the opinions of the individuals creating that site, often presented as hard fact. Other points of view that may discredit or disagree with those opinions can only be accessed through additional online research.

Although the ability to assess the accuracy and reliability of online information is now a vital skill for children and youth, the nature of the Internet can make it difficult for people to evaluate the credibility of organizations sponsoring Web sites. Both the reputable and the disreputable are on the Web, and many Web users lack the experience, knowledge, and skills to distinguish between them. Increasingly, Web development tools have made it easier for members of hate groups to create sites that visually resemble those of reputable organizations. Consequently, these groups can easily portray themselves as legitimate voices of authority.

Generally, people locate specific Web sites in one of three ways: by connecting from another site via a link, through Web directories, and by using one of a number of online search engines. If children follow links from legitimate sites, they are unlikely to end up at a hate site without being aware of the nature of the site. Mainstream sites rarely link to hate sites, and those that do, typically do so in an educational context, so readers understand that if they click on the link, they will be taken to an extremist site.

Web directories, which contain categorized lists of specific sites and their Web addresses, rarely provide descriptions about the sponsors or content of listed sites. While some directories accurately classify hate sites as such, others describe these sites using some of the misleading terms that extremists themselves employ, such as "White Pride" and "Racialist." In one leading Web directory, students can find Holocaust denial sites under the term "Revisionism," the same euphemism that Holocaust deniers use to infer legitimacy for their beliefs. Some Web directories have separate versions which include only those sites that are appropriate for children, such as Yahooligans by Yahoo! These child-friendly directories are designed to be free of addresses for hate sites and other inappropriate content.

While many Web directories provide useful information for identifying hate sites, most search engines do not. Search engines, unlike Web directories, provide users with listings that are based on a computer algorithm, without the added benefit of human assessment and evaluation. Search engines tend to classify Web sites on the basis of how sites describe themselves. Although search engines are indispensable for conducting online research, providing extensive listings of Web sites associated with a particular term, children need instruction to prepare them for the possibility of encountering hate and misinformation while conducting online searches. Many hate sites purposefully describe themselves in misleading terms so that search engines will include their sites in search results for legitimate, benign terms, such as "Civil War" or "Holocaust history."

[. . .]

Can Hate on the Internet Be Eliminated?

Technologically and legally, it is likely that removing hate speech from the Internet is almost impossible. Decentralized by design, the Internet is a worldwide network that consists of thousands of computers with high-speed connections. Often described as an "information superhighway," the Internet crosses international borders, has thousands of unpoliced on-ramps, and has no uniform rules of the road. Because the Internet is global, the laws of the most permissive country have historically set the tone. In general, it is the United States, with its cherished right of free speech, that tends to govern the freedoms afforded online speech. U.S. citizens must often struggle to reconcile their belief in the Constitutional right of free speech with the recognition that the Constitution provides the same rights to all, including hate groups. The protection of these freedoms results in an environment where legitimate dialogue exists alongside hate. A number of people with extremist views from other countries exploit these American freedoms and store their hate sites on computers in the U.S., thus avoiding more stringent laws in their home countries.

The First Amendment shields the majority of hate speech from government regulation. Unless blanket statements of hate, such as "I hate Blacks," contain specific threats, they are protected under the First Amendment. This is true even if such statements mention specific names and cause distress to those individuals. Additionally, in a 1997 Supreme Court decision, *Reno* v. *ACLU*1, lawmakers clarified that traditional First Amendment protection of free speech did extend to speech on the Internet.

The First Amendment does not protect all speech. Speech that is threatening or harassing, for example, may be legally actionable. Threats are generally defined as an individual's declaration of intent to hurt another person. Threatening speech is by far the most likely type of unprotected hate speech to be prosecuted. To be prosecuted, threats must be believable and directed at a specific person, organization or institution. Courts will look at the context in which a statement was made to determine if it is threatening. Prosecution of threatening speech is one measure that has led to some success in the battle against hate on the Internet.

The nature of the Internet, however, complicates the prosecution of threatening hate speech. By using any one of a number of services that provide almost complete anonymity, people intent on promoting bigotry may send repeated emails to a person without revealing their identity. A prosecutable message may easily and anonymously be transmitted to multiple computers in other countries, even if both the sender and the recipient of the message live in the United States. It is not unusual for foreign companies, responsible for computers that are used to transmit such messages, to refuse to provide information to law enforcement agencies in the United States. For example, in the incident described earlier in this publication, in which an 11-year-old Jewish child received multiple e-mail messages from "Adolph, Jr.," many of the messages contained death threats. The Internet Service Provider used to transmit these messages from the Netherlands refused to respond to inquiries about the incident, and authorities were unable to determine the source of the messages. Even when Internet Service Providers want to help investigators, they may be unable to provide the information necessary to identify the culprit. Such companies keep logs of the activities on their computers for a limited time only. If an investigation begins even a week after a potentially criminal message was sent, the relevant records may have already been deleted.

Though most of the thousands of Internet Service Providers that exist in the United States do not regulate hate speech *per se*, some contractually prohibit users from sending bigoted messages on their services, even when that speech is legally permissible. Such prohibitions do not violate the First Amendment because they are stipulations of private contracts with users and do not involve government action. The effectiveness of this strategy is very limited, however, as subscribers who lose their Internet accounts for contract violation may easily sign up with another service that has more permissive regulations. Furthermore, many companies that provide Internet service in the United States have little incentive to regulate the speech of their users because the Telecommunications Act of 1996 specifically states that Internet Service Providers cannot be held criminally liable for the speech of subscribers.

Source: *Hate on the Internet: A Response Guide for Educators and Families*. Washington, DC: Partners Against Hate, 2003.

Hate Violence in 2013

Published by the National Coalition of Anti-Violence Programs (NCAVP), a major national coalition that monitors hate crimes against the LGBT community, this excerpt from their 2013 report includes a statistical summary and analysis of these crimes. The NCAVP claims their reporting "represents the most in-depth information to date on anti-LGBTQ and HIV-affected hate violence available throughout the U.S. including: detailed demographic information on survivors and victims of violence of these crimes." The FBI statistics are not as comprehensive nor are they as intently analyzed.

Executive Summary

In 2013 overall reports of anti-LGBTQ and HIV-affected hate violence and anti-LGBTQ and HIV-affected homicides stayed relatively consistent to 2012, with slight decreases. NCAVP's 2013 hate violence report continues to document multi-year trends revealing that anti-LGBTQ and HIV-affected hate violence disproportionately impacts transgender women, LGBTQ and HIV-affected communities of color, transgender people, and transgender people of color. Also consistent with previous years, White gay cisgender[1] men represented the largest group of hate violence survivors and victims in 2013, showing that hate violence remains a pervasive and persistent issue for all LGBTQ

---

[1]Cisgender is a term used to identify individuals whose gender identity and gender expression matches the sex they were assigned at birth. NCAVP replaced the term non-transgender with "cisgender" in the 2012 report in order for the report language to reflect contemporary language used in the LGBTQ community.

and HIV-affected people. These findings continue to shed light on the importance of violence prevention initiatives, strategic responses to violence, research, and accurate reporting of hate violence as it affects LGBTQ and HIV-affected communities.

Key Findings

Reported Incidents

In 2013, reports of anti-LGBTQ and HIV-affected hate violence stayed relatively consistent with 2012, with a slight .74% decrease (2,016 total reports in 2012, and 2,001 total reports in 2013). However, for NCAVP member organizations that reported data both in 2012 and 2013, the number of incidents actually increased. NCAVP member organization Sean's Last Wish reported data in 2012 and not in 2013, while the Civil Rights Commission of Puerto Rico reported for the first time in 2013. Total number of incidents, disregarding the data from Sean's Last Wish in 2012 and by the Civil Rights Commission of Puerto Rico in 2013, increased by 3%, from 1,926 incidents in 2012 to 1,984 incidents in 2013. In addition, 2013 also saw an increase in the severity of hate violence incidents, with substantial increases in the number of hate violence incidents involving physical and sexual violence.

Hate Violence Homicides

In 2013, anti-LGBTQ and HIV-affected homicides decreased by 28% from 2012 (25 hate violence homicides in 2012 to 18 hate violence homicides in 2013). While NCAVP documented a decrease in homicides in 2013, the total homicides for 2013 remains amongst the highest ever recorded by NCAVP. Severe violence against people of color, transgender, and gender non-conforming LGBTQ and HIV-affected people remains alarmingly high. 89% of all homicide victims in 2013 were people of color, yet LGBTQ and HIV-affected people of color only represented 55% of total survivors and victims. The overwhelming majority of homicide victims (78%) were Black and

African American, 11% of homicide victims were Latin@, and 11% of homicide victims were White. More than half (72%) of victims were transgender women, while 67% of homicide victims were transgender women of color, yet transgender survivors and victims only represent 13% of total reports to NCAVP, highlighting a disproportionate impact of homicide against transgender people. 28% of homicide victims were men, all of whom identified as gay.

Most Impacted Communities

Transgender women survivors were:

- 4 times more likely to experience police violence compared to overall survivors.
- 6 times more likely to experience physical violence when interacting with the police compared to overall survivors.
- 2 times more likely to experience discrimination and 1.8 times more likely to experience harassment compared to overall survivors, and 1.5 times more likely to experience threats and intimidation compared to overall survivors.
- 1.8 times more likely to experience sexual violence when compared to overall survivors.

Transgender survivors were:

- 3.7 times more likely to experience police violence compared to cisgender survivors and victims.
- 7 times more likely to experience physical violence when interacting with the police compared to cisgender survivors and victims.
- 1.8 times more likely to experience discrimination compared to cisgender survivors and victims.
- 1.4 times more likely to experience threats and intimidation compared to cisgender survivors and victims.

- 1.5 times more likely to experience harassment when compared to cisgender survivors.
- 1.7 times more likely to experience sexual violence when compared to cisgender survivors.

Transgender people of color survivors were:

- 2.7 times more likely to experience police violence and 6 times more likely to experience physical violence from the police compared to White cisgender survivors and victims.
- 1.5 times more likely to experience discrimination, 1.5 times more likely to experience threats and intimidation, and 1.5 times more likely to experience sexual violence compared to White cisgender survivors and victims.
- 1.8 times more likely to experience hate violence in shelters.

Transgender men survivors were:

- 1.6 times more likely to experience violence from the police and 5.2 times more likely to experience physical violence perpetrated by the police.
- 1.5 times more likely to experience injuries as a result of hate violence and 4.3 times more likely to be the target of hate violence in shelters when compared with other survivors.

LGBTQ and HIV-affected undocumented survivors were:

- 1.7 times more likely to report to the police and 1.4 times more likely to experience police violence.
- 3.4 times more likely to experience sexual violence and 3.5 times more likely to experience any physical violence.
- 2.0 times more likely to experience injury as a result of hate violence and 1.7 times more likely to require medical attention.

LGBTQ and HIV-affected people of color survivors were:

- 1.5 times more likely to experience physical violence compared to White LGBTQ survivors and were 1.4 times more likely to experience violence in the street or a public area.
- 1.7 times more likely to experience hate violence at the workplace when compared to other survivors.
- 1.7 times more likely to be injured and 2.0 times more likely to require medical attention as a result of hate violence when compared with other survivors.

LGBTQ and HIV-affected Black survivors were:

- 1.4 times more likely to experience any physical violence, 2.0 times more likely to experience threats and intimidation, and 1.4 times more likely to be harassed in public areas.
- 1.4 times more likely to be injured and 2.0 times more likely to require medical attention.

LGBTQ and HIV-affected Latin@ survivors were:

- 1.7 times more likely to experience discrimination, and 1.5 times more likely to be injured.
- 1.5 times more likely to experience police violence, and 1.9 times more likely to report to the police.
- 2.1 times more likely to experience hate violence incidents at the workplace.

Gay men survivors were:

- 1.4 times more likely to report to the police.
- 1.4 times more likely to experience physical violence.
- 1.6 times more likely to experience hate violence incidents in public areas.

- 1.4 times more likely to experience injury as a result of hate violence and 1.7 times more likely to require medical attention.

Lesbian survivors were:

- 1.4 times more likely to experience discrimination and harassment.
- 1.2 times more likely to experience sexual violence, and 1.8 times more likely to experience violence in the workplace

Cisgender women survivors were:

- 1.6 times more likely to experience sexual violence and 1.6 times more likely to experience hate violence in the workplace.

Hate Violence Survivor and Victim Demographics

In 2013, gay survivors and victims represented the highest percentage of total reports (50%). This is consistent with 2012's findings, where gay survivors represented 45% of overall victims and survivors. Lesbian survivors represented 19% of survivors in 2013, a decrease from 2012's findings (21%). Heterosexual survivors represented 14% of survivors in 2013, a decrease from 18% in 2012.[2] Bisexual survivors represented 9% of survivors in 2013, consistent with 2012 (9%). Men accounted for 37% of total hate violence survivors, an increase from 2012 (30%). Women represented the second highest (24%) gender identity category in 2013, with a slight decrease from 2012 (25%). Transgender survivors represented 13% of survivors, a significant increase from 2012 (11%). There was also an absolute increase in the number of transgender survivors who reported to NCAVP in 2013, from 305 in 2012 to 344

---

[2]Within NCAVP's data, "heterosexual" includes multiple identities and most likely represents more transgender people than within heterosexual communities in the United States.

individual survivors in 2013 which represents a 12.79% change from 2012. 8% of survivors were undocumented immigrants.

Police Response

Only 45% of survivors reported their incidents to the police, a slight decrease from 2012 (56%). 32% of survivors reported hostile attitudes from the police in 2013, an increase from 2012 (27%). Of the survivors who interacted with the police and experienced hostility and police misconduct, 55% reported being unjustly arrested by the police, consistent with data from 2012 (57%). Excessive force accounted for 28% of police misconduct, which is exactly consistent with 2012 (28%). Entrapment accounted for 8% of police misconduct, down from 12% in 2012. Police raids accounted for 8% of police misconduct, a large increase from 2012 (3%).

Police Classification

In 2013, 24% of hate violence incidents reported to the police were classified as bias crimes, a substantial decrease from 2012 (77%).

Recommendations for Policymakers and Funders

End the Root Causes of Anti-LGBTQ and HIV-affected Violence through Ending Poverty and Anti-LGBTQ and HIV-affected Discrimination.

• Federal, state, and local governments should pass non-discrimination laws such as the Employment Non-Discrimination Act, the Repeal HIV Discrimination Act, and enact policies that protect LGBTQ and HIV-affected communities from discrimination based on sexual orientation, gender identity, gender expression, and HIV-status.

• Federal, state, and local governments should end laws and policies which criminalize homelessness, HIV status, participation in sex work, and drug possession to increase safety for the most severely impacted LGBTQ and HIV-affected survivors and victims of hate violence.

- Policymakers and legislators should pass laws and policies to address LGBTQ and HIV-affected youth experiences of bullying, harassment, and violence in schools, foster care, family court, shelters, and the juvenile justice system by passing an LGBTQ-inclusive Runaway and Homeless Youth Act, funding trainers familiar to work with these agencies on LGBTQ and HIV-affected cultural competency trainings, and support restorative justice models in schools.
- Policymakers and law enforcement should end policies which profile and police people engaged in survival crimes, and support harm reduction services to support people engaged in survival crimes.
- The United States Interagency Council on Homelessness should establish an LGBTQ and HIV-affected specific research agenda to research policies and programs to address hate violence against LGBTQ and HIV-affected homeless people.
- Federal and state policymakers should raise the minimum wage to increase low-income and low-wage workers to be able to meet basic needs and increase their safety.

End the Homophobic, Transphobic, and Biphobic Culture That Fuels Violence.

- Policymakers and funders should support public education and awareness campaigns to reduce and end homophobia, biphobia, and transphobia.
- Policymakers and public figures should promote safety for LGBTQ and HIV-affected people by denouncing homophobic, biphobic, and transphobic statements, laws, and programs.
- Policymakers should prohibit offenders of anti-LGBTQ and HIV-affected hate violence from using "Gay and Transgender panic" defenses.
- Policymakers should support alternative sentencing programs including individual and group intervention programs,

community service with LGBTQ and HIV-affected organizations, and LGBTQ and HIV-affected antiviolence education programs to encourage behavior change for hate violence offenders.

- Federal, state, and local governments should reduce reporting barriers for LGBTQ and HIV-affected survivors including removing laws and policies that prevent survivors from accessing law enforcement.

- Federal, state, and local governments should mandate trainings that increase first responders' and non-LGBTQ and HIV-affected direct service providers' knowledge and competency on serving LGBTQ and HIV-affected survivors of violence.

- Federal, state, and local governments should pass laws and policies that prevent LGBTQ and HIV-affected students from experiencing bullying, harassment, and violence in schools such as the Student Non-Discrimination Act and the Safe Schools Improvement Act.

End Police Profiling and Police Violence against LGBTQ and HIV-affected People.

- Federal, state, and local governments should enact polices that prohibit police profiling such as the federal End Racial Profiling Ban that includes provisions on sexual orientation, gender identity, gender expression, immigration status, housing status, and race.

- Policymakers should ensure that police officers are investigated and held accountable for homophobic, biphobic, and transphobic harassment and violence.

- Federal, state, and local governments should enact humane, LGBTQ-inclusive immigration reform policies which create a pathway to residency and citizenship for undocumented immigrants and end "enforcement-only" policies such as the Secure Communities (S-Comm), and 287(g) programs, while expanding Deferred Action for Childhood Arrivals (DACA) to include adult immigrants.

- The Center for Disease Control and the Department of Justice should issue guidance condemning reliance on the use of condoms as evidence of prostitution law violations to improve the public safety and public health of LGBTQ and HIV-affected people. State and local law enforcement agencies should prohibit the use of condoms as evidence of prostitution law violations.

- Local law enforcement agencies should prohibit policing protocols and practices that use searches to assign gender for detainees.

- Policymakers should enact policies that address homophobic, transphobic, and biphobic violence within jails, detention centers, and prisons.

- Policymakers should continue to implement the Prison Rape Elimination Act (PREA) in immigration detention centers.

Collect Data and Expand Research on LGBTQ and HIV-affected Communities Overall, Particularly Data and Research on LGBTQ and HIV-affected Communities' Experiences of Violence.

- Federal, state, and local governments should collect and analyze data that includes sexual orientation and gender identity, whenever any demographic information is requested, to more effectively analyze data on LGBTQ and HIV-affected hate violence survivors and victims.

- Federal surveys that collect data on incidents of violence, including the FBI's Uniform Crime Report and the United States Department of Justice's National Crime Victimization Survey, should include questions regarding the sexual orientation and gender identity of both survivors and offenders.

Increase Funding for LGBTQ and HIV-affected Anti-violence Support and Prevention.

- Policymakers and funders should support research on effective LGBTQ and HIV-affected hate violence prevention strategies and models.

- Federal, state, and local governments should fund programs that increase government support for LGBTQ and HIV-affected anti-violence programs, by including LGBTQ and HIV-affected specific funding in all federal, state, and local anti-violence funding streams.

- Federal, state, and local governments should recognize that violence against LGBTQ and HIV-affected people, particularly transgender communities of color, as a public health crisis and support initiatives to prevent this violence.

- Public and private funders should support programs that provide training and technical assistance on serving LGBTQ and HIV-affected survivors of violence to anti-violence grantees.

- Public and private funders should support community-based hate violence prevention initiatives to target programming within communities that are disproportionately affected by violence or underreporting their incidents of violence.

- Private funders including foundations, corporate donors, and individual donors should fund strategies to support LGBTQ and HIV-affected survivors separate from the criminal legal system including community accountability and transformative justice.

- Public and private funders should fund data collection and research on LGBTQ and HIV-affected communities' experiences of violence.

Introduction

The 2013 LGBTQ and HIV-affected hate violence report highlights annual and multi-year trends grounded in contemporary research to give policymakers, LGBTQ and HIV-affected communities, and anti-violence practitioners a wide-ranging viewpoint on the current dynamics of homophobic, biphobic, and transphobic hate violence. It represents the most in-depth information to date on anti-LGBTQ and HIV-affected hate violence available throughout the U.S. including: detailed demographic information on survivors and victims of violence, information on hate violence offenders, and data on police and medical response to anti-LGBTQ and HIV-affected incidents of violence. Data on LGBTQ and HIV-affected communities in the United States is extremely limited, making it challenging for NCAVP to compare its data on LGBTQ and HIV-affected survivors to data on overall LGBTQ and HIV-affected communities. Current data that exists suggests that between 20–25% of lesbian and gay people experience hate crimes within their lifetimes.[3] Unfortunately, data on the prevalence of hate violence against queer, bisexual, transgender, and HIV-affected people is virtually non-existent. The U.S. Census and the American Community Survey, the main data collection surveys for the federal government, and the National Crime Victimization Survey, the federal survey on violence in the U.S., contains no questions on sexual orientation or gender identity. The only comparable data to NCAVP's hate violence report is the "Hate Crime Statistics" report annually released by the FBI's Criminal Justice Information Services Division. This report documents hate crimes motivated by bias against sexual orientation that local law enforcement agencies report to the FBI annually, although only 13.3% of the 13,022 participating law enforcement agencies reported hate crime data to the FBI in 2012. The FBI is currently working to collect information on hate crimes data motivated on the basis of gender identity in accordance with the Matthew Shepard, James Byrd Jr. Hate Crime Prevention Act, but this information is not currently

---

[3]Hate Crime Victimization Among Lesbian, Gay, and Bisexual Adults: Prevalence, Psychological Correlates, and Methodological Issues http://psychology.ucdavis.edu/rainbow/html/violence.PDF

published.[4] In 2013 NCAVP documented over 600 more survivors and victims of hate violence than the FBI in 2012 (1,376 survivors and victims compared to 2,001 survivors and victims).[5] While the FBI tracks hate crimes and NCAVP tracks hate violence including incidents that may not be reported to law enforcement or incidents that law enforcement may not classify as a hate crime, NCAVP still finds the stark difference between these incidents disconcerting.

In January, 2013 the Centers for Disease Control and Prevention (CDC) released a report titled: "The National Intimate Partner Violence and Sexual Violence Survey (NISVS): 2010 findings on Victimization by Sexual Orientation."[6] This groundbreaking report is the first nationally representative prevalence estimate of sexual violence, stalking, and intimate partner violence among those who identify as lesbian, gay, or bisexual in the United States. In many instances of stalking, intimate partner violence, and specifically sexual violence against LGBTQ and HIV-affected communities, anti-LGBTQ bias is utilized. In this study, participants were asked to identify their sexual orientation and/or gender identity. Transgender and gender non-conforming people were not represented in the NISVS findings because the sample size was too small and based on self-reporting. This suggests the need for more explicit inclusion of gender identity and expression in future studies; specifically the inclusion of gender identity and sexual orientation in national surveys, like the FBI's Uniform Crime Report and the Department of Justice's National Crime Victimization Survey, that collect data on hate crimes and hate violence. The study

---

[4]FBI Criminal Justice Information Services Division 2011 Hate Crimes Report. Accessed from http://www.fbi.gov/about-us/cjis/ucr/hate-crime/2010/tables/table-4-offenses-offense-type-by-bias-motivation-2010.xls on April, 4 2014.
[5]Ibid.
[6]Centers For Disease Control and Prevention. The National Intimate Partner and Sexual Violence Survey: 2010 Findings on Victimization by Sexual Orientation. Accessed from http://www.cdc.gov/violenceprevention/pdf/nisvs_sofindings.pdf on April 4th, 2013.

highlights that the lifetime prevalence of rape by any offender against bisexual women was 46.1%, 13.1% for lesbian women and 17.4% for heterosexual women.[7] In addition, 1 in 3 bisexual women (36.6%) have experienced stalking victimization during their lifetime.[8] NCAVP welcomes the increased federal attention on the experiences of LGBTQ and HIV-affected survivors and victims and that federal data collection systems are becoming increasingly more inclusive.

Despite this groundbreaking progress, the lack of comprehensive data about LGBTQ and HIV-affected communities and violence results in policymakers, advocates, practitioners, and LGBTQ and HIV-affected communities having less information on the dynamics of anti-LGBTQ and HIV-affected hate violence. This reduces LGBTQ and HIV-affected communities' ability to create programs that increase safety and support for LGBTQ and HIV-affected survivors and limits LGBTQ and HIV-affected anti-violence programs' ability to measure and evaluate the impact of their programs. Programs experience challenges measuring their impact without this prevalence data because they cannot compare and contrast their programmatic rates of violence with overall rates of hate violence for LGBTQ and HIV-affected communities. It also affects anti-violence programs' ability to tailor programming to the communities who are most severely impacted by violence.

Recognizing the unique and critical role that NCAVP's hate violence report serves, NCAVP continually strives to ensure that this report is accessible to multiple audiences, reflects the current lived experiences of LGBTQ and HIV-affected communities, and provides practical tools to assist anti-violence programs and policymakers working to end anti-LGBTQ and HIV-affected hate violence. In 2013 NCAVP continued the data enhancement project, which originally started in 2010.

---

[7]Ibid.
[8]Ibid.

This project allowed NCAVP to highlight the specific impact of hate violence and intimate partner violence on transgender communities and LGBTQ and HIV-affected communities of color, among many other communities, within our annual reports. In addition, in 2013 NCAVP collected data on the socioeconomic condition of survivors, and plans to publish this data in 2014 reports. NCAVP, in 2013, increased the amount of variables and person-level analysis compared to previous years and continues to create new analytical categories to understand the intersections of identity and hate violence. The increasing severity of hate violence LGBTQ and HIV-affected communities face only reinforces NCAVP's need to find new ways to document and analyze hate violence to support critical legislative, policy, and cultural change.

Gender Identity of Offenders

In 2013, male offenders were the majority of the perpetrators of hate violence, representing 72.45% of reports of hate violence offenders, a large increase from 2012 (43.49%). Women made up 18.25% of offenders, an increase from 2012 (9.52%). These increases in the number of male and female perpetrators are due to the decrease in the reporting of the number of offenders identified as cisgender, although it would be safe to assume that a large majority of those offenders identified as men and women are also cisgender individuals. Transgender, intersex, and other self-identified offenders account for less than 1% of offenders in instances of hate violence. These findings suggest, similar to age, that offenders are more likely to target people of the same identity they hold, except for hate violence incidents involving transgender survivors, who usually identify the person who acted violently against them as cisgender. This is the second year that NCAVP has collected this data, and we believe that the data, while reflecting the survivors and victims' perceptions, is more accurate for men and cisgender offenders than for other gender identities. This data gives policymakers and practitioners important information on the need to target hate violence prevention programs towards cisgender men.

Racial and Ethnic Identity of Offenders

In 2013 most instances of hate violence against LGBTQ and HIV-affected communities (39.09%) were committed by offenders perceived to be White by survivors, while in 2012 White offenders accounted for 27.30% of total offenders. Black and Latina@ offenders account for 34.14% and 20.68% of offenders respectively. In 2012 Black offenders were identified in 40.7% of incidents while Latin@ offenders accounted for 25.11% of overall offenders. In 3.68% of hate violence incidents, the perpetrators were not identified as clearly belonging to a particular ethnic or racial category and were identified as "self-identified or other" by survivors which is consistent with data from 2012. Asian/Pacific Islander, Arab/Middle Eastern and Native American offenders make up a combined total of less than 3% of offender racial identities. It is important to note that offender race is based on the survivor's perception of the offenders' racial identity, and data in this category often does not show any particular trends from one year to the next.

Age of Offenders

In 2013 30.70% of offenders were between 19–29, a decrease from 2012 (45.5%). Ages 30–39 and 40–49 both represent 12.60% of reports, which represents a decrease for both age categories from 18.67% and 14.79% respectively. The number of youth offenders, between the ages of 15–18 also decreased from 13.12% in 2012 to 10.46% in 2013. In contrast, the number of offenders over the age of 50 increased sharply from accounting approximately 7% of offenders in 2012 to more than 9% in 2013. The range of reported ages of offenders mirrors that of LGBTQ and HIV-affected survivors of hate violence, suggesting that offenders are likely to be close in age with the survivors. This data also shows the need for hate violence prevention strategies and LGBTQ and HIV-affected education programs targeted at youth and young adults.

Total Number of Offenders

In 2013 68.75% of survivors were attacked by one offender, a slight increase from 2012 (62.80%). Also in 2013, 23.08% of survivors reported 2–5 offenders, which is fairly consistent with 2012 (18.90%), and only 2.40% of survivors reported 10 or more offenders, a large decrease from 2012 (16.10%). Furthermore, 5.77% of survivors reported 6–9 offenders, which is an increase from 2012 (2.20%). The increase in multiple offenders is likely reflecting more accurate reporting by NCAVP members. NCAVP members often observe that more than other types of violence, hate violence is more likely to involve group violence. Scholars observe that hate violence is often fueled by a sense of peer approval,[9] which increases the amounts of offenders. Anti-LGBTQ and HIV-affected group violence may be particularly common due to a need on the part of offenders to assert their heterosexuality in front of their peers. This "peer mentality" can make hate violence incidents more severe and in some cases more deadly.[10]

Offender Relationships

Data collected by NCAVP from 2013 indicates that in 46.95% of cases of hate violence, the offender was someone whom the survivor already knew, which contradicts the popular belief that hate violence is usually perpetrated by strangers.

In 2013, landlords, tenants, and neighbors represented the most common category of known offenders (25.83%), a slight increase from 2012 (24.26%). Employers and co-workers represent 15.53% of known offenders, which is consistent with

[9]"Hate Crimes: Characteristics of Incidents, Victims, and Offenders," McDevitt, J., et al. Accessed from: http://www.sagepub.com/upm-data/14238_Chapter6.pdf on April 16, 2014.
[10]Ibid.

2012 when 15.99% of known offenders were employees and co-workers. Relatives and family represent 14.95% of known offenders, another increase from 2012 (13.74%). Within known offenders, other relationships represented 14.37% of total reports, a slight increase from 2012 (11.78%), which indicates that these categories are not exhaustive. Acquaintances and friends represent 9.87% of known offenders, remaining fairly consistent with 2012 data (8.98%). The police and other law enforcement combined represent less than 2% of hate violence offenders, a notable decrease from the previous year (6.45%). Ex-lovers, ex-partners, lovers and partners, service providers, roommates, and first responders each represent 5% or less of known offenders.

These findings reflect the diversity of hate violence offenders showing that LGBTQ and HIV-affected people experience hate violence from a range of people in their lives, from landlords, from employers, within families, and from law enforcement. The increase in hate violence from employers, co-workers, and landlords points to the need for non-discrimination policies for LGBTQ and HIV-affected people to prevent workplace and housing based hate violence. For some LGBTQ and HIV-affected, communities, the pervasive experiences of hate violence and discrimination can result in long-term economic consequences.

In 2013, 87.34% of unknown offenders were strangers, an increase from 2012 (73.01%). Only 9.90% of unknown offenders were police, a significant decrease from 2012 (23.93%). In 1.25% of cases where the offender was indicated as unknown, the violence was reported to be related to pick-up/hook-up violence which remains consistent with 2012 (1.53%). To address pick-up/hook-up related hate violence, the Buckeye Region Anti-Violence Organization, New York City Anti-Violence Project, and other NCAVP members are engaged in targeted outreach through online dating and hook-up sites. First responders, other unknown relationships, and other law enforcement combined made up less than 1% of total unknown offenders.

Source: National Coalition of Anti-Violence Programs. Lesbian, Gay, Bisexual, Transgender, Queer, and HIV-Affected Hate Violence in 2013: 2014 Release Edition. New York: NCAVP. Available online at http://www.avp.org/storage/documents/2013_ncavp_hvreport_final.pdf Used by permission of the National Coalition of Anti-Violence Programs.

Vulnerable to Hate: A Survey of Hate Crimes Committed against Homeless People in 2013

Published by the National Coalition for the Homeless in June 2014, this excerpt "has the main objective of educating lawmakers, advocates, and the general public about the problem of hate crimes and violence against homeless people. The hope is to instigate change and ensure protection of civil rights for everyone, regardless of their economic circumstances or housing status."

Executive Summary

In the past 15 years (1999–2013), the National Coalition for the Homeless (NCH) has documented 1,437 acts of violence against homeless individuals by housed perpetrators. These crimes are believed to have been motivated by the perpetrators' biases against homeless individuals or by their ability to target homeless people with relative ease. *VULNERABLE TO HATE: A Survey of Hate Crimes Committed against Homeless People in 2013* is the 15th annual report documenting violence against people experiencing homelessness, including an array of atrocities from murder to beatings, rapes, and even mutilation.

NCH found startling data in the number and severity of attacks. However, the reports also acknowledge that, since the homeless community is treated so poorly in our society, many more attacks go unreported. Hate crimes against the homeless community are part of an issue that is in growing need of public attention.

Over the last 15 years, NCH has determined the following:

- 1,437 reported acts of violence have been committed against homeless individuals.

- 375 of the victims have lost their lives as a result of the attacks.
- Reported violence has occurred in 47 states, Puerto Rico, and Washington, DC.
- Perpetrators of these attacks were generally male and under the age 30; most commonly they were teenage boys.

Specifically, in 2013:

- 85% of all perpetrators were under the age of 30.
- 93% of all perpetrators were male.
- 65% of all victims were 40 years old or older.
- 90% of all victims were male.
- 18 of the 109 attacks resulted in death.

VULNERABLE TO HATE: A Survey of Hate Crimes Committed against Homeless People in 2013 documents the known cases of violence against individuals experiencing homelessness by housed individuals in 2013. The report includes descriptions of the cases, current and pending legislation that would help protect homeless people, and recommendations for advocates to help prevent violence against homeless individuals.

Purpose Statement

The main objective of this report is to educate lawmakers, advocates, and the general public about hate crimes and violence against homeless people, in order to bring about change and ensure the protection of civil rights for everyone, regardless of economic circumstances or housing status. As part of its mission, the NCH is committed to creating the systemic and attitudinal changes necessary to end homelessness. A large component of these changes must include the societal guarantee of safety and protection, as well as a commitment by lawmakers to combat hate crimes and other violent acts against people who experience homelessness.

Methodology

The data on violent acts committed against the homeless population was gathered from a variety of sources. A number of narratives were taken from published national and local news reports. Homeless advocates and local service providers across the country provided information about incidents in their local communities. Lastly, this report relied on the voices of homeless persons and formerly homeless people, who self-reported incidents they experienced first-hand.

Every reported incident was subject to a rigorous factchecking process, designed to evaluate and verify the accuracy of the reported events. This process entailed multiple follow-up discussions with those closely involved with the incident. Cross-comparisons were also made with other news sources reporting the incident.

While the motive for each attack was not always evident from the information available, in many cases, there was confirmation that these violent acts were perpetrated because of a bias against the victim based his or her housing status. Other attacks were deemed opportunistic, and committed merely because the homeless person, due to the nature of homelessness, was in a vulnerable position that turned him or her into an easy target. Only attacks perpetrated by housed individuals against un-housed individuals were evaluated. Crimes committed by homeless people against other homeless persons were excluded from this report.

Although the NCH has made every effort to verify the facts regarding each incident included in this report, new information about cases may become available after its publication. For this reason, the NCH constantly researches and reviews all facts related to the included data. As additional evidence emerges about prior, new, or previously unknown cases, it is the policy of NCH to adjust tabulations based on the new information.

Now and Then: Hate Crimes against the
Homeless 1999–2013

The FBI does not currently recognize a protected status for people experiencing homelessness. Over the past 15 years, the NCH has recorded 1,437 incidents of crimes committed against this unprotected group. In 2013 alone, the NCH became aware of 109 attacks, 18 of which resulted in death. While this report provides alarming statistics, it is important to note that people experiencing homelessness are often treated so poorly by society that attacks are forgotten or unreported.

In this country, hate crimes are committed against a group of vulnerable people who are at constant risk because they live in public spaces. Many of our local communities do not have shelter space or adequate affordable housing to meet their needs. According to the U.S. Department of Housing and Urban Development, on a single night in 2013 there were 610,042 homeless people in the United States, including 387,845 who were homeless as individuals and 222,197 who were homeless in families.

Violence against the homeless by housed individuals is an alarming trend that has often increased from year to year and certainly has not decreased in occurrence from 1999 to 2013. In 2013, the same number of fatal attacks (18) occurred as in 2012 and 30 percent more nonlethal attacks were committed.

This reality worsens when one considers the fact that many violent acts against homeless populations go unreported and therefore, the true number of incidents is likely to be substantially higher.

Source: Stoops, Michael. Vulnerable to Hate: A Survey of Hate Crimes & Violence Committed against Homeless People in 2013. Washington, DC: National Coalition for the Homeless, 2014. Used by permission of the National Coalition for the Homeless.

Kennedy Introduces the Hate Crimes Amendment

This speech in defense of hate crime statutes was given by the late Senator Edward Kennedy, who cosponsored the initial legislation that later culminated in the Matthew Shepard hate crimes law.

I'd like to speak for a moment regarding the Hate Crimes Amendment—at a time when our ideals are under attack by terrorists in other lands, it is more important than ever to demonstrate that we practice what we preach, and that we are doing all we can to root out the bigotry and prejudice in our own country that leads to violence here at home. Now more than ever, we need to act against hate crimes and send a strong message here at home and around the world that we will not tolerate crimes fueled by hate.

Since the September 11th attacks, we've seen a shameful increase in the number of hate crimes committed against Muslims, Sikhs, and Americans of Middle Eastern descent. Congress has done much to respond to the vicious attacks of September 11th. We're doing all that we can to strengthen our defenses against hate that comes from abroad. We've spent billions of dollars in the War on Terrorism to ensure that international terrorist organizations such as al' Qaeda are not able to carry out attacks within the United States. There is no reason why Congress should not act to strengthen our defenses against hate that occurs here at home.

In Iraq and Afghanistan, our soldiers are fighting for freedom and liberty—they are on the front line fighting against evil and hate. We owe it to our troops to uphold those same principles here at home.

Hate crimes are a form of domestic terrorism. They send the poisonous message that some Americans deserve to be victimized solely because of who they are. Like other acts of terrorism, hate crimes have an impact far greater than the impact on the individual victims. They are crimes against entire communities, against the whole nation, and against the fundamental ideals on which America was founded. They are a violation of all our country stands for.

We're united in our effort to root out the cells of hatred around the world. We should not turn a blind eye to acts of hatred and terrorism here at home. We should not shrink now from our role as the beacon of liberty to the rest of the world. The national interest in condemning bias-motivated violence in the United States is strong, and so is our interest in condemning bias-motivated violence occurring world-wide. When the Senate approves this amendment, we will send a message about freedom and equality that will resonate around the world.

Mr. President, hate crimes violate everything our country stands for. They send the poisonous message that some Americans deserve to be victimized solely because of who they are. These are crimes committed against entire communities, against the nation as a whole and the very ideals on which our country was founded.

The time has come to stand up for the victims of these senseless acts of violence—victims like Matthew Shepard, for whom this bill is named, and who died a horrible death in 1998 at the hands of two men who singled him out because of his sexual orientation. Nine years after Matthew's death—nine years—we still haven't gotten it done. How long are we going to wait?

Senator Smith and I urge your support of this bipartisan bill. The House has come through on their side and passed the bill. Now it's time for the Senate to do the same. This year, we can get it done. We came close twice before. In 2000 and 2002, a majority of Senators voted to pass this legislation. In 2004, we had 65 votes for the bill and it was adopted as part of the Defense Authorization Bill. But—that time—it was stripped out in conference.

The President has threatened to veto this legislation, but we can't let that threat stop us from doing the right thing. Let's display the same kind of courage that came from David Ritcheson, a victim of a brutal hate crime that scarred him both physically and emotionally. This spring, David testified before the House Judiciary Committee. He courageously described the horrific attack against him the year before—after what had been an enjoyable evening with other high school students near his home in Spring, Texas.

Later in the evening however, two persons attacked him and one attempted to carve a swastika into his chest. He was viciously beaten and burned with cigarettes, while his attackers screamed terrible epithets at him. He lay unconscious on the ground for 9 hours, and remained in a coma for several weeks. After a very difficult recovery, David became a courageous and determined advocate. Tragically, though, this life-changing experience exacted its toll on David and recently, he took his own life. He had tried so hard to look forward, but he was still haunted by this brutal experience.

My deepest sympathy and condolences go out to David's family and friends coping with this tragic loss. David's death shows us that these crimes have a profound psychological impact. We must do all we can to let victims know they are not to blame for this brutality, that their lives are equally valued. We can't wait any longer to act.

Our amendment is supported by a broad coalition of 210 law enforcement, civic, disability, religious and civil rights groups, including the International Association of Chiefs of Police, the Anti-Defamation League, the Interfaith Alliance, the National Sheriff's Association, the Human Rights Campaign, the National District Attorneys Association and the Leadership Conference on Civil Rights. All these diverse groups have come together to say now is the time for us to take action to protect our fellow citizens from the brutality of hate-motivated violence. They support this legislation, because they know it is a balanced and sensible approach that will bring greater protection to our citizens along with much needed resources to improve local and state law enforcement.

Our bill corrects two major deficiencies in current law. Excessive restrictions require proof that victims were attacked because they were engaged in certain "federally protected activities." And the scope of the law is limited, covering hate crimes based on race, religion, or ethnic background alone.

The federally protected activity requirement is outdated, unwise and unnecessary, particularly when we consider the unjust outcomes of this requirement. Hate crimes now occur in a variety of circumstances, and citizens are often targeted during routine activities that should be protected. All victims should be protected—and it's simply wrong that a hate crime—like the one against David Ritcheson—can't be prosecuted federally because it happened in a private home.

The bill also recognizes that some hate crimes are committed against people because of their sexual orientation, their gender, their gender identity, or their disability. Passing this bill will send a loud and clear message. All hate crimes will face federal prosecution. Action is long overdue. There are too many stories and too many victims.

We must do all we can to end these senseless crimes, and I urge my colleagues to support cloture on this amendment and to support its passage as an amendment to the DOD authorization bill.

Source: Kennedy, Ted. "The Matthew Shepard Act." Congressional Record, 110th Congress. Senate, September 25, 2007. Washington, DC: Government Printing Office, S12026.

Obama on the Matthew Shepard and James Byrd Jr. Hate Crimes Prevention Act

After Congress passed the Matthew Shepard and James Byrd Jr. Hate Crimes Prevention Act in 2009, President Obama spoke of the historic nature of this new law.

Hello, everybody. Good to see you. Yes. Thank you so much, and welcome to the White House. There are several people here that I want to just make mention of because they helped to make today possible: we've got Attorney General Eric Holder and the Department of Justice crowd; a champion of this legislation and a great Speaker of the House, Nancy Pelosi; my dear friend, senior Senator from the great State of Illinois, Dick Durbin; the outstanding chairman of Armed Services, Carl Levin; Senator Arlen Specter; chairman of the Judiciary Committee in the House, Representative John Conyers; Representative Barney Frank; Representative Tammy Baldwin; Representative Jerry Nadler; Representative Jared Polis; all the Members of Congress who are here today. We thank you.

Mr. David Bohnett and Mr. Tom Gregory and the David Bohnett Foundation—they are partners for this reception—thank you so much, guys, for helping to host this; and finally and most importantly, because these were really the spearheads of this effort, Dennis, Judy, and Logan Shepard, as well as Betty Byrd Boatner and Louvon Harris, sisters of James Byrd, Jr. To all the activists, all the organizers, all the people who helped make this day happen, thank you for your years of advocacy and activism, pushing and protesting that made this victory possible.

You know, as a nation we've come far on the journey towards a more perfect union. And today, we've taken another step forward. This afternoon, I signed into law the Matthew Shepard and James Byrd, Jr. Hate Crimes Prevention Act.

This is the culmination of a struggle that has lasted more than a decade. Time and again, we faced opposition. Time and again, the measure was defeated or delayed. Time and again, we've been reminded of the difficulty of building a nation in which we're all free to live and love as we see fit. But the cause endured and the struggle continued, waged by the family of Matthew Shepard, by the family of James Byrd, by folks who held vigils and led marches, by those who rallied and organized and refused to give up, by the late Senator Ted Kennedy who fought so hard for this legislation and all who toiled for years to reach this day.

Now, you understand that we must stand against crimes that are meant not only to break bones, but to break spirits, not only to inflict harm, but to instill fear. You understand that the rights afforded every citizen under our Constitution mean nothing if we do not protect those rights, both from unjust laws and violent acts. And you understand how necessary this law continues to be.

In the most recent year for which we have data, the FBI reported roughly 7,600 hate crimes in this country. Over the past 10 years, there were more than 12,000 reported hate crimes based on sexual orientation alone. And we will never know how many incidents were never reported at all.

And that's why, through this law, we will strengthen the protections against crimes based on the color of your skin, the faith in your heart, or the place of your birth. We will finally add Federal protections against crimes based on gender, disability, gender identity, or sexual orientation. And prosecutors will have new tools to work with States in order to prosecute to the fullest those who would perpetrate such crimes, because no one in America should ever be afraid to walk down the street holding the hands of the person they love. No one in America should be forced to look over their shoulder because of who they are or because they live with a disability.

At root, this isn't just about our laws; this is about who we are as a people. This is about whether we value one another, whether we embrace our differences rather than allowing them to become a source of animus. It's hard for any of us to imagine the mindset of someone who would kidnap a young man and beat him to within an inch of his life, tie him to a fence, and leave him for dead. It's hard for any of us to imagine the twisted mentality of those who'd offer a neighbor a ride home, attack him, chain him to the back of a truck, and drag him for miles until he finally died.

But we sense where such cruelty begins: the moment we fail to see in another our common humanity, the very moment when we fail to recognize in a person the same fears and hopes, the same passions and imperfections, the same dreams that we all share.

We have for centuries strived to live up to our founding ideal of a nation where all are free and equal and able to pursue their own version of happiness. Through conflict and tumult, through the morass of hatred and prejudice, through periods of division and discord we have endured and grown stronger and fairer and freer. And at every turn, we've made progress not only by changing laws but by changing hearts, by our willingness to walk in another's shoes, by our capacity to love and accept even in the face of rage and bigotry.

In April of 1968, just 1 week after the assassination of Martin Luther King, as our Nation mourned in grief and shuddered in anger, President Lyndon Johnson signed landmark civil rights legislation. This was the first time we enshrined into law Federal protections against crimes motivated by religious or racial hatred, the law on which we build today.

As he signed his name, at a difficult moment for our country, President Johnson said that through this law "the bells of freedom ring out a little louder." That is the promise of America. Over the sound of hatred and chaos, over the din of grief and anger, we can still hear those ideals, even when they are faint, even when some would try to drown them out. At our best we seek to make sure those ideals can be heard and felt by Americans everywhere. That work did not end in 1968. It certainly does not end today. But because of the efforts of the folks in this room, particularly those family members who are standing behind me, we can be proud that that bell rings even louder now and each day grows louder still.

So thank you very much. God bless you, and God bless the United States of America.

Source: Barack Obama: "Remarks on the Enactment of the Matthew Shepard and James Byrd, Jr. Hate Crimes Prevention Act," October 28, 2009. Online by Gerhard Peters and John T. Woolley, *The American Presidency Project*. http://www.presidency.ucsb.edu/ws/?pid=86813.

Federal Hate Crimes Laws

The two following documents are taken from the U.S. Code: the first states the federal government's jurisdiction over hate crimes; the second document asserts the government mandate to support educational efforts and training in the elementary and secondary schools to prevent hate crimes.

18 U.S. Code § 249—Hate Crime Acts

(a) In General.—

    (1) Offenses involving actual or perceived race, color, religion, or national origin.—

Whoever, whether or not acting under color of law, willfully causes bodily injury to any person or, through the use of fire, a firearm, a dangerous weapon, or an explosive or incendiary device, attempts to cause bodily injury to any person, because of the actual or perceived race, color, religion, or national origin of any person—

(A) shall be imprisoned not more than 10 years, fined in accordance with this title, or both; and

(B) shall be imprisoned for any term of years or for life, fined in accordance with this title, or both, if—

    (i) death results from the offense; or

    (ii) the offense includes kidnapping or an attempt to kidnap, aggravated sexual abuse or an attempt to commit aggravated sexual abuse, or an attempt to kill.

(2) Offenses involving actual or perceived religion, national origin, gender, sexual orientation, gender identity, or disability.—

(A) In general.— Whoever, whether or not acting under color of law, in any circumstance described in subparagraph (B) or paragraph (3), willfully causes bodily injury to any person or, through the use of fire, a firearm, a dangerous weapon, or an explosive or incendiary device, attempts to cause bodily injury to any person, because of the actual or perceived religion, national origin, gender, sexual orientation, gender identity, or disability of any person—

    (i) shall be imprisoned not more than 10 years, fined in accordance with this title, or both; and

    (ii) shall be imprisoned for any term of years or for life, fined in accordance with this title, or both, if—

    (I) death results from the offense; or

    (II) the offense includes kidnapping or an attempt to kidnap, aggravated sexual abuse or an attempt to commit aggravated sexual abuse, or an attempt to kill.

(B) Circumstances described.— For purposes of subparagraph (A), the circumstances described in this subparagraph are that—

(i) the conduct described in subparagraph (A) occurs during the course of, or as the result of, the travel of the defendant or the victim—

(I) across a State line or national border; or

(II) using a channel, facility, or instrumentality of interstate or foreign commerce;

(ii) the defendant uses a channel, facility, or instrumentality of interstate or foreign commerce in connection with the conduct described in subparagraph (A);

(iii) in connection with the conduct described in subparagraph (A), the defendant employs a firearm, dangerous weapon, explosive or incendiary device, or other weapon that has traveled in interstate or foreign commerce; or

(iv) the conduct described in subparagraph (A)—

(I) interferes with commercial or other economic activity in which the victim is engaged at the time of the conduct; or

(II) otherwise affects interstate or foreign commerce.

(3) Offenses occurring in the special maritime or territorial jurisdiction of the united states.—Whoever, within the special maritime or territorial jurisdiction of the United States, engages in conduct described in paragraph (1) or in paragraph (2)(A) (without regard to whether that conduct occurred in a circumstance described in paragraph (2)(B)) shall be subject to the same penalties as prescribed in those paragraphs.

(4) Guidelines.—All prosecutions conducted by the United States under this section shall be undertaken pursuant to guidelines issued by the Attorney General, or the designee of the Attorney General, to be included in the United States Attorneys' Manual that shall establish neutral and objective criteria for determining whether a crime was committed because of the actual or perceived status of any person.

(b) Certification Requirement.—

(1) In general.— No prosecution of any offense described in this subsection may be undertaken by the United States, except under the certification in writing of the Attorney General, or a designee, that—

(A) the State does not have jurisdiction;

(B) the State has requested that the Federal Government assume jurisdiction;

(C) the verdict or sentence obtained pursuant to State charges left demonstratively unvindicated the Federal interest in eradicating bias-motivated violence; or

(D) a prosecution by the United States is in the public interest and necessary to secure substantial justice.

(2) Rule of construction.— Nothing in this subsection shall be construed to limit the authority of Federal officers, or a Federal grand jury, to investigate possible violations of this section.

(c) Definitions.— In this section—

(1) the term "bodily injury" has the meaning given such term in section 1365 (h)(4) of this title, but does not include solely emotional or psychological harm to the victim;

(2) the term "explosive or incendiary device" has the meaning given such term in section 232 of this title;

(3) the term "firearm" has the meaning given such term in section 921 (a) of this title;

(4) the term "gender identity" means actual or perceived gender-related characteristics; and

(5) the term "State" includes the District of Columbia, Puerto Rico, and any other territory or possession of the United States.

(d) Statute of Limitations.—

(1) Offenses not resulting in death.— Except as provided in paragraph (2), no person shall be prosecuted, tried, or punished for any offense under this section unless the indictment for such offense is found, or the information for such offense is instituted, not later than 7 years after the date on which the offense was committed.

(2) Death resulting offenses.— An indictment or information alleging that an offense under this section resulted in death may be found or instituted at any time without limitation.

20 U.S. Code § 7133—Hate Crime Prevention

(a) Grant authorization

From funds made available to carry out this subpart under section 7103 (2) of this title the Secretary may make grants to local educational agencies and community-based organizations for the purpose of providing assistance to localities most directly affected by hate crimes.

(b) Use of funds

(1) Program development
Grants under this section may be used to improve elementary and secondary educational efforts, including—

(A) development of education and training programs designed to prevent and to reduce the incidence of crimes and conflicts motivated by hate;

(B) development of curricula for the purpose of improving conflict or dispute resolution skills of students, teachers, and administrators;

(C) development and acquisition of equipment and instructional materials to meet the needs of, or otherwise be part of, hate crime or conflict programs; and

(D) professional training and development for teachers and administrators on the causes, effects, and resolutions of hate crimes or hate-based conflicts.

(2) Application

In order to be eligible to receive a grant under this section for any fiscal year, a local educational agency, or a local educational agency in conjunction with a community-based organization, shall submit an application to the Secretary in such form and containing such information as the Secretary may reasonably require.

(3) Requirements

Each application under paragraph (2) shall include—

(A) a request for funds for the purpose described in this section;

(B) a description of the schools and communities to be served by the grants; and

(C) assurances that Federal funds received under this section shall be used to supplement, and not supplant, non-Federal funds.

(4) Comprehensive plan

Each application shall include a comprehensive plan that contains—

(A) a description of the hate crime or conflict problems within the schools or the community targeted for assistance;

(B) a description of the program to be developed or augmented by such Federal and matching funds;

      (C) assurances that such program or activity shall be administered by or under the supervision of the applicant;

      (D) procedures for the proper and efficient administration of such program; and

      (E) fiscal control and fund accounting procedures as may be necessary to ensure prudent use, proper disbursement, and accurate accounting of funds received under this section.

(c) Award of grants

    (1) Selection of recipients

The Secretary shall consider the incidence of crimes and conflicts motivated by bias in the targeted schools and communities in awarding grants under this section.

    (2) Geographic distribution

The Secretary shall attempt, to the extent practicable, to achieve an equitable geographic distribution of grant awards.

    (3) Dissemination of information

The Secretary shall attempt, to the extent practicable, to make available information regarding successful hate crime prevention programs, including programs established or expanded with grants under this section.

(d) Reports

The Secretary shall submit to Congress a report every 2 years that shall contain a detailed statement regarding grants and awards, activities of grant recipients, and an evaluation of programs established under this section.

Source: U.S. Code. http://uscode.house.gov/.

Further Research

Since the publication of the first edition of this book, the literature on hate crimes has burgeoned, making it difficult to compile a comprehensive listing even for materials published since 1999. Since many books on this topic often provide important and, occasionally, unique historical and analytical information not easily accessible elsewhere, this list includes many previously listed titles in addition to the many recent new books. Most of the magazine and journal citations, however, cover material published from 1999 through 2014. The following list is necessarily selective and will provide the student and researcher with annotated citations to significant and diverse publications on the topic.

Books

Allport, Gordon. *The Nature of Prejudice*. Menlo Park, CA: Addison-Wesley, 1979 (originally published in 1954).

> A pioneering work by a Harvard psychologist on the social and psychological nature of bigotry.

Barkun, Michael. *Religion and the Racist Right: The Origins of the Christian Identity Movement*. Chapel Hill: University of North Carolina Press, 1994.

From left, Judy Shepard, cofounder of Matthew Shepard Foundation, and Ellen Kahn, Director of Children, Youth and Families Program at Human Rights Campaign (HRC), speak on stage at HRC's Time to Thrive Conference, on February, 14, 2014, in Las Vegas. (AP Photo for Human Rights Campaign/Jeff Bottari)

A survey and analysis of the Christian Identity movement, a racist and anti-Jewish ideology whose adherents claim is a religion.

Bell, Jeannine. *Policing Hatred: Law Enforcement, Civil Rights and Hate Crime*. New York: New York University Press, 2002.

This ethnographic study analyzes the way law enforcement officers enforce hate crime laws and discusses the societal impacts of their efforts.

Bellant, Russ. *Old Nazis, the New Right and the Republican Party*. Boston: South End, 1991.

A disturbing investigation of the heretofore unknown ties of former Nazis who immigrated to this country after World War II and established ties to mainstream political groups.

Blee, Kathleen. *Inside Organized Racism: Women in the Hate Movement*. Berkeley: University of California Press, 2002.

Author of an earlier work on women in the Ku Klux Klan (see later), University of Pittsburgh sociology professor Kathleen Blee provides unique insight on women involved in contemporary violently racist movements. After interviewing a few dozen participants over a two-year period, she learned that the common stereotype of these women—poor, uneducated, raised in abusive families, and mainly recruited by boyfriends or husbands—was not usually true.

Blee, Kathleen. *Women of the Klan: Racism and Gender in the 1920s*. Berkeley: University of California Press, 1991.

This historical volume examines the involvement of women in the most notorious racist organization in the United States. The author interviewed many former members living in the Midwest and learned that some of these women were involved with women's suffrage and other progressive movements.

Bussey, Jennifer A. *Hate Crimes*. Detroit: Greenhaven Press, 2007.

> This anthology of essays on hate crimes contains a large number of primary documents—including speeches, court cases, personal reflections, and newspaper accounts—that discuss this topic from earlier times to the present. The essays by historians and contemporary scholars add useful background information.

Chanes, Jerome A. *Antisemitism: A Reference Handbook*. Santa Barbara, CA: ABC-CLIO, 2004.

> This volume surveys the historical, political and sociological manifestations of anti-Jewish prejudice and violence in more than fifty countries. The work includes an extensive introductory essay, a chronology of significant events, movements and legislation, print and nonprint surveys of the topic, and a list of organizations combating this age-old hatred. Chanes, a U.S. Jewish communal leader, also discusses governmental, judicial and other efforts to counteract anti-Semitism.

Cleary, Edward J. *Beyond the Burning Cross: The First Amendment and the Landmark R.A.V. Case*. New York: Random House, 1994.

> This work offers an extensive discussion of the legal ramifications of the Supreme Court case involving a hate crime in St. Paul, Minnesota, in 1992.

Coates, James. *Armed and Dangerous: The Rise of the Survivalist Right*. New York: Hill and Wang, 1995.

> An investigative reporter for the *Chicago Tribune*, Coates has written an informative survey of the main organizations and individuals on the violent wing of the extreme political right in the United States. A preface to this edition updates events since its initial publication in 1987. Especially noteworthy is the bibliographic notes section, which

provides access to a wide variety of relevant newspaper and magazine articles and books published in the 1980s.

Comstock, Gary David. *Violence against Lesbians and Gay Men.* New York: Columbia University Press, 1991.

This study provides statistical data on the extent of antigay violence nationwide and offers a theoretical framework to examine its origins. The book includes a chapter on police violence and empirical data on perpetrators. Also contains extensive footnotes and a bibliography.

Dees, Morris, and Steve Fiffer. *Hate on Trial: The Case against America's Most Dangerous Neo-Nazi.* New York: Villard Books, 1993.

The story of the lawsuit brought by a founder of the Southern Poverty Law Center against Tom Metzger, a neo-Nazi, who instigated the murder of an Ethiopian student in Portland, Oregon. Metzger and his skinhead group were required to pay a multimillion-dollar settlement to the family of the murdered African immigrant.

Dees, Morris, and Steve Fiffer. *A Lawyer's Journey: The Morris Dees Story.* Chicago: American Bar Association, 2001.

Originally published in 1991 as *A Season for Justice.* This volume brings Dees's autobiography up to date as of 2001 and includes new material on Dees's most recent legal victory over the Aryan Nations in Idaho.

Dobratz, Betty A., and Stephanie L. Shanks-Meile. *White Power, White Pride: The White Separatist Movement in the United States.* New York: Twayne, 1997.

This work examines the white separatist movement through extensive interviews with more than 100 active participants. The authors attended rallies and other gatherings to chronicle the history and strategies of the movement.

Dray, Philip. *At the Hands of Persons Unknown: the Lynching of Black America.* New York: Modern Library, 2003.

This history of lynching in America describes its prevalence in the southern United States, and discusses the crusade by both black and white Americans to eliminate this murderous problem.

Dyer, Joel. *Harvest of Rage: Why the Oklahoma City Bombing Is Only the Beginning.* Boulder, CO: Westview Press, 1997.

Dyer surveys the rise of violent antigovernment and extremist hate groups to better understand the attitudes that resulted in the horrific bombing of the federal building in Oklahoma City in 1995 which killed168 people.

Ezekiel, Raphael S. *The Racist Mind: Portraits of American Neo-Nazis and Klansmen.* New York: Vintage, 1995.

A former senior research scientist at the Harvard School of Public Health, Ezekiel spent four years conducting extensive interviews with members of a neo-Nazi group and leaders of racist organizations in order to understand the origin of their views.

Ferrell, Claudine L. *Nightmare and Dream: Anti-Lynching in Congress, 1917–1922.* New York: Garland, 1986.

Originally a doctoral dissertation, this work surveys legislative initiatives in Congress to end the wave of southern lynchings during the early part of the 20th century.

Flint, Colin, ed. *Spaces of Hate: Geographies of Discrimination and Intolerance in the U.S.A.* New York: Routledge, 2004.

This anthology provides a geographic perspective on hate-motivated activity. The authors are primarily social science professors who adapt postmodern concepts and jargon—critical race, postcolonial, and whiteness theories—to analyze hate crimes and other types of bigotry.

Foster, Arnold. *Square One.* New York: Donald I. Fine, 1988.
A memoir by the former general counsel of the Anti-Defamation League describes his lifelong battle against anti-Semitism and his concern for the welfare and rights of the Jewish people.

Foxman, Abraham H. and Christopher Wolf. *Viral Hate: Containing Its Spread on the Internet.* New York: Palgrave Macmillan, 2013.
This book discusses the anonymous nature of the Internet and how it helps spread bigotry, bullying, and other hateful and violent activities. The book recommends steps for establishing legal policies to control this problem.

Gaylin, Willard. *Hatred: The Psychological Descent into Violence.* New York: Public Affairs, 2003.
Gaylin, a psychoanalyst and author of more than a dozen works, debunks the widespread "therapeutic trivialization of morality." In this brilliant and thought-provoking critique, he condemns societal attitudes that attempt to excuse the murderous actions of terrorists and bigots because of their alleged grievances or family background.

Gerstenfeld, Phyllis B., and Diana R. Grant. *Crimes of Hate: Selected Readings.* Thousand Oaks, CA: Sage Publications, 2004.
This anthology includes essays from a variety of academic fields, including criminology, sociology, psychology, and political science.

Gerstenfeld, Phyllis B., and Diana R. Grant. *Hate Crimes: Causes, Controls and Controversies.* Thousand Oaks, CA: Sage Publications, 2013.
Designed as a college textbook with exercises and discussion questions, this third edition is a companion volume to *Crimes of Hate: Selected Readings* (see above) that provides

an overview of the history and effectiveness of hate crime legislation, the activities of violent hate groups, and the international dimensions of the problem. Well-organized and well-designed, this volume serves as an excellent primer.

Greene, Melissa Fay. *The Temple Bombing*. Reading, MA: Addison-Wesley, 1996.

Engaging and well written, this work chronicles the bombing of the oldest synagogue in Atlanta on October 12, 1958. The author did an enormous amount of research to recount the worst anti-Jewish incident in southern history since the lynching of Leo Frank in 1915.

Hall, Patricia Wong, and Victor M. Hwang. *Anti-Asian Violence in North America: Asian-American and Asian Canadian Reflections on Hate, Healing and Resistance*. Walnut Creek, CA: AltaMira Press, 2001.

This anthology discusses a variety of problems affecting North Americans of Asian ancestry, including civil rights, ethnic identity, and, especially, hate crimes, economic scapegoating, and Internet racism. An introductory essay briefly surveys the history of anti-Asian violence in the United States and Canada and includes a directory of organizations (such as Asian, Jewish, and antiracist) that combat racial bigotry and intolerance.

Hamm, Mark S. *American Skinheads: The Criminology and Control of Hate Crime*. Westport, CT: Praeger, 1993.

This volume examines the social and psychological dimensions of the skinhead movement and, through interviews with some members, analyzes its development. According to the author, "Not all acts of terrorism can be considered hate crimes, and hate crimes are not necessarily terrorism unless such prejudiced violence has a political or social underpinning."

Hamm, Mark S. *Hate Crime: International Perspectives on Causes and Control.* Highland Heights, KY: Academy of Criminal Justice Sciences, Northern Kentucky University; and Cincinnati, OH: Anderson, 1994.

Hamm, Mark S. *In Bad Company: America's Terrorist Underground.* Boston: Northeastern University Press, 2002.
> Hamm, a professor of criminology at Indiana State University, provides an exhaustive survey of the Aryan Republic Army, a little-known paramilitary radical right-wing gang associated with Oklahoma City bomber Timothy McVeigh.

Hate Groups: Opposing Viewpoints. Compiled by Mary E. Williams, book ed. Farmington Hills, MI: Greenhaven, 2004.
> This anthology primarily consists of previously published articles from magazines, books, newspaper articles, and columns; a list of organizations; and a bibliography.

Hentoff, Nat. *Free Speech for Me—But Not for Thee: How the American Left and Right Relentlessly Censor Each Other.* New York: HarperCollins, 1992.
> Hentoff, a prolific writer on civil liberties, presents an absolutist interpretation of the First Amendment to the U.S. Constitution.

Herek, Gregory M., and Kevin T. Berrill. *Hate Crimes: Confronting Violence against Lesbians and Gay Men.* Newbury Park, CA: Sage Publications, 1992.
> The first major monograph on antigay violence in the United States, this anthology includes an overview of the topic, essays on perpetrators and victims, and suggestions for public policy responses. Data and analysis from the first national study conducted by the National Gay and Lesbian Task Force in 1984 are presented.

Jacobs, James B., and Kimberly Potter. *Hate Crimes: Criminal Law and Identity Politics.* New York: Oxford University Press, 1998.

Jacobs, a New York University law professor and preeminent critic of hate crimes legislation, along with his coauthor, argue that these laws are both subjective and unnecessary and also infringe on basic First Amendment rights. An important critical contribution to the hate crimes debate.

Jenness, Valerie, and Kendal Broad. *Hate Crimes: New Social Movements and the Politics of Violence.* New York: Aldine de Gruyter, 1997.

This work examines why bias-motivated violence has recently become a serious issue and the reason some minority constituencies have been categorized as victims while others have gone relatively unnoticed. A sociopolitical analysis, the book also discusses the response to violence against gays and women.

Jenness, Valerie, Kendal Broad, and Ryken Grattet. *Making Hate a Crime: From Social Movement Concept to Law Enforcement.* New York: Russell Sage Foundation, 2004.

The authors analyze, from a sociological perspective, the symbolic importance of hate crime laws but also raise questions about their effectiveness in combating hate-motivated violence.

Jimenez, Stephen. *The Book of Matt: Hidden Truths about the Murder of Matthew Shepard.* Hanover, New Hampshire: Steerforth Press, 2013.

The savage murder of Matthew Shepard, a gay 21-year-old Wyoming college student in 1998, galvanized many Americans—both gay and straight—to publicly confront the extreme hate and violence directed against the gay community. Jimenez had questions about the nature of the crime and over the course of a thirteen-year investigation traveled to twenty states and Washington, D.C. to interview more than a hundred sources. His exhaustive investigation also plunged him into the violent underworld of drug trafficking. Jimenez wanted to find out—what he claimed was the untold story—about the circumstances behind this brutal murder. The author's conclusion was that it was a drug-related and not an anti-gay crime. His book quickly evoked furious reactions from many critics who claimed the book tried to whitewash anti-gay violence. Jimenez, who also happens to be gay, unapologetically defended his thesis and the importance of finding the facts behind this violent and terrible crime.

Johnson, Sandra E. *Standing on the Ground: A Triumph over Hate Crime in the Deep South.* New York: St. Martin's Press, 2002.

A poignant journalistic account of a 1995 racist arson attack on the St. John Baptist Church in Dixiana, South Carolina, and the valiant work of two women—Barbara Simmons, an African American, and Ammie Murray, a white—to rebuild the church.

Kelly, Robert J., ed. *Bias Crime: American Law Enforcement and Legal Responses.* Chicago: Office of International Criminal Justice, University of Illinois at Chicago, 1993.

This anthology covers various methods used by police and other law enforcement officials to prosecute violent hate crimes. Although much of the material covers the mid- to late 1980s, it still provides a useful overview for government attorneys, prosecutors, and other public officials.

King, Joyce. *Hate Crime: The Story of a Dragging in Jasper, Texas.* New York: Knopf, 2003.

Written by a Dallas-based broadcast journalist, this volume recounts the savage racist murder of James Byrd Jr., an African American, on June 7, 1998. The author describes the background of the three white murderers, who met while in a Texas prison. (See also Temple-Raston.)

Kotlowitz, Alex. *The Other Side of the River: A Story of Two Towns, a Death, and America's Dilemma*. New York: Nan A. Talese/Doubleday, 1998.

When the Coast Guard pulled the body of Eric McGinnis, a black teenager, out of southwestern Michigan's St. Joseph's River in May 1991, the mostly white residents of St. Joseph assumed the drowning was accidental. But African Americans in Benton Harbor, a mostly black town on the other side of the river, believed that whites chased him into the water for dating a white girl and that the crime was covered up by the white-dominated St. Joseph police force. Written by the author of the award-winning book *There Are No Children Here*, this work deals brilliantly with how differing perceptions of events are filtered through one's racial background.

Kressel, Neil J. *Mass Hate: The Global Rise of Genocide and Terror*. New York: Westview Press, 2002.

Written by a psychology professor and licensed psychologist, this work is a revised and updated edition of his earlier 1996 volume. Kressel surveys the horrors of mass slaughter and genocide throughout the twentieth century and the alarming rise of Islamic terrorism.

Lamy, Philip. *Millennium Rage*. New York: Plenum Press, 1996.

This work discusses the growth of extreme right-wing groups and militias as the year 2000 approached. The author, a professor at Castleton State College in Vermont, examines the growth of this movement and its influence.

Langer, Elinor. *A Hundred Little Hitlers: The Death of a Black Man, the Trial of a White Racist and the Rise of the Neo-Nazi Movement in America*. New York: Henry Holt, 2003.

> A thoroughly researched study of the skinhead murder of an Ethiopian immigrant, Mulugeta Seraw, in Portland, Oregon, on November 13, 1988. The author interviewed the murderers and discusses the successful Southern Poverty Law Center lawsuit against their organization, White Aryan Resistance.

Lawrence, Frederick M. *Punishing Hate: Bias Crimes under American Law*. Cambridge, MA: Harvard University Press, 2002.

> Lawrence, formerly a Boston University law school professor and former Brandeis University president, examines the legal basis for hate crime statutes and strongly advocates for the enactment of these laws. Some legislators and legal scholars have praised this volume as a landmark contribution in support of these criminal laws.

Levin, Jack, and Jack McDevitt. *Hate Crimes Revisited*. Boulder, CO: Westview Press, 2002.

> This volume updates the authors' earlier 1993 volume, with special emphasis on the impact of the 9/11 Arab terrorist attack.

MacLean, Nancy. *Behind the Mask of Chivalry: The Making of the Second Ku Klux Klan*. New York: Oxford University Press, 1994.

> This work discusses the rebirth of the KKK, its attitude toward white women, blacks, Catholics, Jews, and immigrants, and how it foments terror through lynching and other violent crimes.

Marcus, Kenneth L. *Jewish Identity and Civil Rights in America*. New York: Cambridge University Press, New York, 2010.

This book discusses the complex legal and policy issues involved with civil rights protections for Jewish students. Written by a former staff director at the U.S. Commission on Civil Rights, this volume examines the extent of the problem and suggests some solutions.

Martinez, Thomas, with John Guinther. *Brotherhood of Murder*. New York: McGraw-Hill, 1988.

A first-person account by a former member of the neo-Nazi group The Order. After Martinez revealed the organization's activities to federal law enforcement agencies, his ex-comrades threatened his life.

Metress, Christopher, ed. *The Lynching of Emmett Till: A Documentary Narrative*. Charlottesville, VA: University of Virginia, 2002.

Containing more than one hundred documents, this work includes news accounts, memoirs and literary works about the murder of fourteen-year-old Emmett Till on August 28, 1955. (See also Whitfield.)

Michael, George. *Confronting Right-Wing Extremism and Terrorism in the U.S.A.* New York: Routledge, 2003.

An expansion of a doctoral dissertation, this work surveys the rise of the far right since 1990. It includes interviews with some of the far right's leaders and also with former government officials and human rights activists.

Neiwart, David A. *Death on the Fourth of July: The Story of a Killing, a Trial, and Hate Crime in America*. New York: Palgrave Macmillan, 2004.

On July 4, 2000, a group of drunken white males—who dressed like skinheads—yelled racial epithets at some Asian Americans shopping at a convenience store in Ocean Shores, Washington. A violent fight erupted and one of the white men was fatally stabbed. Written by a freelance journalist, this work reports the details of the murder and examines the broader social and legal issues surrounding hate crimes.

Newton, Michael and Judy, eds. *Ku Klux Klan: An Encyclopedia*. New York: Garland, 1991.
Probably the only event worth commemorating on the 125th anniversary of the "world's oldest, most persistent terrorist organization" is the publication of this useful reference source. Meticulous and diligent researchers, the Newtons have compiled an essential guide for students and researchers.

Newton, Michael and Judy, eds. *Racial and Religious Violence in America: A Chronology*. New York: Garland, 1991.
An outstanding reference source, this work provides a unique chronology of many bias-motivated violent incidents throughout U.S. history.

Perry, Barbara. *Hate and Bias Crime: A Reader*. New York: Routledge, 2003.
This anthology examines hate groups and hate crimes from a wide range of academic disciplines, including sociology, criminology and criminal justice, psychology and social psychology, political science and law.

Perry, Barbara. *Hate Crimes*. New York: Praeger, 2009.
This five-volume set addresses the wide variety and incidence of hate crimes, exposing their impacts on individual communities and society. The contributing authors to this extensive anthology discuss online hate crimes, hate-based music, anti-Latino hostilities, school-based anti-hate initiatives, and legislative, educational, social

policy, and community organizational responses to the various forms of hate crime, among other topics.

Perry, Barbara. *In the Name of Hate: Understanding Hate Crimes.* New York: Routledge, 2001.

The author, a former professor of criminology at Northern Arizona University, uses a theoretical framework called "structured action theory" to analyze hate crimes. Her analysis contends that hate crime is an "instrument that defends the gendered and racialized social ordering of American culture."

Perry, Barbara. *Silent Victims: Hate Crimes against Native Americans.* Tucson: University of Arizona Press, 2008.

This book contends that hate crimes against Native Americans are common but mostly go unreported. The author interviewed almost 300 individuals and recorded their accounts of bias-related crimes directed against Native Americans.

Quarles, Chester L. *Ku Klux Klan and Related American Racialist and Antisemitic Organizations: A History and Analysis.* Jefferson, NC: McFarland, 1999.

Quarles, a professor of political science at the University of Mississippi, describes the membership, ideology, and philosophy of this notorious hate group, including its formerly secret oaths.

Ridgeway, James. *Blood in the Face: The Ku Klux Klan, Aryan Nations, Nazi Skinheads, and the Rise of a New White Culture.* New York: Thunder's Mouth Press, 1995.

In this updated second edition, a former *Village Voice* journalist surveys the rise of violent racist groups throughout the country. The book is well illustrated with photographs and artwork; especially noteworthy is a chart showing the interrelationships among the various groups and individuals. The author has filmed a documentary in conjunction with this work.

Robins, Robert S., and Jerrold M. Post. *Political Paranoia: The Psychopolitics of Hatred.* New Haven: Yale University Press, 1997.

Written by a political scientist and psychiatrist, this work surveys the phenomenon of the paranoid personality and how it generates various political and social movements. Hitler, Stalin, Christian Identity, and the Nation of Islam are some of the topics discussed in this wide-ranging work.

Sargent, Lyman Tower, ed. *Extremism in America: A Reader.* New York: New York University Press, 1995.

This unique anthology contains the actual texts of the hard-to-locate publications, articles, and tracts issued from both ends of the political spectrum—the far left and the far right. The work is conveniently organized by topic, including race, gender, economics, and education.

Sherry, Mark. *Disability Hate Crimes: Does Anyone* Really *Hate Disabled People?* Burlington, VT: Ashgate, 2010.

The author, a University of Toledo professor, focuses on disability hate crimes in the United Kingdom where these violent acts have received much British governmental attention for some time. Only recently have U.S. law enforcement agencies recognized that crimes against the disabled warrant special attention and need to be recorded in separate statistical categories of bias-motivated crimes.

Sims, Patsy. *The Klan.* Lexington: University Press of Kentucky, 1996.

A survey of the history and recent activities of this notorious organization based on interviews with current members.

Smith, Brent L. *Terrorism in America: Pipe Bombs and Pipe Dreams.* New York: State University of New York Press, 1994.

The author, a professor of criminal justice and sociology at the University of Alabama, provides empirical data and analysis on left-wing and right-wing terrorist groups in the United States.

Stanton, Bill. *Klanwatch: Bringing the Ku Klux Klan to Justice.* New York: Grove Weidenfeld, 1991.

The former director of the Southern Poverty Law Center's Klanwatch project chronicles the history of the organization's "multi-pronged anti-Klan program," which included filing lawsuits, publishing educational materials, and monitoring the activities of the KKK. Engagingly written, the book contains several photographs.

Swigonski, Mary E., et al. *From Hate Crimes to Human Rights: A Tribute to Matthew Shepard.* Binghamton, NY: Harrington Park Press, 2001.

Originally published as an issue of the *Journal of Gay and Lesbian Social Service* (vol. 3, no.1/2, 2001), this separately published monograph covers a wide variety of gay- and lesbian-related topics, including hate crimes.

Temple-Raston, Dina. *A Death in Texas: A Story of Race, Murder, and a Small Town's Struggle for Redemption.* New York: Henry Holt, 2003.

Similar to the Joyce King book (see above), this work describes the brutal lynching of James Byrd Jr., an African American, by three white racists, on June 7, 1998. The author interviewed law enforcement and townspeople in the small Texas town of Jasper, where this internationally reported crime occurred.

Tunnell, Kenneth D. *Political Crime in Contemporary America: A Critical Approach.* New York: Garland Publishing, 1993.

This volume contains a chapter by Wayman C. Mullins, editor of the *Journal of Police and Criminal Psychology*, entitled "Hate Crime and the Far Right."

Vollers, Maryanne. *Ghosts of Mississippi: The Murder of Medgar Evers, the Trials of Byron De La Beckwith, and the Haunting of the New South*. Boston: Little Brown, 1995.

Vollers provides background to the murder conviction of a white supremacist in the 1963 murder of Medgar Evers, leader of the National Association for the Advancement of Colored People (NAACP). After two mistrials, Beckwith was convicted in 1992.

Wade, Wyn Craig. *The Fiery Cross: The Ku Klux Klan in America*. New York: Simon and Schuster, 1987.

A journalistic history, this work traces the activities and influence of the KKK throughout U.S. history.

Walker, Samuel. *Hate Speech: The History of an American Controversy*. Lincoln: University of Nebraska Press, 1994.

The author, a professor of criminal justice at the University of Nebraska at Omaha, surveys the history of hate speech from the 1920s to the present and the varying views of organizations about suppressing such speech, from the American Civil Liberties Union to the American Jewish Committee and the National Association for the Advancement of Colored People (NAACP).

Whitfield, Stephen J. *A Death in the Delta: The Story of Emmett Till*. New York: Free Press, 1988.

This meritorious work deserves wider recognition. The book recounts the story of a black teenager who was murdered in Money, Mississippi, in 1955 for allegedly whistling at a white female. Many historians view this incident as the beginning of the modern civil rights movement. (See also Metress.)

Wolfe, Zachary J. *Hate Crimes Law.* Eagan, Michigan: Thomson Reuters, 2014+

This annual updated publication covers constitutional issues related to federal hate crime statutes, federal criminal civil rights statutes used to prosecute hate crimes, federal sentencing issues, state criminal law, and also discusses potential areas for constitutional challenges.

Articles

Abrams, Kathryn. "Fighting Fire with Fire: Rethinking the Role of Disgust in Hate Crimes." *California Law Review* 90, no. 5 (October 2002): 1423–1465.

Abrams analyzes the community-based responses to hate crimes in the United States and the role of disgust as a response to hate crimes.

"Accused Killer of Three Is Linked to Racist Writing." *New York Times*, March 3, 2000, A12.

A black man accused of killing three people and wounding two in a shooting rampage in Wilkinsburg, Pennsylvania, had antiwhite writings in his apartment and singled out whites during the attack.

Alter, Jonathan. "A Question of Anti-Semitism." *Newsweek*, October 7, 2002, 45.

Alter, a *Newsweek* editor, analyzes how anti-Israel campus politics, along with other such political activities throughout the world, may help encourage the dangerous perceptions of some Palestinian Arabs who want to destroy the state of Israel.

"Although Scapegoated, Muslims, Sikhs and Arabs Are Patriotic, Integrated—and Growing." *Time*, October 1, 2001, 72–75.

> This essay discusses the scapegoating of some non-Christian Americans following the 9/11 terrorist attacks.

Anderson, James F., et al. "Preventing Hate Crime and Profiling Hate Crime Offenders." *Western Journal of Black Studies* (Fall 2002): 140–149.

> Proposes methods for preventing hate crimes and profiling hate crime offenders in the United States and suggests educational campaigns in cultural diversity awareness and racial tolerance.

"Anti-Semitism: An Enduring Virus." *The Economist*, November 22, 2003, 44.

> This editorial analyzes the rise of anti-Jewish incidents and observes that many Jews in Israel and throughout the world feel that this alarming phenomenon is not incited by the conflict with Palestinian Arabs. Instead, the conflict is used as a "convenient excuse for the anti-Semites."

"Black, Jewish Congress Members Condemn Rash of Hate Crimes." *Jet*, August 16, 1999, 4.

> This article looks at a petition denouncing an outbreak of hate crimes, including the firebombing of three synagogues in California, that was signed by 55 black and Jewish members of Congress.

Bragg, Rick. "In One Last Trial, Alabama Faces Old Wound." *New York Times*, May 12, 2002, A1.

> Bragg discusses the pending murder trial of Bobby Frank Cherry for his role in the bombing death of four girls at the Sixteenth Street Baptist Church in Birmingham, Alabama, in 1963.

Carless, Will. "Family of a Murdered Immigrant Was in Crisis," *New York Times*, April 6, 2012, 11.

Shaima Alawadi, an Iraqi-born mother of five, was found bludgeoned to death with a threatening note near her bed, which was assumed to be a hate crime. But court documents revealed that there were several family crises including possible divorce and a daughter resisting an arranged marriage. Authorities were investigating the possible involvement of her family in the murder.

Clemetson, Lynette. "The New Victims of Hate." *Newsweek*, November 6, 2000, 61.

Clemetson discusses the increase in violent attacks against Asian-Americans and their reluctance to report these crimes.

Clemetson, Lynette. "A Slaying in 1982 Maintains Its Grip on Asian-Americans." *New York Times*, June 18, 2002, A1.

This front page article focuses on the commemoration of the June 19, 1982, killing of Chinese American Vincent Chin in Detroit, Michigan, and the crime's profound impact on Asian American politics and identity.

Clines, Francis X. "Slaying of a Gay Black Spurs Call for Justice." *New York Times*, July 13, 2000, A16.

Clines covers the demonstrations held in Fairmont, West Virginia—a state with no hate crime law—following the murder of Arthur Warren, an African American gay man.

Cloud, John. "Is Hate on the Rise?" *Time*, July 19, 1999, 33.

Although many hate groups have not achieved great financial or political power, some experts believe hate-motivated violence is on the rise, in part because these groups are using powerful new tools like the Internet to attract new followers. Rabbi Abraham Cooper of the

Simon Wiesenthal Center notes that many racist organizers know they will never have a mass movement, but with the help of the Internet, they will be able to recruit people who are ready to violently act out their beliefs.

Dao, James. "Indictment Makes Start at Lifting a 40-Year-Old Cloud over a Mississippi County." *New York Times*, January 8, 2005, A11.

After a Mississippi prosecutor gathered new criminal evidence, Edgar Ray Killen, a former leader of the local Ku Klux Klan chapter, is charged with the murder of three civil rights workers, Andrew Goodman, Michael H. Schwerner and James E. Chaney, in Philadelphia, Mississippi in 1964. Killen was originally charged with federal civil rights violations in 1967 but the jury was deadlocked and he was released from prison.

Decter, Midge. "Crimes du Jour: Hate Crime Laws." *National Review*, September 13, 1999, 22–24.

A well-known conservative author claims that many people who once advocated leniency toward certain crimes on grounds of the mental or emotional state of the offender now support stern laws against hate crimes.

Dees, Morris S. "Hate Crimes Address, September 22, 1999." *Vital Speeches of the Day*, February 1, 2000, 247–252.

In an address to Eureka College in Eureka, Illinois, the director of the Southern Poverty Law Center discusses cases of discrimination that have involved the Ku Klux Klan and skinheads.

Dinnerstein, Leonard. "Is There a New Anti-Semitism in the United States?" *Society*, January/February 2004, 53–58.

Professor Dinnerstein, who has written widely about the history of anti-Jewish attitudes and incidents in the United States analyzes the current political climate for American Jews.

Duimovich, Samuel. "A Critique of the Hate Crime Prevention Act Regarding Its Protection of Gays and Lesbians (and How a Private Right Could Fix It)." *Southern California Review of Law and Social Justice* 23.2 (2014): 295–327.

> According to the FBI, hate crimes based on sexual orientation have not seen a credible drop in incidents since sexual orientation was included as a protected class. This article analyzes the weaknesses in the Hate Crime Prevention Act to show why it is not as effective as it could be in preventing hate crimes.

Duncan, D., and M. Hatzenbuehler. (2014). "Lesbian, Gay, Bisexual, and Transgender Hate Crimes and Suicidality among a Population-Based Sample of Sexual-Minority Adolescents in Boston." *American Journal of Public Health*, 104(2), 272–278.

> This journal article examined whether past-year suicidality among sexual-minority adolescents was more common in neighborhoods with a higher prevalence of hate crimes targeting lesbian, gay, bisexual, and transgender (LGBT) individuals. Participants' data came from a racially/ethnically diverse population-based sample of ninth- through twelfth-grade public school students in Boston, Massachusetts.

Egan, Timothy. "A Racist Attack, a Town Plagued." *New York Times*, October 15, 2000, 24.

> Egan explores issues of racial hatred in relation to manslaughter charges facing Asian American Min Duc Hong for the death of Christopher Kinison in Ocean Shores, Washington, on July 4, 2000.

Elder, Larry. "When the Bad Guy Is Black." *Human Events*, March 31, 2000, 13.

> Elder criticizes the double standard of mass media regarding hate crimes in the United States in the case of Ronald Taylor, an African American who deliberately shot and killed whites.

Feder, Don. "Hate-Crime Laws Penalize Ideas in Name of Tolerance." *Human Events*, September 3, 1999, 10.

A conservative columnist questions the legal basis for enforcement of hate crimes legislation.

Feder, Don. "Hate Crimes' Laws Would Criminalize Thought." *Human Events*, August 26, 2002, 18.

This essay questions the philosophical basis of hate crime laws.

Firestone, David. "Trial in Gay Killing Opens; Conspiracy of Hate Is Cited." *New York Times*, August 4, 1999, A8.

Firestone looks at Charles Monroe Butler Jr., who admitted to conspiring to kill Billy Jack Gaither, a gay man, and rejected a plea agreement for the murder case.

Fries, Jacob H. "Complaints of Anti-Arab Bias Crimes Dip, but Concerns Linger." *New York Times*, December 22, 2001, B8.

Fries reports on the decrease in the number of hate crimes committed against Arab Americans and Muslims in the United States as of December 2001, three months after the terrorist attacks in September of that year.

Gill, Aisha K., and Hannah Mason-Bish. "Addressing Violence against Women as a Form of Hate Crime: Limitations and Possibilities." *Feminist Review* 105 (2013): 1–20.

The potential benefits and limitations of extending the provisions of the British hate crime legislation to violence against women (VAW) are explored. Results of a survey of stakeholders working in the VAW sector indicate that they favored an inclusion of a gender category in hate crime legislation that would challenge incorrect assumptions and problematic stereotypes.

Goodstein, Laurie, and Gustav Niebuhr. "Attacks and Harassment of Arab-Americans Increase." *New York Times*, September 14, 2001, A14.

Goodstein and Niebuhr report that although President Bush condemned attacks against Muslim and Arab Americans, harassment and violent attacks continued to take place in several parts of the United States.

Goodstein, Laurie, and Tamar Lewin. "Victims of Mistaken Identity, Sikhs Pay a Price for Turbans." *New York Times*, September 19, 2001, A1.

Goodstein and Lewin look at the murder of Balbir Singh Sodhi, a turban-wearing Sikh who was murdered in Mesa, Arizona, and his co-religionists, who experienced harassment and physical attacks throughout the United States.

Gootman, Elissa. "Hate Motives Are Argued in Beating of Mexicans." *New York Times*, August 3, 2001, B5.

Gootman discusses an attack on Mexican immigrant day laborers in Suffolk County, New York.

"Guilty Plea Is Entered for Anti-Semitic Acts." *New York Times*, March 18, 2001, 19.

An article about Alex James Curtis, a 25-year-old publisher of a white supremacist Internet newsletter, who pleaded guilty to civil rights violations for threatening Rep. Bob Filner (D-CA), a Jewish congressman, and other officials and vandalizing two synagogues. Under the plea agreement, he would serve no more than three years in prison.

Hammer, Joshua. "The 'Gay Panic' Defense." *Newsweek*, November 8, 1999, 40–42.

Hammer reports on the start of the Laramie, Wyoming, murder trial of Aaron McKinney in the October 1998 death of Matthew Shepard, to which accomplice Russell Henderson had previously pleaded guilty.

Hardi, Joel. "P.R. 101: Don't Joke About Hate Crimes." *Chronicle of Higher Education*, May 26, 2000, A12.
Article on a comment made by the University of Iowa's vice president for university relations, Ann Rhodes, which was interpreted as biased.

Harris, Hamil R. "Ex-Klansman Found Guilty of 1963 Church Bombing." *The New Crisis*, July–August 2001, 7–9.
This article examines the criminal case against Thomas E. Blanton, found guilty nearly 40 years later of a 1963 church bombing in Alabama that claimed the lives of four African American children.

"Hate Crimes Up against Muslims." *New York Times*, November 26, 2002, A16.
A report on the findings of the Federal Bureau of Investigation on the increase in 2001 of hate crimes in the United States against Muslims and people who are or appear to be of Middle Eastern descent.

"Hatred Unexplained." *The Economist*, July 10, 1999, 2.
This article discusses the three-day, two-state shooting spree that began on July 2, 1999, by 21-year-old university student and member of the World Church of the Creator Benjamin Smith, who killed an African American and a Korean and injured nine Jews, blacks, and Asians.

Hemingway, Mark. "The Media's Double Standard." *The Weekly Standard*, August 19, 2013, 9–10.
The relative lack of media reaction to the shooting by gay rights supporter Floyd Lee Corkins at the headquarters of

the anti–same sex marriage group, the Family Research Council, indicates a media double standard on hate crimes.

Herek, Gregory M., et al. "Victim Experiences in Hate Crimes Based on Sexual Orientation." *Journal of Social Issues*, June 2002, 319–340.

Using interview data from a sample of 450 lesbian, gay, and bisexual adults, this article discusses the varieties of victim experiences. An important factor on deciding whether to report antigay crimes was the fear that the perpetrator would not be punished.

Horowitz, Craig. "The Return of Anti-Semitism." *New York*, December 15, 2003, 28–33.

The author discusses the alarming increase in anti-Jewish incidents and hostile rhetoric around the world.

Husselbee, L. Paul, and Larry Elliott. "Looking beyond Hate: How National and Regional Newspapers Framed Hate Crimes in Jasper, Texas, and Laramie, Wyoming." *Journalism & Mass Communication Quarterly*, Winter 2002, 833–853.

The article examines two infamous and nationally reported hate crimes directed against an African American and a gay student.

Hutchinson, Earl Ofari. "The Price of Black Silence on Certain Hate Crimes." *Christian Science Monitor*, March 8, 2000, 9.

Hutchinson discusses the racially motivated shootings in Pennsylvania of five white men by one black man. The author claims that black leaders and organizations should have quickly condemned the shootings.

Janofsky, Michael. "Gay Man's Death Led to Epiphany for Wyoming Officer." *New York Times*, September 30, 2000, A9.

A profile of David S. O'Malley, commander of the investigations unit of the Laramie, Wyoming, police department, who discusses how the murder of Matthew Shepard led to his campaign for national hate crimes legislation.

Janofsky, Michael. "Parents of Gay Obtain Mercy for His Killer." *New York Times*, November 5, 1999, A1.

A front page article about the parents of murdered gay Wyoming student Matthew Shepard, who requested that Aaron McKinney be spared the death sentence.

Jenness, Valerie. "Managing Differences and Making Legislation: Social Movements and the Racialization, Sexualization, and Gendering of Federal Hate Crime Law in the U.S., 1985–1998." *Social Problems*, November 1999, 548–571.

A sociological analysis of the emergence and evolution of federal hate crime laws, including the Hate Crimes Statistics Act, the Violence against Women Act, and the Hate Crimes Sentencing Enhancement Act.

Justice and the Suffolk County Police, *New York Times*, September 26, 2011, 28.

Discusses charges that the Suffolk County, New York police tolerate hate crimes against undocumented aliens.

Kim, Richard. "The Truth about Hate Crimes Laws." *Nation*, July 12, 1999, 20.

The author believes that national lesbian and gay organizations are expending too much effort trying to pass hate crime laws. Instead, he advocates local community organizing and forming coalitions with other minority advocacy groups.

Lappin, Shalom. "Israel and the New Anti-Semitism." *Dissent*, Spring 2003, 18–24.

A prolific analyst notes that although much of the criticism directed against Israel since September 2000 is legitimate, the growing antagonism stems in part from strong hostility to the existence of a Jewish state and also a widespread European attitude that Israel is no longer a nation of victims.

Lee, Felicia R. "ABC News Revisits Student's Killing and Angers Some Gays." *New York Times*, November 26, 2004, A33.

The ABC news program *20/20* claims in an investigative report that the widely publicized murder of Matthew Shepard, a Wyoming gay student, was not a hate crime but a botched robbery committed by men high on drugs.

Lee, Stephen. "U.S. Intervention in the Middle East, the 'War on Terror' and Domestic Hate Crimes: An Amerasia Journal Chronology." *Amerasia Journal* 27/28, no. 3/1 (2001/2002): 295–319.

Lee presents a chronology of domestic hate crimes since the terrorist attack on September 11, 2001, and the U.S. war against the Taliban-ruled Afghanistan.

Leo, John. "Faking the Hate." *U.S. News & World Report*, June 5, 2000, 22.

This essay discusses fraudulent reports of race and gender crimes on college campuses in the United States, including alleged hate crimes at the University of Massachusetts and other institutions that were revealed to be hoaxes.

Leo, John. "Not Fit to Print?" *U.S. News & World Report*, April 16, 2001, 14.

Jesse Dirkhising, a 13-year-old Arkansas boy, was drugged, tied to a bed, raped, tortured, and suffocated in September 1999 by two gay men. The columnist claims this story received far less media attention than the Matthew Shepard murder.

McCarty, James F. "Jury Finds 16 Amish Guilty in Beard-cutting Attacks." *Christian Century*, October 17, 2012, p.18.

>Details about the conviction of the U.S. Amish bishop who, along with his family members assaulted and cut the beards of members of a neighboring Amish community outside of Cleveland.

McNeil, Donald G. "France Vows Harsh Action after More Synagogues Burn." *New York Times*, April 2, 2002, A3.

>Article about the alarming increase of anti-Jewish violence in France. Among other incidents, a gunman fired at a kosher butcher shop, vandals set fire to a Strasbourg synagogue, and hooded men crashed a car into a Lyon synagogue.

McPhail, Beverly A. "Gender-Bias Hate Crimes." *Trauma, Violence & Abuse*, April 2002, 125–144.

>The author, a doctoral student at the University of Texas School of Social Work, surveys the history of the initial exclusion, then inclusion, of gender in the hate crime laws and also discusses its implications for social work research, practice, and policy.

McPhail, Beverly A. "Hating Hate: Policy Implications of Hate Crime Legislation." *Social Service Review*, December 2000, 635–653.

>McPhail believes it is important for social workers to be actively involved in the debate about hate crime laws.

Michaelson, Jay. "Can Suicide Be a Hate Crime." *Newsweek*, March 19, 2012, 17.

>Discusses the trial of Dharun Ravi, a college student on trial for a hate crime and invasion of privacy related to the suicide of fellow student Tyler Clementi, who committed suicide after a video posted by Ravi depicted him in a gay sex act.

Mikton, Christopher et al. "Systematic Review of the Effectiveness of Interventions to Prevent and Respond to Violence against Persons with Disabilities." *Journal of Interpersonal Violence* November 2014, 3207–3226

> Persons with disabilities make up some 15 percent of the world's population and are at higher risk of violence. Yet there is currently no systematic review of the effectiveness of interventions to prevent violence against them. The aim of this review was to systematically search for, appraise the quality of, and synthesize the evidence for the effectiveness of interventions to prevent and mitigate the consequences of all the main forms of interpersonal violence against people with all types of disabilities.

Milloy, Ross E. "Texas Senate Passes Hate Crimes Bill that Bush's Allies Killed." *New York Times*, May 8, 2001, A16.

> Texas legislators passed the James Byrd Jr. Hate Crimes Act with provisions to include crimes against gays and lesbians.

Mitchell, Corrie. "FBI Widens List of Groups Subject to Hate Crimes." *Christian Century*, July 10, 2013, 17–18.

> On June 5, 2013, the FBI widened its tracking of hate crimes to a larger number of ethnic and religious groups including Arab Americans, Orthodox Christians, Buddhists, Hindus, Sikhs, Mormons and Jehovah's Witnesses.

"More Insulted and Attacked after Sept. 11." *New York Times*, March 11, 2002, A12.

> A report on the increasing number of attacks on South Asian immigrants in the United States after the September 11, 2001, tragedy, based on information from a survey by the National Asian Pacific American Legal Consortium.

Murphy, Dean E. "Survey Finds an Increase in Anti-Semitic Incidents." *New York Times*, March 21, 2001, B2.

> A survey by the Anti-Defamation League shows that anti-Jewish incidents in New York City rose by about 49 percent in 2000, an increase the group said might be a spillover from the conflict in the Middle East.

Murphy, Dean E. "Three Are Charged in Death of Man Who Dressed Like a Woman." *New York Times*, October 19, 2002, A11.

> Reports on the hate crime charges filed against several men for the death of Eddie Araujo, a transgendered man, in Newark, California.

Newman, Maria. "Victims of Hate Crime Calls High Court Ruling a 'Slap in the Face.'" *New York Times*, June 27, 2000, B5.

> Newman discusses the effect of the U.S. Supreme Court's decision to reverse a New Jersey lower court decision on a hate crimes case.

Niebuhr, Gustav. "Abhorring Terror at an Ohio Mosque." *New York Times*, September 22, 2001, A11.

> Niebuhr examines a story of forgiveness by the worshippers at a Parma, Ohio, mosque. After a perpetrator deliberately crashed his car into the mosque, the imam and the congregants forgave him for his violent attack.

Nieves, Evelyn. "Slain Arab-American May Have Been Hate-Crime Victim." *New York Times*, October 6, 2001, A8.

> Nieves looks at the case of Abdo Ali Ahmed, a Yemeni Muslim who was murdered in his Reedley, California, grocery store. No money was stolen during the crime.

Noelle, Monique. "The Ripple Effect of the Matthew Shepard Murder: Impact on the Assumptive Worlds of Members of the Targeted Group." *American Behavioral Scientist*, September 2002, 27–51.

This research article investigates the psychological impact of the Shepard murder, a widely publicized antigay hate crime in 1998, on nonvictims who are also gay.

Nolan III, James J., et al. "The Hate Crime Statistics Act of 1990: Developing a Method for Measuring the Occurrence of Hate Violence." *American Behavioral Scientist*, September 2002, 136–154.

A report on the Hate Crime Statistics Act of 1990, which helped establish the mechanisms for identifying and collecting data on the occurrence of hate crimes in this country.

Poussaint, Alvin F. "They Hate. They Kill. Are They Insane?" *New York Times*, August 26, 1999, A17.

Harvard Medical School psychiatrist Poussaint urges the American Psychiatric Association to designate extreme racism as a mental health problem and advocates that clinicians use guidelines for recognizing delusional racism.

Pruzan, Adam. "What Is a Hate Crime? Media Bias in Coverage." *The American Enterprise*, January/February 2000, 10.

The author compares and contrasts the coverage in the *New York Times* of a gun attack at the North Valley Jewish Community Center in Los Angeles, California, and of the murder of seven people at a Baptist church in Fort Worth, Texas.

Rabinowitz, Dorothy. "The Hate-Crimes Bandwagon." *Wall Street Journal*, June 27, 2000, A30.

This WSJ columnist and editor raises questions about the politicization of hate crimes legislation.

"Report Calls for Better Prevention for Hate Crimes." *National Catholic Reporter*, November 29, 2002, 9.

This article discusses a Human Rights Watch report issued on November 14, 2002, which called for better prevention of hate crimes.

Rose, Suzanna M., and Mindy B. Mechanic. "Psychological Distress, Crime Features, and Help-Seeking Behaviors Related to Homophobic Bias Incidents." *American Behavioral Scientist*, September 2002, 14–27.
A psychological study of victims of antigay hate incidents.

Rutenberg, Jim. "Against Hate Crimes." *New York Times*, January 10, 2001, E10.
The reporter covers the decision by MTV to preempt all of its regular programming for 17-and-a-half hours—with no commercial interruptions—as it scrolls the names of victims of hate crimes and recounts the stories behind the crimes.

Santora, Marc. "Woman Is Charged with Murder as a Hate Crime in a Fatal Subway Push." *New York Times*, December 30, 2012, 15.
This article reports on the arrest of Erika Menendez who was charged with second-degree murder for pushing Sunando Sen, a 46 year-old Indian immigrant, onto a New York City subway track because she believed him to be a Hindu or Muslim.

Saulny, Susan. "Man Who Killed Two outside Gay Bar Remains Mentally Ill, a Jury Finds." *New York Times*, June 14, 2001, B8.
Saulny reports a ruling by a New York State Supreme Court jury that Ronald K. Crumpley, who shot and killed two people and wounded six others outside a Greenwich Village gay bar in 1980, was still mentally ill.

Sherry, Mark. "Hate Crimes against Disabled People." *Social Alternatives*, October 2000, 23–30.

This article examines underreported hate crimes directed against the disabled. The author claims these incidents often go unrecognized because the crime is often referred to as "abuse" or "neglect" and such "euphemisms deny the validity" of its magnitude.

Sterngold, James. "Supremacist Who Killed Postal Worker Avoids Death Sentence." *New York Times*, January 24, 2001, A13.

The author looks at Buford O. Furrow, who sprayed automatic gunfire in a Los Angeles Jewish community center filled with children in 1999, then confessed to murdering a Filipino letter carrier. Furrow planned to plead guilty to sixteen felony counts in return for a sentence that would allow him to avoid the death penalty.

"Student Accused of Sending Hate E-Mails." *New York Times*, October 3, 1999, 50.

A report on a Bridgewater-Raritan High School student in New Jersey who was charged with sending 108 racially-charged e-mail hate messages.

Sullivan, Andrew. "What's So Bad about Hate?" *New York Times Magazine*, September 26, 1999, 50.

Sullivan, the former editor of the *New Republic* analyzes the complex legal and philosophical issues of hate speech and hate crime.

Tatchell, Peter. "Why Can Blacks Bash Gays?" *New Statesman*, October 14, 2002, 14–15.

This British magazine discusses the homophobic lyrics found in the song "Chi Chi Man," performed by the

Jamaican music group TOK and hate crimes and violence against gay people.

Tavernise, Sabrina. "Bomb Attack Shows That Russia Hasn't Rooted Out Anti-Semitism." *New York Times*, June 1, 2002, A1.

Tavernise notes that despite the efforts of President Vladimir Putin to eradicate anti-Jewish attitudes resulting in frequent violence directed at Russian Jews, it is still present at the local level and among ordinary Russians.

Tavernise, Sabrina. "Russian Parliament Passes a Hate-Crime Bill Backed by Putin." *New York Times*, June 28, 2002, A9.

Tavernise reports on a Kremlin-backed bill that was passed by the lower house of the Russian Parliament to fight hate crimes and attacks by fascist groups.

"Texas: Man Executed for Hate Crime." *New York Times*, September 22, 2011, 22.

Lawrence Russell Brewer, a white racist gang member, was executed for the dragging death of James Byrd Jr., a black man from east Texas. Mr. Byrd was chained to the back of a pickup truck in 1998 in one of the most brutal hate crimes in recent Texas history. Defense attorney attempts to forestall the execution were unsuccessful.

Thomas, Jo. "New Face of Terror Crimes: 'Lone Wolf' Weaned on Hate." *New York Times*, August 16, 1999, A1.

Thomas reports that, after examining recent hate crimes—including bombings, shootings, and robberies—federal and state investigators have determined that no evidence exists of an organized coordination among violent right-wing groups and individuals against racial and religious minorities.

Tsesis, Alexander. "Contextualizing Bias Crimes: A Social and Theoretical Perspectives." *Law & Social Inquiry*, Winter 2003, 315–340.

An analysis of the arguments supporting hate crimes legislation and a review of *Punishing Hate: Bias Crimes under American Law*, by Frederick M. Lawrence.

"Two Attacked at Mosque." *New York Times*, March 18, 2001, 19.

A report about two Muslim men who were injured, one critically, when they were attacked outside a Sparks, Nevada, mosque in what the police called a possible hate crime. An Associated Press story published in the March 21, 2001, issue of the *Las Vegas Review Journal* notes that police investigators later claimed it was a "robbery-motivated assault," not a hate crime.

"United States: Suspect in Murder of Lesbian Hikers Apprehended after Six Years." *Off Our Backs*, May/June2002, 7.

This issue of *Off Our Backs* reports on the apprehension of Darrel David Rice for the murder of lesbian hikers and also discusses hate crimes directed against lesbians.

Watts, Meredith W. "Aggressive Youth Cultures and Hate Crime: Skinheads and Xenophobic Youth in Germany." *American Behavioral Scientist*, December 2001, 600–616.

Watts notes that bias crime in Germany increased dramatically after unification in 1990 and remained at a relatively high level for the rest of the decade. Hatred of foreigners and other targeted groups not only seems linked to violent elements of youth culture but appears to be stimulated by local and international right-wing and fascist networks.

Williams, Timothy. "The Hated and the Hater: Both Touched by Crime." *New York Times*, July 19, 2001, 15.

> Believing that a few South Asian men were Arabs and enraged by the 9/11 terrorist attacks, Mark Anthony Stroman killed Vasudev Patel, a Hindu Indian immigrant, and Waqar Hasan, a Pakistani Muslim in a series of murderous attacks in Arizona.

Wisse, Ruth R. "On Ignoring Anti-Semitism." *Commentary*, October 2002, 26–33.

> Harvard professor Ruth Wisse warns about the dangers of ignoring anti-Jewish attitudes and violence and the tragic historical consequences.

Wistrich, Robert S. "The Old-New Anti-Semitism." *National Interest*, Summer 2003, 59–70.

> A distinguished historian and academic adviser to the British television documentary *The Longest Hatred*, Wistrich analyzes the current resurgence of anti-Jewish hatred throughout the world.

Wu, Frank H. "Why Vincent Chin Matters." *New York Times*, June 23, 2012, 19.

> Two white auto workers killed Vincent Chin on June 23, 1982 because they thought he was Japanese, even though he was Chinese, because they attributed their economic plight to the success of the Japanese auto industry at that time.

Wypijewski, Joann. "The Myth of Matthew." *The Nation*, October 28, 2013, 6–8.

> This article reviews *The Book of Matt*, which charges that Matthew Shepard was killed in a drug deal gone awry and was not, as widely believed, an antigay murder.

Reports

The U.S. government, state and municipal entities, and many private organizations publish reports and documents on hate crimes, hate groups, and the growth of bigotry throughout the country. The following selections include some major and important publications issued in the past few decades. Since many government and other documents have been digitized it is most advisable to use the Internet when starting your search.

U.S. Government Documents and Reports

U.S. Congress, House Committee on the Judiciary, 108th Congress, 1st Session (Superintendent of Documents no. Y1.1/8: 108–249). *Condemning Bigotry and Violence against Arab-Americans, Muslim-Americans, South Asian-Americans, and Sikh-Americans: Report, September 3, 2003.*

> This report provides background about the discriminatory backlash crimes in the wake of the September 11, 2001, terrorist attacks and contains the text of a congressional resolution deploring the harassment and violence committed against the abovementioned groups and urging law enforcement authorities to vigorously prosecute these crimes.

U.S. Congress, House Committee on the Judiciary, 106th Congress, 1st session (Superintendent of Documents no. Y4.J89/1: 106/47). *Hate Crimes Violence: (Hearing) August 4, 1999.*

> This hearing considered the passage of the Hate Crimes Prevention Act of 1999 to expand federal jurisdiction over bias-motivated crimes. The witnesses included Frederick M. Lawrence, professor of Law at Boston University; Reuben Greenberg, chief of police of Charleston, South Carolina; an assault victim; and the mother of a murdered victim.

U.S. Congress, House Committee on the Judiciary, 105th Congress, 1st session (Superintendent of Documents no.: Y4.J89/1:105/4). *Implementation of the Church Arson Prevention Act of 1996: Hearing, March 19, 1997.*

This hearing examined how federal agencies implemented this act, including the provisions that clarified and expanded the jurisdiction of U.S. federal law enforcement over offenses involving religious property destruction. Witnesses included Patricia C. Glenn, national coordinator of the Church Burning Response Team of the U.S. Department of Justice; Harold McDougall, an official with the National Association for the Advancement of Colored People (NAACP); and Elder T. Myers, a pastor in a South Carolina church. The report of the hearing also includes the Center for Democratic Renewal's document issued in March 1997, "Fourth Wave: A Continuing Conspiracy to Burn Black Churches."

U.S. Congress, House Committee on the Judiciary, 100th Congress, 2nd session (Superintendent of Documents no.:Y4. J89/1:100/144). *Racially Motivated Violence: Hearings, May 11 and July 12, 1988.*

This hearing considered legislation to establish the Commission on Racially Motivated Violence. The hearing also examined the prevalence of and responses to acts of violence against members of minority groups and surveyed the history of racial prejudice in the United States and the increase of racial tensions in colleges and universities. Witnesses included Rev. C. T. Vivian, chairman of the Center for Democratic Renewal; Benjamin L. Hooks, executive director of the National Association of the Advancement of Colored People; Douglas Seymour, an undercover police agent who infiltrated the Ku Klux Klan in California; and Reginald Wilson, director of the Office of Minority Concerns, American Council on Education.

U.S. Congress, House Committee on the Judiciary, Subcommittee on Civil and Constitutional Rights, 100th Congress, 1st session (Superintendent of Documents no.: Y4.J89/1:100/116). *Anti-Asian Violence: Oversight Hearing, November 10, 1987.*

> This hearing examined the causes of and possible responses to recent violent acts committed against Asians and Asian Americans. Witnesses included Rep. Norman Y. Mineta (D-CA); Rep. Robert T. Matsui (D-CA); Floyd D. Shinomura of the Japanese American Citizens League; James C. Tso, president of the Organization of Chinese Americans; and Arthur Soong, president of the Asian American Legal Defense and Education Fund. The report includes a compilation of articles from 1983 to 1987 on violence against Asian immigrants and Asian Americans in Massachusetts and a February 1987 report issued by the Los Angeles County Commission on Human Relations on ethnic- and religious-motivated violence in that region.

U.S. Congress, House Committee on the Judiciary, Subcommittee on Civil and Constitutional Rights, 103rd Congress, 1st session (Superintendent of Documents no.: Y4.J 89/1:103/51). *Crimes of Violence Motivated by Gender: Hearing, November 16, 1993.*

> The hearing examined proposed legislation that would make crimes of violence motivated by gender actionable under civil rights and hate crimes laws.

U.S. Congress, House Committee on the Judiciary, Subcommittee on Crime and Criminal Justice, 102nd Congress, 2nd session (Superintendent of Documents no.: Y4.J 89/1:102/80). *Bias Crimes: Hearing, May 11, 1992.*

> This hearing focused on crimes motivated by prejudice against the racial, ethnic, religious, or sexual orientation of the victim. The witnesses discussed the Hate Crimes Sentencing Act of 1992, which directs the U.S. Sentencing

Commission to revise sentencing guidelines to increase penalties for hate crimes. Witnesses included Rabbi Melvin Burg, whose Los Angeles synagogue was vandalized; Charles J. Hynes, district attorney of Kings County, Brooklyn, New York; and Gary Stoops of the Federal Bureau of Investigation. Other witnesses represented Asian American, Jewish, and gay and women's rights organizations. The hearing report includes the article "Sticks and Stones Can Put You in Jail, but Can Words Increase Your Sentence? Constitutional and Policy Dilemmas for Ethnic Intimidation Laws," by Professor Susan Gellman, published in the *UCLA Law Review*, December 1991 (see *Anti-Gay Violence: Hearings, October 9, 1986* entry).

U.S. Congress, House Committee on the Judiciary, Subcommittee on Crime and Criminal Justice, 102nd Congress, 2nd session (Superintendent of Documents no.: Y4:J89/1:102/64). *Hate Crimes Sentencing Enhancement Act of 1992: Hearing, July 29, 1992.*

This hearing examined the use of penalty enhancement for hate crimes and the implications on the constitutionality of hate crime laws following the June 1992 Supreme Court decision *R. A. V. v. City of St. Paul*, which struck down a Minnesota hate crime statute. The following witnesses offered varied views on the constitutionality of the proposed legislation: Laurence H. Tribe, a professor at Harvard University Law School; Floyd Abrams, a prominent constitutional law attorney; Robert S. Peck, legislative counsel of the American Civil Liberties Union; and Susan Gellman, assistant public defender, Ohio Public Defender Commission.

U.S. Congress, House Committee on the Judiciary, Subcommittee on Criminal Justice, 99th Congress, 2nd session

(Superintendent of Documents no.: Y4.J89/1:99/132). *Anti-Gay Violence: Hearing, October 9, 1986.*

> This hearing examined the problem of violence against gay men and lesbians. The report includes descriptions of violent acts, the nature and extent of the violence, and surveys of cultural and social prejudicial attitudes toward gay people. Rep. Barney Frank (D-MA) presented a statement and participated in interviewing witnesses, who included Kevin Berrill, director of the Violence Project of the National Gay and Lesbian Task Force; Dr. Gregory M. Herek, a psychology professor; and Robert J. Johnston, chief of the New York City Police Department. In addition, some gay victims of violence told of their own experiences.

U.S. Congress, House Committee on the Judiciary, Subcommittee on Criminal Justice, 99th Congress, 1st session (Superintendent of Documents no.: Y4.J89/1:99/134). *Crimes against Religious Practices and Property: Hearings, May 16 and June 19, 1985.*

> These hearings considered a bill to establish federal penalties for damaging any religious building or cemetery or intimidating any person in the exercise of religious beliefs. Witnesses included Victoria Toensing, deputy assistant attorney general, who objected to the proposed legislation and advocated state, not federal, prosecution of such crimes. Richard Foltin, associate legal director of the American Jewish Committee, testified in support of the legislation.

U.S. Congress, House Committee on the Judiciary, Subcommittee on Criminal Justice, 99th Congress, 2nd session (Superintendent of Documents no.: Y4.J89/1:99/135). *Ethnically Motivated Violence against Arab-Americans: Hearing, July 16, 1986.*

This hearing examined reports of harassment and violence directed against Arab Americans in the United States. Witnesses included Oliver B. Revell III, the executive assistant director of the FBI; David Sadd, executive director of the National Association of Arab Americans; and David M. Gordis, executive vice president of the American Jewish Committee. The report included testimony of Rep. Mary Oakar (D-OH) and Rep. Nick Joe Rahall (D-WV).

U.S. Congress, House Committee on the Judiciary, Subcommittee on Criminal Justice, 99th Congress, 1st session (Superintendent of Documents no.: Y4.J89/1:99/137). *Hate Crime Statistics Act: Hearing, March 21, 1985.*

The first congressional hearing held to discuss passage of a law requiring the U.S. Justice Department to collect and publish statistics on crimes motivated by racial, ethnic, or religious prejudice. Witnesses in support of this legislation included Elaine Jones of the Legal, Defense, and Education Fund of the National Association for the Advancement of Colored People (NAACP); Jerome Bakst of the Anti-Defamation League of B'nai B'rith; and Rep. Mario Biaggi (D-NY). Opponents of the legislation discussed the anticipated difficulties of determining the motivation for certain crimes and the problems of incorporating these statistics into the Uniform Crime Reporting program administered by the U.S. Department of Justice. These witnesses included William M. Baker, assistant director of the Office of Congressional and Public Affairs of the FBI, and Steven R. Schlesinger, director of the Bureau of Justice Statistics. Other witnesses included Rep. Norman Y. Mineta (D-CA) and Rep. Barbara B. Kennelly (D-CT), who testified on crimes of violence against members of ethnic, racial, and religious minorities.

U.S. Congress, House Committee on National Security, 104th Congress, 2nd session (Superintendent of Documents no.:

Y4.Se2/1 A:995–96). *Extremist Activity in the Military: Hearing, June 25, 1996.*

> This hearing examined the participation of current or former U.S. Army personnel in antigovernment hate groups and militia organizations. It also studied the murder of an African American couple in Fayetteville, North Carolina, by soldiers of the 82nd Airborne Division based at Fort Bragg, who were affiliated with white supremacist groups.

U.S. Congress, Senate Committee on the Judiciary, 104th Congress, 2nd session (Superintendent of Documents no.: Y4.J 89/2:S.hrg.104–851). *Church Burnings: Hearing, June 27, 1996, on the Federal Response to Recent Incidents of Church Burnings in Predominantly Black Churches across the South.*

> This hearing surveyed the rash of arson against black churches and acts of violence against other houses of worship. It also examined the federal investigation and prosecution of the perpetrators and the financial support given to assist in rebuilding the burned buildings.

U.S. Congress, Senate Committee on the Judiciary, 106th Congress, 1st session (Superintendent of Documents no.: Y4.J89/2: 106–517). *Combating Hate Crimes: Promoting a Responsive and Responsible Role for the Federal Government, May 11, 1999.*

> This hearing discussed the passage of the Hate Crimes Prevention Act of 1999 to expand federal jurisdiction of bias-motivated crimes related to interstate commerce. The witnesses offered different opinions on the constitutionality and desirability of this proposed legislation.

U.S. Congress, Senate Committee on the Judiciary, 104th Congress, 2nd session (Superintendent of Documents no. Y4.J89/2:S.hrg 104–842). *Combating Violence against Women: Hearing, May 15, 1996.*

> This hearing examined the implementation of the Violence against Women Act (VAWA) of 1994, providing

protection for women against violent crime. Witnesses included Sen. Kay Bailey Hutchinson (R-TX); U.S. Attorney General Janet Reno; Kathryn J. Rogers, executive director of the National Organization for Women (NOW) Legal Defense and Education Fund; and Denise Brown, director of the Nicole Brown Simpson Charitable Foundation.

U.S. Congress, Senate Committee on the Judiciary, 106th Congress, 1st session (Superintendent of Documents no.: Y4.J89/2: 106–803). *Hate Crime on the Internet, September 14, 1999.*

This hearing explored the issues related to the use of the Internet to promote prejudice and bias-motivated crimes. The witnesses included Rabbi Abraham Cooper, the associate director of the Simon Wiesenthal Center; Howard Berkowitz, the national chairman of the Anti-Defamation League; and Joseph T. Roy, an official of the Southern Poverty Law Center.

U.S. Congress, Senate Committee on the Judiciary, 100th Congress, 2nd session (Superintendent of Documents no.: Y4.J89/2:S.hrg.100–1069). *Hate Crime Statistics Act of 1988: Hearing, June 21, 1988.*

This hearing considered the proposed legislation to require the U.S. Department of Justice to collect and publish statistics on crimes motivated by racial, ethnic, or religious prejudice. The witnesses endorsing the legislation included Alan M. Schwartz, director of the Research and Evaluation Department of the Anti-Defamation League of B'nai B'rith; Patricia Clark, director of the Klanwatch project of the Southern Poverty Law Center; Joan C. Weiss, executive director of the National Institute against Prejudice and Violence; William Yoshino, midwestern region director of the Japanese American Citizens League;

and Kevin Berrill, director of the Anti-Violence Project of the National Gay and Lesbian Task Force.

U.S. Congress, Senate Committee on the Judiciary, 105th Congress, 2nd session (Superintendent of Documents no.: Y4.J89/2: 105–904). *Hate Crimes Prevention Act of 1998: Hearing July 8, 1998.*

This hearing discussed proposed legislation to expand the federal jurisdiction to allow the prosecution of crimes motivated by prejudice against a victim's sexual orientation, gender, or disability and to eliminate the stipulation that victims must be engaged in a federally protected activity in order to have federal prosecution.

U.S. Congress, Senate Committee on the Judiciary, 103rd Congress, 2nd session (Superintendent of Documents no.: Y4. J 89/2: S.hrg. 103–1078). *Hate Crimes Statistics Act: Hearing, June 28, 1994.*

This hearing reviewed the implementation of the Hate Crime Statistics Act of 1990, requiring that the FBI collect and publish statistics on crimes motivated by racial, ethnic, or religious prejudice. The report also examined educational efforts of private organizations to promote tolerance and to prevent hate crimes. One witness was Steven Spielberg, the acclaimed motion picture director and producer, who discussed his perspectives on the making of the award-winning movie *Schindler's List* and its educational value. Other witnesses included Robert Machleder, chairman of the New York Regional Board of the Anti-Defamation League; Sara Bullard, education director of the Southern Poverty Law Center; and Deedee Corradini, mayor of Salt Lake City, Utah, representing the U.S. Conference of Mayors.

U.S. Congress, Senate Committee on the Judiciary, 104th Congress, 2nd session (Superintendent of Documents no.:

Y4.J89/2: S.hrg. 104–845). *Reauthorization of the Hate Crime Statistics Act: Hearing, March 19, 1996.*

This hearing considered amending the Hate Crime Statistics Act of 1990 to permanently reauthorize the FBI programs to collect and publish statistics on crimes motivated by race, ethnicity, sexual orientation, disability, or religious prejudice. The witnesses included Charles W. Archer, assistant director of the FBI's Criminal Justice Information Services Division; Emanuel Cleaver II, mayor of Kansas City, Missouri, who represented the U.S. Conference of Mayors; Stephen Arent, vice chairman of the National Civil Rights Committee of the Anti-Defamation League; and Karen M. Lawson, executive director of the Leadership Conference Education Fund. The report includes the FBI document "Summary Reporting System: National Incident-Based Reporting System; Hate Crime Data Collection Guidelines" and the 1994 Covington and Burlington law firm report "D.C. Bias-Related Crime Act: An Unused Weapon against Violent Crime," prepared for the National Asian Pacific American Bar Association.

U.S. Congress, Senate Committee on the Judiciary, 102nd Congress, 1st session (Superintendent of Documents no. Y4.J89/2:S.hrg. 102–369). *Violence against Women: Victims of the System; Hearing, April 9, 1991.*

This hearing considered the Violence against Women Act of 1991, in particular to amend various acts to revise and expand protections against rape and other violent crime. The witnesses included Bonnie J. Campbell, attorney general of Iowa; Roland W. Burris, attorney general of Illinois; and Cass R. Sunstein, a professor at the University of Chicago Law School. The subsequent document includes a committee staff report entitled "Violence against Women: The Increase of Rape in America, 1990," with tables and graphs.

U.S. Congress, Senate Committee on the Judiciary, Subcommittee on the Constitution, 102nd Congress, 2nd session (Superintendent of Documents no.: Y4.J89/2: S.hrg. 102–1131). *Hate Crimes Statistics Act: Hearing, August 5, 1992.*

> This hearing reviewed the implementation of the Hate Crime Statistics Act of 1990 by the FBI, state crime reporting agencies, and local law enforcement agencies under the direction of the U.S. Department of Justice. Witnesses included G. Norman Christensen, assistant director of the Criminal Justice Information Services Division of the FBI; Jack McDevitt, coauthor of *Hate Crimes;* and Elsie L. Scott, deputy commissioner of training for the New York City Police Department, representing the National Organization of Black Law Enforcement Executives. Also called to speak were Harold Gershowitz, chairman of the Chicago Regional Board of the Anti-Defamation League; and Elizabeth R. Ouyang, staff attorney for the Asian American Legal Defense and Education Fund, who expressed concern about the possible underreporting of hate crimes against Asian Americans. This report also included the FBI document "Hate Crime Data Collection Guidelines: Uniform Crime Reporting" and the 1991 annual report issued by the Massachusetts Executive Office of Public Safety, entitled "Hate Crime/ Hate Incidents in Massachusetts."

U.S. Congress. Senate. Subcommittee on Constitution, Civil Rights and Human Rights; Committee on the Judiciary. *Hate Crimes and the Threat of Domestic Extremism, September 19, 2012.*

> This hearing was inspired by congressional concerns that not enough was being done to combat the threat of violent domestic extremists or to protect the vulnerable communities that extremists may target. According to the Bureau of Justice Statistics, there were an estimated 195,000 hate crimes per year between 2003 and 2009.

U.S. Congress. Senate. Committee on the Judiciary. *The Matthew Shepard Hate Crimes Prevention Act of 2009, June 25, 2009.* (SuDoc no. Y4.J89/2:S.HRG.111–464)

> Hearing to consider S. 909, the Matthew Shepard Hate Crimes Prevention Act of 2009, to establish certain hate crimes as new Federal offenses, and to authorize the Department of Justice to make grants to State, local, and tribal governments to investigate and prosecute hate crimes, including crimes manifesting prejudice based on gender or gender identity and hate crimes affecting juveniles. Includes supplementary material: American-Arab Anti-Discrimination Committee; "Report on Hate Crimes and Discrimination Against Arab Americans: 2003–2007"; Leadership Conference on Civil Rights Education Fund; "Confronting the New Faces of Hate: Hate Crimes in America", 2009; Parshall, Craig L.; "Tyranny over the Mind: A Legal and Policy Analysis of H.R. 1592 and S. 1105 (Hate Crimes Legislation)", May 14, 2007; Southern Poverty Law Center Intelligence Project; "Terror from the Right: 75 Plots, Conspiracies and Racist Rampages Since Oklahoma City.

U.S. Congress. House. Committee on the Judiciary. *Jena 6 and the Role of Federal Intervention in Hate Crimes and Race-Related Violence in Public Schools, October 16, 2007.* (Sudoc Number: Y4.J89/1:110–162)

> Hearing to examine role of Federal intervention in racially motivated incidents in public schools, in light of recent events in Jena, Louisiana, in which racial tensions among high school students led to hate crimes and violence that resulted in disproportionate punishments among black and white students.

U.S. Congress. Joint Commissions and Temporary Committees. Commission on Security and Cooperation in Europe. *Hate Crimes, November 6, 2007.* (Sudoc Number: Y4.SE2:H28)

A transcript of Commission on Security and Cooperation in Europe briefing on combating hate crimes and discrimination in Europe and Russia.

U.S. Congress. Senate. Subcommittee on Crime and Drugs; Committee on the Judiciary. *Crimes Against America's Homeless: Is the Violence Growing?, September 29, 2010.* (Sudoc Number: Y4.J89/2:S.HRG.111–915)

Hearing before the Subcomittee on Crime and Drugs to examine trends in violent crimes against the homeless. According to HUD's latest report to Congress, approximately 640,000 persons were homeless on any given night in 2009, and roughly 1.5 million people, or one out of every 200 Americans, spent at least one night in a shelter during 2009. According to National Coalition for the Homeless numbers, bias-motivated crimes against the homeless are pervasive and growing. The previous year was the deadliest one for attacks on homeless people.

U.S. Department of Justice, Bureau of Justice Assistance. *A Policymaker's Guide to Hate Crimes,* 1997.

This report surveys the scope and nature of hate crimes and the response to the problem by federal, state, and local government agencies.

U.S. Department of Justice, Federal Bureau of Investigation. *Hate Crime Statistics.* An annual report mandated by the Hate Crime Statistics Act of 1990.

The FBI is the major U.S. government agency collecting, tabulating, and publishing official data on the extent of hate crimes nationwide.

U.S. Department of Justice. Federal Bureau of Investigation. Hate Crime Data Collection Guidelines and Training Manual, 2015. http://www.fbi.gov/about-us/cjis/ucr/hate-crime-data-collection-guidelines-and-training-manual.pdf

The official U.S. government guidelines for defining groups vulnerable to hate crime victimization and also discusses the techniques of training law enforcement officials for analyzing and investigating these crimes.

Weekly Compilation of Presidential Documents, Remarks at the Dedication of Mount Zion A.M.E. Church in Greeleyville, South Carolina, June 17, 1996: 1038–1042.

The text of remarks by President Bill Clinton in which he promises to prosecute those responsible for the church burnings and to assist communities in rebuilding their houses of worship.

Weekly Compilation of Presidential Documents, Statement on the Attack on Jewish Students in Brooklyn, New York, March 2, 1994, March 7, 1994: 418.

The text of a statement in which President Bill Clinton condemns the shooting incident directed against Hasidic Jewish students riding across the Brooklyn Bridge.

Weekly Compilation of Presidential Documents, Statement on Hate Crimes Legislation, October 18, 1999: 2024–2025.

The text of a statement given by President Bill Clinton on October 13, 1999, which deals with the hate crimes legislation.

Weekly Compilation of Presidential Documents, Letter to the Speaker of the House of Representatives on the Proposed "Hate Crimes Prevention Act," July 17, 2000: 1627.

The text of a letter given by President Bill Clinton on July 12, 2000, which deals with the proposed Hate Crimes Prevention Act.

Weekly Compilation of Presidential Documents, Statement on Senate Action on Hate Crimes Legislation, June 26, 2000: 1416–1418.

The text of a statement given by President Bill Clinton on June 20, 2000.

Weekly Compilation of Presidential Documents, Remarks on Proposed Hate Crimes Legislation, May 1, 2000: 920–923.
The text of remarks given by President Bill Clinton on April 25, 2000.

Organization Reports

Nongovernmental organizations and associations have published important studies on hate crimes and extremist organizations. Since the last edition of this book, many of these publications are available electronically on various organizations' Web sites.

Anti-Defamation League (ADL), http://www.adl.org

The Anti-Defamation League, the oldest Jewish civil and human rights organization in the U.S., offers an extensive number of publications on its Web site. These publications cover anti-Semitism, racism, homophobia, interethnic and intergroup relations, hate groups, law enforcement activities to combat hate crimes, among many other topics.

International Association of Chiefs of Police (IACP), http://www.theiacp.org/

The IACP has published many useful publications on hate crimes covering many topics including a guide for law enforcement officers involved in the investigation and prevention of these crimes.

Nonprint Resources

In recent years, a growing amount of material on hate crimes has been appearing in nonprint format, including videos, films, television, and the Internet. This section includes information about some useful and informative sources. The availability of these videos constantly changes so please check the Internet to find the current distributor.

Anti-Gay Hate Crimes

Media Type: DVD

Running Time: 50 minutes

Release Date: 2008

Distributor: New Video Group

Originally broadcast on the A& E television network, this documentary surveys the activities of the most vocal groups opposed to the so-called "homosexual agenda".

Assault on Gay America: The Life and Death of Billy Jack Gaither

Media Type: VHS

Running Time: 60 minutes

Release Date: 2000

In February 1999, in Sylacauga, Alabama, Billy Jack Gaither was murdered by a white supremacist who later testified that he killed the thirty-year-old computer programmer because he was "queer." This film explores the roots of homophobia in the United States and examines how these beliefs and fears contribute to the recent rise in violence against gays and lesbians.

Beyond Hate

Media Type: DVD

Running Time: 91 minutes

Release Date: 2013

Originally aired on PBS in 1991, Bill Moyers examines the origins and dimensions of hate through the eyes of world leaders, human rights activists, Arabs and Israelis, high school students, youth gangs, and U.S. white supremacist groups.

Boys Don't Cry

Media Type: DVD

Running Time: 208 minutes

Distributor: Twentieth Century Fox Home Entertainment

Release Date: 2010

This major Hollywood movie depicts the true story of a transgendered youth living as a man in rural Nebraska who assumes the name Brandon Teena and is later murdered.

The Brandon Teena Story

Media Type: DVD

Running Time: 88 minutes

Release Date: 2008

Distributor: New Video Group

A true story about transgendered teen Brandon Teena and the hostile reaction he received in a Nebraska town. Teena arrived in rural Falls City, Nebraska, in 1993, where he found new friends. Three weeks later, he was raped and beaten by these friends, who had discovered that Brandon was actually a woman. The film was named best documentary at the 1998 Berlin Film Festival and the 1998 Vancouver Film Festival and was the inspiration of the Oscar-winning movie *Boys Don't Cry.*

Brotherhood of Hate

Media Type: VHS

Running Time: 52 minutes

Release Date: 2000

This film documents one family's legacy of hate, showing how it was handed down from one generation to the next. It is the story of eight brothers raised to be white supremacist warriors.

Bum Hunting

Media Type: DVD and videodisc

Running Time: 12 minutes

Release Date: 2006

This short film documents a disturbing trend of teenage violence directed at homeless people.

Hate across America

Media Type: VHS

Running Time: 50 minutes

Release Date: 1996

This film surveys the history of violent hate crimes, from the murder of three civil rights workers in Mississippi in 1964 to the present day.

Hate Crime

Media Type: VHS

Running Time: 58 minutes

Release Date: 1999

This film highlights two communities that are having some success in solving the problem of hate crimes. Following the burning of African American churches in South Carolina, law enforcement officials arrested members of the Ku Klux Klan (KKK). One of the black churches filed a lawsuit against the KKK and won a $38 million judgment against the Klan from a racially mixed jury. The second case features a high school class on tolerance, developed by teacher Joe Moros, that has changed the social climate at San Clemente High School in California, where tensions among whites, Hispanics, blacks, and Asian Americans led to brutal violence and killing in the 1990s.

Hate Groups USA

Media Type: VHS

Running Time: 48 minutes

Release Date: 1999

Originally a BBC broadcast entitled *The Heart of Darkness*, this documentary contains interviews with some leading racist leaders as well as government officials and civil rights leaders who try to combat their hateful activities.

Hate.com: Extremists on the Internet

Media Type: VHS

Running Time: 42 minutes

Release Date: 2000

This documentary discusses the use of the Internet to spread messages of hate and violence and contains segments on the leaders of racist movements, including Don Black, founder of Stormfront; Matt Hale, founder of the World Church of the Creator; Richard Butler, founder of Aryan Nations and Christian Identity; and Dr. William Pierce, founder of the National Alliance and author of *The Turner Diaries*. The film also profiles so-called lone wolves—individuals apparently without organizational support who perpetrated violent hate crimes—including Timothy McVeigh, Benjamin Smith, the lynchers of James Byrd Jr., and others.

Journey to a Hate-Free Millennium: Stories of Compassion and Hope

Media Type: DVD

Running Time: 78 minutes

Release Date: 2000

This film discusses some infamous hate crimes in the United States. Victims as well as students, teachers, celebrities, and others affected by these incidents are interviewed.

Last Lynching

Media Type: DVD and videodisc

Running Time: 44 minutes

Release Date: 2009

Explores the history of lynching, including a schoolteacher whose grandfather witnessed the lynching of five

African-Americans in 1916 and law student and later Congressman Artur Davis who helped prosecute the KKK for a 1981 lynching in Mobile, Alabama.

Licensed to Kill

Media Type: DVD

Running Time: 77 minutes

Release Date: 2007

Rarely seen videotaped interviews with the men who have beaten and killed gay people. Including news reports and police files. Originally broadcast on PBS in 1998.

The Matthew Shepard Story: Death in the High Desert

Media Type: VHS

Running Time: 46 minutes

Release Date: 2001

This film discusses the events surrounding the murder of Matthew Shepard (1976–1998), who was murdered in Laramie, Wyoming, because he was gay. The video includes profiles of the murderers and excerpts from their confessions. It also explores the impact on the community and the legal issues concerning a fair trial for the accused murderers.

Responding to Hate Crimes: A Roll Call Training Video for Police Officers

Media Type: VHS

Running Time: 20 minutes

Release Date: 2000

Cost: Contact Bureau of Justice Assistance

This video explains the differences between a hate incident and a hate crime and how law enforcement officials should address community concerns.

Shadow of Hate

Media Type:

Running Time: 40 minutes

Release Date: 2012

An historical overview of religious, ethnic, and racial intolerance in the United States.

South

Media Type: VHS

Running Time: 70 minutes

Release Date: 1999

Director Chantal Akerman changed the focus of this film, originally intended as a documentary on the American South, to examine the gruesome lynching of James Byrd Jr., an African American, in Jasper, Texas.

Two Spirits

Media Type: DVD

Running Time: 51 minutes

Release Date: 2009

This movie examines the role of two-spirit people in the Navajo culture. Fred Martinez, a *nadleehi* or a" male-bodied person with a feminine essence" was murdered in a hate crime at the age of sixteen. This film examines the views of Native Americans on gender and sexuality.

Two Towns of Jasper

Media Type: VHS

Running Time: 90 minutes

Release Date: 2007

This video examines the different reactions in the white and black communities to the lynching of James Byrd Jr., an

African American, by three white men in Jasper, Texas in 1998.

Understanding Hate Crimes

Media Type: VHS

Running Time: 47 minutes

Release Date: 2000

A dramatization of the impact on a community after a junior high school student is abducted and beaten to death for being gay. While fellow students prepare a memorial service for the boy they hardly knew, they begin to question the forces that led to the murder. Comments from a variety of professionals are interspersed throughout.

Antibias Videos

The Anti-Defamation League (ADL) is one of the largest producers and distributors of human relations materials, including videos, books, teachers' discussion guides, and classroom program activities.

Several dozen ADL videos are easily accessible on YouTube (https://www.youtube.com/user/ADLNational) and the ADL Web site (http://www.adl.org). These videos cover a wide range of topics including hate crimes, interfaith and intergroup relations, promoting tolerance, combatting racism, anti-Semitism and homophobia, Israel and the Middle East, among many other subjects. These videos are aimed at students, teachers, community groups, church and synagogues, social workers among other professionals.

Because the number of individual violent hate crimes committed in the United States during the past few decades is too large to include in a single list, the following chronology is necessarily selective. Although most of the cited incidents occurred in the United States a few hate crimes committed outside the country were included to demonstrate that the problem is worldwide. Individual victims from various racial, religious, and sexual minority groups are cited in this chapter, which explains why a broad range of human and civil rights groups and ethnic defense organizations have been galvanized to promote anti-hate crimes legislation to deter bias incidents. The chronology also contains notable events in the legislative and judicial history of hate crimes laws.

The chronology begins in 1955, the year Emmett Till was lynched in Mississippi, an event many historians consider the beginning of the modern civil rights movement. In the spring of 2004, the U.S. Department of Justice reopened this historic case to investigate new information about other possible perpetrators.

Many of the listed crimes committed before 1979 have been adapted from the outstanding reference work *Racial and Religious Violence in the United States: A Chronology* (New York: Garland, 1991) by Michael and Judy Ann Newton. Recent

---

On September 25, 2014, protestors gathered in Philadelphia's John F. Kennedy Plaza, also known as Love Park, to demonstrate support for adding sexual orientation to Pennsylvania's hate crime law. The renewed call for the legislation came in response to the September 11 beating of a gay couple that left two local men with injuries requiring hospitalization. (AP Photo/Matt Rourke)

material has been adapted from the invaluable "Hate Incidents" webpage compiled by Michelle Bramblett which is posted on the Southern Poverty Law Center Web site.

1955

May 7   The Reverend George W. Lee, an official of the National Association for the Advancement of Colored People (NAACP), is shot and killed on a highway in Belzoni, Mississippi.

August 13   Lamar Smith, a vocal supporter for black voter registration, is shot and killed on the lawn of the county courthouse in Brookhaven, Mississippi.

August 28   Emmett Till, a fourteen-year-old black boy, is kidnapped, shot, and drowned in a river near Money, Mississippi, for allegedly whistling at a white man's wife. His killers are acquitted after a controversial trial. This notorious incident is often considered the catalyst for the modern civil rights movement. Two books published in 2002 and 2003 and a television documentary reveal possibly new information on this case.

October 22   John Reese, a 16-year-old African American, is killed and two other black youths are wounded by white gunmen at a café in Mayflower, Texas. The attack is one of several violent incidents aimed at discouraging the black community from building a new school.

1956

January 30   A bomb explodes at the Montgomery, Alabama, home of the Reverend Martin Luther King Jr.

February 3–4   The admission of black student Autherine Lucy to the University of Alabama sparks a riot from local Ku Klux Klan (KKK) members and white students. Another riot occurs on February 6, which led university administrators to suspend and later expel Lucy from the university. In April 1988, the university revoked her expulsion and she re-enrolled. More than 35 years later, Autherine Lucy received an MA degree in elementary education at the University of Alabama.

April 11   Six Klan members assault singer Nat "King" Cole during a performance at the Birmingham, Alabama, municipal auditorium.

1957

January 23   Willie Edwards, a black truck driver, is abducted by Klan members in Montgomery, Alabama. They accuse Edwards of attacking white women and force him at gunpoint to leap from a river bridge. His death, considered accidental until 1976, is charged as a homicide when a Klan member confesses to the crime. Three other Klan members are indicted, but the charges are dismissed when the prosecution fails to prove that the cause of Edwards's death was drowning. In 1998 Montgomery district attorney Ellen Brooks orders an exhumation, and the coroner finds the death was indeed caused by drowning.

1958

March 16   The Jewish Community Center in Nashville, Tennessee, is dynamited.

June 29   A black miner removes a package of dynamite from a Baptist church in Birmingham, Alabama, whose pastor is civil rights leader Reverend F. L. Shuttlesworth. The dynamite explodes in the street, breaking windows in a four-block area.

July 7   An early morning explosion damages the home of the Reverend Warren Carr, the white chairman of the Durham, North Carolina, Human Relations Committee, a local group devoted to improving racial relationships.

August 24–25   Two formerly all-white schools in Deep Creek, North Carolina, are destroyed by fire after they were scheduled to be integrated.

October 12   The Temple, a synagogue in Atlanta, is bombed at 3:30 a.m., causing an estimated $200,000 in damage. The blast tears an eighteen-square-foot hole in a side entrance of the building and shatters windows of a nearby building and apartment house. Twenty minutes after the blast, a caller says it was the "last empty building I'll blow up in Atlanta." The bombings and phone calls parallel similar attacks on synagogues in Miami and Jacksonville, Florida, and Birmingham, Alabama, during this time.

1959

April 25   Mack Parker, a black truck driver, is taken from his jail cell, where he was being held for suspected rape, and is lynched by a mob of whites in Poplarville, Mississippi. An area prosecutor refuses to accept evidence by the Federal Bureau of Investigation (FBI) naming several of the lynchers. When the state trooper who arrested Parker offers his gun to the husband of the rape victim so that he can shoot Parker, the husband refuses because his wife's description of the perpetrator is unclear.

1960

January 7–8   Teenage vandals are arrested in a wave of anti-Jewish vandalism at synagogues and other buildings in New York, Philadelphia, Chicago, Boston, and more than a dozen other cities.

April 23   William Moore, a northern white civil rights advocate, is shot and killed in Attalla, Alabama, during a one-man civil rights march from Tennessee to Mississippi. On April 27, a local white man is charged with the murder.

1961

September 25   Herbert Lee, a cotton farmer and black voter registration organizer, is shot and killed by E. H. Hurst in the town of Liberty, Mississippi. Hurst, a white neighbor and state legislator, is never brought to trial.

1962

April 9   Roman Ducksworth, a black soldier, is shot and killed by a white policeman for refusing to sit in the back of a bus in Taylorsville, Mississippi.

1963

June 8   The county sheriff and police chief of Winona, Mississippi, and three other whites are indicted on federal charges of brutalizing black prisoners.

June 12   Medgar Evers, a black NAACP leader, is killed by a sniper in the driveway of his home in Jackson, Mississippi. The FBI finds that the murderer is Byron De La Beckwith, a member of the Ku Klux Klan and White Citizens' Council. However, two trials for the murder result in hung juries. In 1967 Beckwith runs for governor of Mississippi with the backing of the Klan. After prosecutors try Beckwith a third time, he is convicted on February 5, 1994, and sentenced to life imprisonment at the Central Mississippi Correctional Facility.

September 4   The home of Arthur Shores, a black attorney in Birmingham, Alabama, is bombed a second time, touching off a riot that results in one death and 18 injuries. On the same day, 125 members of the National States Rights Party, a neo-Nazi racist organization, scuffle with police outside a recently integrated school.

September 15   A bomb explodes at the Sixteenth Street Baptist Church in Birmingham, Alabama, during Sunday services. Four black girls are killed: Addie Mae Collins, Cynthia Wesley, Carole Robertson, and Denise McNair. Another person is blinded. African Americans riot in response to the explosion. Alabama state troopers, under the command of Al Lingo, a "good friend" of the Klan, try to disperse the rioters. During the outbreak, a police officer kills Johnny Robinson, a black youth. Another black youth, 13-year-old Virgil Ware, is also fatally shot by two white youths.

1964

January 31   Louis Allen, a witness to the 1961 murder of Herbert Lee, is shot and killed in the front yard of his home in Liberty, Mississippi.

April 7 The Reverend Bruce Klunder, a white minister from Cleveland, Ohio, is crushed to death by a bulldozer while protesting the construction of a segregated school.

May 2 Henry Dee and Charlie Moore, two African American teenagers, are abducted by Klan members in Meadville, Mississippi. Two months later, their bodies are pulled from a nearby river. Although murder charges are filed against two Ku Klux Klan members, the charges are later dismissed.

June 10 A white mob hurling bricks and sulfuric acid breaks through police lines to attack black demonstrators in St. Augustine, Florida. Police use tear gas to disperse the rioters.

June 21 Civil rights workers Michael Schwerner, James Chaney, and Andrew Goodman are arrested for allegedly speeding in Philadelphia, Mississippi. They are released to a waiting group of Klan members, who murder the men on a rural road and bury them in an earthen dam. On August 4, their bodies are recovered. Although the state of Mississippi refuses to file murder charges, the seven Klan members are later convicted of federal civil rights violations.

June 25 A black church in Longdale, Mississippi, is damaged by a firebomb.

June 26 Arsonists burn a black church in Clinton, Mississippi.

July 6 Two black churches in Raleigh, Mississippi, are burned to the ground.

July 10 Three rabbis active in black voter registration programs in Hattiesburg, Mississippi, are assaulted with metal clubs. On August 8, two white men plead guilty to the attacks, pay $500 fines, and receive 90-day suspended sentences.

July 11 Klan members in Colbert, Georgia, ambush a carload of black army reserve officers returning home from summer training exercises. Lt. Col. Lemuel Penn is killed by shotgun blasts; his companions escape unharmed. Two Klan members are acquitted of murder charges, but both are later sentenced to prison for federal civil rights violations.

1965

February 10   Deputies armed with electric prods force civil rights marchers out of Selma, Alabama, leaving them stranded more than a mile from town.

February 17   A voter registration headquarters is set on fire by Ku Klux Klan members in Laurel, Mississippi.

February 18   Jimmy Lee Jackson, a black civil rights worker, is beaten and fatally shot in Marion, Alabama, when state law enforcement officers attack about 400 black demonstrators. While Jackson lies in a Selma, Alabama, hospital, police serve him an arrest warrant. He dies on February 26.

March 9   In Selma, Alabama, violent racists attack the Reverend James Reeb, a Boston minister active in the civil rights movement. He is fatally beaten. The defendants are acquitted by a jury that had earlier discussed their verdict with Sheriff Jim Clark, a professed racist.

March 21   A desegregated cafe is firebombed in Vicksburg, Mississippi.

March 25   Viola Liuzzo, a white civil rights worker from Detroit, is ambushed and killed by Klan members in Lowndesboro, Alabama.

March 29   Members of the Klan hurl a tear gas grenade at blacks in Bogalusa, Louisiana.

May 13   An African American church in Oxford, Alabama, is bombed.

May 17   A gas station and a motel owned by vocal Klan opponents are bombed in Laurel, Mississippi.

June 2   Oneal Moore and Creed Rogers, two black sheriff's deputies, are ambushed while on patrol in Bogalusa, Louisiana; Rogers is wounded, and Moore is fatally injured. On June 5, gunshots are fired at the home of the law enforcement official investigating the murder. Although Klan member Ray McElveen was arrested for the murder, he was released a few weeks later because local authorities claimed not to have enough evidence for a trial. Since that time, no one has been arrested or prosecuted for these crimes. In June 2002, 100 people gathered in Moore's hometown to honor his memory and his surviving partner, Creed Rogers, who was then eighty years old. In 2007, David "Creed" Rogers passed away without ever learning who killed his partner. In 2009, the case was re-opened by the Cold Case Initiative.

June 16   Klan members shoot at a black-owned nightclub and also at the state vice president of the NAACP in separate incidents in Laurel, Mississippi.

July 1   In Laurel, Mississippi, Klansmen burn the headquarters of a civil rights organization and thirteen homes occupied by civil rights workers.

July 15   Willie Brewster, a black man, is shot and killed in Anniston, Alabama, by night riders following a rally organized by the National States Rights Party.

July 16   While police stand and watch, white mobs attack black protesters in Bogalusa, Louisiana. After the seventh assault, police arrest two white attackers. On July 17, whites spray water and hurl rocks and bottles at black demonstrators. In Greensboro, Alabama, about 75 black demonstrators are attacked by a white mob armed with clubs, hammers, and rubber hoses. Seventeen demonstrators require hospitalization.

July 18   An African American church in Elmwood, Alabama, is burned. Arsonists also burn two black churches in Greensboro, Alabama. The Imperial Wizard of the Klan, Sam Bowers, boasts that the Klan is responsible for more than 16 arson fires in Laurel, Mississippi.

July 27   Two black homes are firebombed in Ferriday, Louisiana. The office of the Congress of Racial Equality (CORE) is firebombed in New Orleans, Louisiana.

July 31   The headquarters of the Council of Federated Organizations, in Columbia, Mississippi, is damaged by fire and subjected to gunfire in a predawn attack.

August 20   Jonathan Daniels, a white seminary student on leave from the Episcopal Theological School in Cambridge, Massachusetts, is shot and killed by a part-time deputy sheriff and Klan member in Hayneville, Alabama. Robert F. Morrisoe, a Catholic priest from Chicago, is also seriously wounded in the same attack.

August 23 The Reverend Donald A. Thompson, a Unitarian minister who is involved in civil rights work in Jackson, Mississippi, is seriously wounded in an ambush.

August 26 At a rally in Plymouth, North Carolina, Klan members beat 27 black protesters.

August 27 George Metcalfe, an NAACP official, is maimed when a bomb explodes in his car in Natchez, Mississippi. Although FBI agents find Klan members responsible, no one is prosecuted for the explosion.

September 26 A black church in Jones County, Mississippi, is burned by arsonists.

October 4 In Crawfordsville, Georgia, the Grand Dragon of the KKK assaults a black demonstrator.

November 18 Gunshots are fired at four civil rights workers in Victoria, Virginia, injuring one person.

November 29 Three persons are injured from a car bomb planted near a black-owned grocery store in Vicksburg, Mississippi, close to the site of a local civil rights meeting.

December 15 Lee Culbreath, a black newspaper carrier, is shot and killed by two white men in Hamburg, Arkansas. Police charge two Klan members with the murder.

December 31 A store owned by John Nosser—the mayor of Natchez, Mississippi, and a vocal opponent of the Klan—is destroyed by arson.

1966

January 2 An African American church in Newton, Georgia, is burned. Anonymous callers threaten the life of the local sheriff if he investigates the incident.

January 3 Samuel Younge Jr., a black college student, is shot and killed in Tuskegee, Alabama, for trying to use a "whites only" restroom.

January 10   After volunteering to pay the poll taxes for black voters, civil rights activist Vernon Dahmer is fatally burned in a firebomb attack in his Hattiesburg, Mississippi, home. Imperial Wizard Sam Bowers of the Ku Klux Klan is to be tried four times for the murder; the trials resulted in deadlocked juries. On August 21, 1998, a multiracial jury convicted Bowers of murder and arson.

January 30   The Atlanta-based Southern Regional Council issues a report stating that southern whites had killed a total of fourteen blacks and civil rights workers in 1965 and three blacks thus far in 1966.

February 24   A recently integrated high school in Elba, Alabama, is damaged by two dynamite blasts.

April 2   Bombs explode at two swimming pools in Baton Rouge, Louisiana, that were scheduled to be integrated facilities.

April 9   Bombs destroy a black church in Ernul, North Carolina.

June 6   Civil rights worker James Meredith is wounded by three gunshots during a one-person "march against fear" in Hernando, Mississippi. The hospital treating Meredith receives threats from a caller describing himself as a Klan member.

June 10   Ben White, an elderly black man, is kidnapped, shot, and killed in Natchez, Mississippi, by Klan members who believe the murder will attract the Reverend Martin Luther King Jr. to the area. The Klan members are acquitted of murder charges on December 9, 1967. White's relatives file a civil suit for wrongful death and win more than $1 million in damages on November 13, 1968. The defendant, Ernest Avants, avoided paying any money by placing his assets in his first wife's name.

June 17   News reporters covering a civil rights rally in Greenwood, Mississippi, escape injury after two poisonous snakes are tossed into their vehicle.

June 21   Civil rights marchers are assaulted by white mobs in Philadelphia, Mississippi, while police watch.

June 24   A mob of whites pelt the Reverend Martin Luther King Jr. and other demonstrators with eggs and missiles in Philadelphia, Mississippi. Arsonists destroy a Catholic church in Carthage, Mississippi.

July 1   Klan members bomb a store in Milwaukee, Wisconsin, owned by the former president of the Wisconsin Civil Rights Congress.

July 3   Klan members pelt police with stones in Lebanon, Ohio, after two Klan members are arrested for violating the state's antimask law.

July 10   Two whites are arrested after firing a submachine gun at a federal officer and two civil rights workers outside an African American church in Grenada, Mississippi.

July 18   Jeering whites assault civil rights marchers in Jacksonville, Florida.

July 20   A black-owned store in Jacksonville, Florida, is firebombed.

July 28   Following a rally of the National States Rights Party, white gangs invade a black neighborhood in Baltimore, Maryland. Three members are charged with inciting a riot and are sentenced to a two-year prison term.

July 30   Charles Triggs, a black bricklayer, is shot and killed by two white gunmen in Bogalusa, Louisiana.

July 31   White mobs stone a civil rights procession led by the Reverend Martin Luther King Jr. in Chicago. Fifty-four persons are injured, including two police officers.

September 12–13   A mob of almost 400 whites riot in Grenada, Mississippi, in opposition to school integration. Police stand by while blacks and news reporters are beaten with ax handles, chains, and steel pipes. Two black youths are hospitalized with serious injuries.

September 24   Arsonists destroy the Cleveland, Ohio, home of the Reverend John Compton, a black minister.

October 5   A black church in Richmond, Virginia, is bombed.

November 8   Violent incidents against blacks participating in local elections occur in Lowndes County, Alabama, and in Amite County, Mississippi.

November 20   James Motley, a black man, is beaten to death in a jail cell in Wetumpka, Alabama. A jury acquits Sheriff Harvey Conner of murder on April 12, 1967.

1967

January 10   Vandals desecrate more than 100 graves at two Jewish cemeteries in New Orleans, Louisiana.

April 25   Bombs damage the home of the mother of Judge Frank Johnson in Birmingham, Alabama. Judge Johnson, a vocal opponent of the Ku Klux Klan, had issued several decisions in support of school integration.

May 14   A black-owned home in a predominantly white suburb of Cleveland, Ohio, is bombed.

July 18   FBI agents arrest 12 whites, including at least seven Klan members, for violent racist acts committed over a 21-month period in Rowan and Cabarrus counties, North Carolina. In a separate incident in Greensboro, North Carolina, two Klan members are jailed for a cross burning.

August 28   White mobs shouting "We want slaves!" and "Get yourself a nigger!" stone NAACP demonstrators in Milwaukee, Wisconsin. Marchers are again attacked the next day and the local NAACP Freedom House is destroyed by arsonists. Milwaukee Mayor Henry Maier issues a proclamation banning evening demonstrations and rallies.

September 18   Temple Beth Israel in Jackson, Mississippi, is bombed. As FBI agents pursue suspects, their vehicle is rammed from the rear by a carload of armed Klan members.

October 6   Snipers fire into the home of an NAACP worker in Carthage, Mississippi.

November 21   The home of Rabbi Perry Nussbaum in Jackson, Mississippi, is bombed. Nussbaum and his wife, Arene, narrowly escape death.

1968

February 8   Three black students—Henry E. Smith, Delano H. Middleton, and Samuel Hammond Jr.—are killed and at least 34 others are wounded when state police fire on rioters at South Carolina State College in Orangeburg. Campus unrest began when college demonstrators started picketing a segregated local bowling alley.

April 4   The Reverend Martin Luther King Jr. is assassinated by a sniper on the eve of a scheduled protest demonstration in support of sanitation workers in Memphis, Tennessee. Rioting erupts in more than 125 U.S. cities over the next week, leaving 46 persons dead, 2,600 injured, and 21,270 arrested. Damage from arson and vandalism is estimated at $45 million.

August 14   The church of the Reverend A. D. King is bombed in Louisville, Kentucky.

August 16–17   Two white men murder the black female proprietor of a tavern in Cincinnati, Ohio. A riot erupts, and one black youth is critically shot while stoning police cars.

November 25   A Hebrew school in the Bronx, New York, is damaged in a suspicious fire. It is the 10th attack on Jewish institutions in New York City in the past three months.

November 27   The Yeshiva of Eastern Parkway in Brooklyn, New York, is destroyed in a fire. Four teenagers under 16 years old are charged with arson. Mayor John Lindsay announces a six-point program for more police surveillance at religious institutions and the creation of a special arson squad.

December 24   Gunshots are fired into the home of a black Office of Economic Opportunity administrator in Monroe, Louisiana. Although a Ku Klux Klan member is arrested, he is set free in February 1969.

1970

January 19   Fire damages a Bronx, New York, synagogue that had been vandalized four times in the past year.

January 28   Vandals paint swastikas and start a fire at the Intervale Jewish Center in the Bronx, New York.

March 3   A mob of whites attack school buses carrying black students to recently integrated schools in Lamar, South Carolina. Three rioters are convicted on February 17, 1971.

August 30   Ten buses scheduled for use in desegregating schools in Pontiac, Michigan, are bombed. Six members of the Ku Klux Klan are arrested, including Robert Miles, a major national neo-Nazi leader. September 10. A bomb with more than a dozen sticks of dynamite is found under a Jacksonville, Florida, school bus and defused.

1973

September 16   Ku Klux Klan member Byron De La Beckwith is arrested; firearms and a time bomb are found in his automobile. Beckwith was planning a raid on the home of A. I. Botnick, a New Orleans Jewish leader. The Louisiana Klan conducts a fund-raising campaign for Beckwith's legal defense, and he is acquitted of all charges on January 16, 1974.

October 2   Evelyn Walker, a white woman, is doused with gasoline and burned to death by black youths after her car breaks down in a black neighborhood in Boston, Massachusetts.

October 6   Kirk Miller, a white cab driver, is the victim of a racially motivated murder in Boston.

October 19   Members of the San Francisco–based Black Muslim splinter group the Death Angels assault white victims Richard and Quita Hague with machetes, killing Quita Hague and leaving her husband severely injured. Members of this violent group reportedly earn their "angel wings" by killing white men and women. The killings begin in October and continue for about six months, resulting in the deaths of 14 men and women and leaving seven wounded. (The case was nicknamed

"Zebra" because a special police task force used the last radio frequency, Z, for communication.)

October 29   Frances Rose, a white woman, is shot and killed in another "Zebra" killing in San Francisco, California. Jessie Cooks, a member of the Death Angels, is arrested near the scene and sentenced to life in prison for the murder.

November 21   The Sephardic Institute for Advanced Learning in New York City is badly damaged and one employee is killed during an arson attack. In the previous few months, five synagogues were damaged in arson attacks in the Flatbush section of Brooklyn.

November 26   The Reverend Edward Pace, a black minister in Gadsden, Alabama, is shot and killed in his home. Bruce Botsford, a Klan member, is convicted of second degree murder by an all-white, all-male jury on March 9, 1974 and sentenced to 30 years in prison.

1974

January 28   Death Angel members kill Tana White and Jane Holly in random, racially motivated attacks in the San Francisco, California, area.

April 14   Ward Anderson and Terry White are shot by Death Angel gunmen at a San Francisco bus stop.

April 19   Frank Carlson, a white grocer, is murdered and his wife is beaten and raped by an African American who claims to be one of the "Zebra" killers. Police arrest seven Death Angel suspects on May 1; four are convicted and sentenced to life in prison.

July 27   Shootings are reported during a local Klan recruiting drive in Kokomo, Indiana.

August 16   Judge Arthur Gamble, who signed the murder indictments against three Klan members involved in the murder of white civil rights activist Viola Liuzzo on March 25, 1965, is injured by a car bomb in Greenville, Alabama.

September 19   Dr. Charles Glatt, who worked for the city of Dayton, Ohio, to prepare school desegregation plans, is shot and killed at work. Police arrest Neal Bradley Long, who had been linked to a series of racially motivated murders of seven local blacks since 1972.

November 11   In the Boro Park section of Brooklyn, New York, two synagogues, a Jewish school, and the homes of two Hasidic Jews are firebombed.

1976

February 26   Four members of the Ku Klux Klan are indicted for the murder of Willie Edwards in Montgomery, Alabama, in 1957 (*see* 1957: January 23). The judge later dismissed the charges. Diane Alexander, the widow of Henry Alexander, who was accused of the crime but never tried, said her husband confessed to the murder before his death in 1992. Mrs. Alexander wrote a letter of apology to Sarah Salter, Mr. Edwards's widow, who then lived in Buffalo, New York, and met her in person on September 4, 1993, to express her remorse.

April 6   In Boston, Massachusetts, Theodore Landsmark, a black attorney, is attacked by a white youth who attempted to stab him with the staff of an American flag. The Pulitzer Prize–winning photograph of this incident is published in newspapers around the world.

September 8   White youths shouting racial epithets randomly attack blacks and Hispanics in Washington Square Park in Greenwich Village, New York. Marcus Mota is killed, and several others are injured. Five youths are sentenced to prison terms ranging from three to twenty-five years.

1977

February 14   Fred Cowan, a professed hater of Jews and blacks and member of the racist National States Rights Party, kills six persons—Frederick Holmes, Joseph E. Hicks, James Greene, Pariyarathu Varghese, Allen McCleod, and Joseph Russo—and wounds five others before committing suicide in New Rochelle, New York. His victims were three blacks, an

Asian Indian immigrant, and two whites, including a policeman. He was previously suspended from work after a conflict
with a Jewish supervisor.

April 15–17   In a series of violent incidents in Elwood, Indiana, Klan members burn crosses and scatter garbage on the
lawns of local residents. The mayor's home is also sprayed with
shotgun pellets.

1978

April 28   Roy Keith Palmer, seventeen, pleaded guilty to
burning down two black churches in Wilkes County, Georgia,
in December 1977. At Palmer's sentencing, a black deacon and
a minister from the destroyed churches asks that the defendant
be treated leniently for the crime.

August 7   Alphonse Manning and Toni Schwenn, an interracial couple, are killed by Joseph Paul Franklin, in Madison,
Wisconsin. Franklin is a former member of the Ku Klux Klan
and the American Nazi Party.

September 5   A white youth wearing a Nazi armband fires on
black picnickers in Jonesville, North Carolina, killing one man
and wounding three. A second victim dies on September 7.
The gunman commits suicide.

October 8   A sniper, later believed to be Joseph Paul Franklin, kills Gerald Gordon while he is leaving a bar mitzvah in
Richmond Heights, a suburb of St. Louis, Missouri.

November 18   Former Klan member Robert Chambliss is
convicted of murder in the bombing of the Sixteenth Street
Baptist Church in Birmingham, Alabama, on September 15,
1963, which killed four black girls.

1979

December   The Anti-Defamation League (ADL) issues its
first *Audit of Anti-Semitic Incidents*.

October 21   Jessie Taylor and Marion Bresette, an interracial
couple, are shot and killed in a parking lot in Oklahoma City.

Joseph Paul Franklin is later charged in the case, but the indictments are dismissed in 1983.

1980

January 8   Joseph Paul Franklin kills Larry E. Reese, an African American man, at a local fast-food restaurant in Indianapolis, Indiana.

August 19   Joseph Paul Franklin, a former member of the Ku Klux Klan and American Nazi Party, murders David Martin and Theodore Fields, two black men who were jogging alongside two white women in a park in Salt Lake City, Utah. Franklin was later connected to other crimes, including the bombing of Beth Shalom synagogue in Chattanooga, Tennessee, on July 29, 1977; the shooting of former National Urban League director Vernon Jordan on May 29, 1980; the murders of Darrell Lane and Dante Evans Brown in a vacant lot in Cincinnati, Ohio, on June 6, 1980; and the murders of Kathleen Mikula and Arthur Smothers in Johnstown, Pennsylvania, on June 15, 1980. Franklin was reportedly involved in the slaying of twenty-one people who were either interracial couples or Jews. He was on death row for 15 years in a Missouri prison and was executed by lethal injection on November 20, 2013.

1981

The Anti-Defamation League drafts the first model hate-crime legislation.

1982

June 19   Vincent Chin, a young Chinese American, is brutally murdered in Detroit by unemployed autoworkers, who apparently believed he was Japanese. The case receives national attention when the judge places the assailants on probation and requires them each to pay only a $3,000 fine.

1984

The National Gay and Lesbian Task Force issues its first report on antigay violence in the United States.

June 18   Alan Berg, a popular Denver, Colorado, radio talk show host, is murdered in a machine-gun attack in the driveway of his home. His assailants are members of a neo-Nazi group.

1985

March 21   The U.S. House of Representatives Committee on the Judiciary holds its first congressional hearing to discuss the passage of a law to require the U.S. Justice Department to collect and publish statistics on hate crimes.

December 24   Charles Goldmark, a Seattle, Washington, attorney, is brutally murdered by a drifter named David Lewis Rice, who had close ties with racist and anti-Jewish groups. Rice thought that Goldmark, a prominent liberal lawyer, "looked Jewish."

1986

July 16   The U.S. House of Representatives Committee on the Judiciary holds hearings to examine reports of harassment and violence directed against Arab Americans.

October 9   The U.S. House of Representatives Committee on the Judiciary holds hearings to examine the problem of violence against gay men and lesbians.

December 20   A gang of white teenagers in the Howard Beach section of Queens, New York, attack Michael Griffith, an African American who was passing through their neighborhood. They beat him and then chase him to his death on a nearby highway. His stepfather, Cedric Sandiford, is also severely beaten.

1987

November 10   The U.S. House of Representatives Committee on the Judiciary holds hearings on the causes of and possible responses to recent violent acts committed against Asians and Asian Americans.

1988

May 11–July 12   The U.S. House of Representatives Committee on the Judiciary holds hearings to consider legislation to establish a Commission on Racially Motivated Violence and to examine the prevalence of violence against members of minority groups.

May 15   Eighteen-year-old Richard Lee Bednarski and his friends look for gay men to harass in Dallas, Texas. Bednarski kills 34-year-old Tommy Trimble and twenty-seven-year old Lloyd Griffin in a gruesome murder. He was found guilty, but Judge Jack Hampton said that killing gays was not a serious crime and gave the defendant a lenient sentence for the murders. His remarks stirred a major controversy, and Hampton was censured by his judicial colleagues. He was later defeated for reelection in December 1992.

June 21   The U.S. Senate Committee on the Judiciary holds hearings to consider proposed legislation to require the U.S. Justice Department to collect and publish statistics on hate crimes.

1989

January 17   Patrick Purdy enters an elementary school yard in Stockton, California, and fires 105 rounds from an AK-47, killing three Cambodian girls (Ram Chun, Sokhim An, and Oeun Lim); a Cambodian boy (Rathanan Or); and a Vietnamese girl (Thuy Tran). The gunman also wounds thirty others, including a teacher, and then kills himself. The 24-year-old Purdy had an obsessive hatred of Cambodians, Indians, Pakistanis, and especially Vietnamese.

July 29   Two brothers in Raleigh, North Carolina, beat to death Ming Hai "Jim" Loo, a 24-year-old Chinese American. Witnesses told police that the men thought Loo was Vietnamese. They apparently sought revenge for their brother who served in the U.S. military in Vietnam and never returned.

August 23   A white gang armed with baseball bats and guns attack four black youths on a street in Bensonhurst, a neighborhood in Brooklyn, New York. Yusuf Hawkins is beaten and shot to death in the attack. Seven suspects are arrested.

November 5   A memorial sculpture made of black granite is dedicated on the grounds of the Southern Poverty Law Center in Montgomery, Alabama. Designed by Maya Lin, who also created the Vietnam Veterans Memorial in Washington, D.C., the sculpture commemorates the more than forty people—black and white; men, women, and children—who were killed during the civil rights movement. More than 600 relatives of the victims attend the dedication.

1990

January 21   James Zappalorti, a gay Vietnam war veteran, is brutally murdered in Staten Island, New York, by two teenagers.

March 15   Henry Lau, a thirty-one-year-old Chinese immigrant, is fatally stabbed on a New York City subway train. Prior to the stabbing, the assailant called Lau an "egg roll."

April 23   President George H. W. Bush signs into law the Hate Crime Statistics Act, which mandates the FBI to compile annual statistics on hate crimes throughout the United States.

August 9   Two skinheads shouting "white power" murder Hung Truong, a 15-year-old Vietnamese youth, in Houston.

1991

March 3   Rodney King, an African American motorist, is beaten by four white Los Angeles police officers after he is stopped for speeding. When police finally reach the car, they deliver more than 50 baton blows and six kicks to King in two minutes, resulting in 11 skull fractures as well as brain and kidney damage. The incident is captured on videotape by a bystander and gains national media attention.

August 19 A Hasidic Jewish driver is involved in a traffic accident in Brooklyn, New York, that kills Gavin Cato, a seven-year-old African American. Following the accident, black youths murder Yankel Rosenbaum, a visiting Australian Jewish scholar. During three days of rioting in the Crown Heights section of Brooklyn, crowds roam the streets, yelling, "Get the Jews."

1992

April 29 A jury in suburban Simi Valley, California, acquits four white Los Angeles police officers on all but one charge stemming from the beating of black motorist Rodney King in March 1991.

April 30–May 3 Following the controversial jury verdict in the Rodney King case, the south central section of Los Angeles is engulfed in widespread burning, looting, and violence. Fifty-eight people are killed in the rioting, 2,383 are injured, and damage estimates range as high as $1 billion. According to Yumi Park, former director of the Korean American Grocers Association, 800 Korean-owned establishments are damaged in the rioting. Tensions between African Americans and Korean Americans had risen following the November 15, 1991, trial of Soon Ja Du, a Korean grocer who had shot to death a 15-year-old black girl, Latasha Harlins. Even though the grocer was convicted of manslaughter, the judge had refused to send her to prison.

May 11 The U.S. House of Representatives Committee on the Judiciary holds hearings on crimes motivated by prejudice against the racial, ethnic, religious, or sexual orientation of the victim.

June 22 In the case of *R. A. V. v. City of St. Paul*, the U.S. Supreme Court strikes down a hate-crime ordinance in St. Paul, Minnesota.

July 29   The U.S. House of Representatives Committee on the Judiciary holds hearings on the use of penalty enhancement for hate crimes and also examines the implications of the June 22, 1992, U.S. Supreme Court decision.

August 5   The U.S. Senate Committee on the Judiciary reviews implementation of the Hate Crime Statistics Act of 1990 by the FBI, state crime reporting agencies, and local law enforcement agencies under the direction of the U.S. Department of Justice.

August 18   Luyen Phan Nguyen, a 19-year-old premed student at the University of Miami, is beaten to death by five men in Coral Springs, Florida, who made disparaging remarks about his Vietnamese ancestry.

October 27   Seaman Allen R. Schindler, serving on a U.S. Navy ship, is brutally murdered by shipmates outside a military base in Sasebo, Japan, after they learn of his homosexuality. One assailant later pleads guilty to murder and his accomplice receives a lighter sentence for cooperating with investigators. The cable station Lifetime airs *Any Mother's Son* in August 1997, a docudrama based on the murder.

1993

January 4   The FBI releases its first official report containing nationwide hate crime statistics for 1991.

June 11   The U.S. Supreme Court unanimously upholds Wisconsin's penalty enhancement hate crimes statute in the case *Wisconsin v. Mitchell.*

November 16   The U.S. House of Representatives Committee on the Judiciary discusses proposed legislation that would make crimes of violence motivated by gender actionable under civil rights and hate crime laws.

December 7   Colin Ferguson, a black Jamaican immigrant, murders Mi Kyung Kim, James Gorycki, Dennis McCarthy, Marita Theresa Magtoto, Amy Federici, and Richard Nettleton on the Long Island Rail Road. He had previously written notes expressing hatred of Asians and whites.

1994

February 5   In his third and decisive trial in Jackson, Mississippi, Byron De La Beckwith is found guilty by a jury of eight blacks and four whites of murdering Medgar Evers on June 12, 1963. (*See* 1963: June 1 and September 16)

March 1   Rashid Baz, a Lebanese immigrant, shoots at a van carrying 15 Hasidic Jewish students over the Brooklyn Bridge. One student, Aaron Halberstam, is killed; another, Nachum Sasonkin, is severely injured. The murderer once vowed to "kill all Jews."

April   National Asian Pacific American Legal Consortium issues its first *Audit of Violence against Asian Pacific Americans.*

September 1   A mosque in Yuba City, California, is gutted in a suspected anti-Muslim arson case.

September 13   The Violent Crime Control and Law Enforcement Act directs the U.S. Sentencing Commission to devise sentencing guidelines to incorporate a federal sentence enhancement for hate crimes. The Violence against Women Act (Title IV of the Violent Crime Control and Law Enforcement Act of 1994) provides civil rights remedies for gender-motivated violence, explicitly stating that all "persons within the United States shall have the right to be free from crimes of violence motivated by gender."(42 United States Code 13981)

1995

December 7   African Americans Michael Jones and Jackie Burden are murdered in a random shooting by soldiers from Fort Bragg, North Carolina, who are affiliated with white supremacist groups.

December 8   During several weeks, picketers demanded that Freddy's Fashion Mart, a store in Harlem, should be owned by blacks, and they made antiwhite and anti-Jewish statements during their protests. Roland Smith, who had previously picketed the Jewish-owned store, enters the store, shoots four people, and then douses the premises with lighter fluid. The ensuing blaze kills seven people: Garnette Ramautar, Mayra Rentas, Cynthia Martinez, Angelina Marrero, Luz Ramos, Kareem Brunner, and Olga Garcia. Smith also dies in the blaze.

1996

January 29   Thien Minh Ly, a 24-year-old Vietnamese-American, is kicked, stomped, and stabbed more than a dozen times on a tennis court in Tustin, California, in a racially motivated attack by white skinheads.

June 25   The U.S. House of Representatives Committee on National Security holds hearings on the participation of current or former U.S. military personnel in antigovernment or racist hate groups.

June 27   The U.S. Senate Committee on the Judiciary holds hearings on the rash of arsons directed against black churches and other acts of violence against houses of worship.

1997

February 23   Ali Abu Kamal, a 69-year-old Palestinian Arab teacher who arrived in the United States in December 1996, opens fire on the 86th floor observation deck of the Empire State Building in New York City, killing Chris Burmeister, a Danish tourist, and wounding six others before taking his own life. In a pouch around Abu Kamal's neck, police found a letter stating his intention to kill as many "Zionists" as possible in their "den" in New York City.

November 18   Oumar Dia, an immigrant from Mauritania, is murdered at a Denver, Colorado, bus stop by Nathan Thill, a skinhead who later said he hated blacks. (Dia, a black African, had fled his native country because he was persecuted by Arabs.) Jeannie VanVelkinburgh, a white woman who comes to his aid, is also shot and is consequently paralyzed from the waist down. Thill pleads guilty to first-degree murder and is serving a life sentence plus 32 years. His accomplice, Jeremiah Barnum, also pleads guilty as an accessory to the murder and is sentenced to 12 years.

1998

February 23   Members of the New Order, a neo-Nazi group, are arrested in their homes in southern Illinois, where police find guns, pipe bombs, and hand grenades. The FBI says the suspects were plotting to bomb the Southern Poverty Law Center in Montgomery, Alabama, and the Simon Wiesenthal Center, the New York headquarters of the Anti-Defamation League. Authorities learned of the plot when the suspects attempted to recruit a man who then became a federal informant. Also on this date, in the largest hate crime judgment in Illinois history, a jury awards $6 million to the family of Ricardo Arroyo of Waukegan, Illinois, who died from injuries inflicted by another motorist. After Arroyo's and the other motorist's cars collide, the assailant kicks Arroyo in the stomach three times and shouts at him, "Mexicans, go back to Mexico!"

March 13   Brian Wilmes falls into a coma after being beaten outside a San Francisco, California, gay bar by an attacker who uttered antigay slurs. In November 1998, a municipal court judge rules that the alleged assailant, Edgard Mora, must stand trial for murder with a hate crime enhancement penalty.

April 5   Five white men in Orange County, California, are beaten by five Iranian males attending an Iranian New Year's party. The Iranian men jump the victims—whose names were not released by police—from behind, yelling, "What are you white guys doing here?" A witness captures the attack on video-tape; the footage shows one of the perpetrators kicking a victim with steel-toed boots.

April 14   In Biddeford, Maine, Anthony Cabana is sent to jail for threatening to "snap" a woman's neck. He is reportedly the first person ever charged in Maine with a gender-based hate crime.

April 27 Steven Goedereis, a gay man, is brutally beaten to death in West Palm Beach, Florida, by two teenagers, Bryan Donahue and William Dodge, who were angered by an allegedly sexually suggestive comment Goedereis made to them.

May 9 In Rutherfordton, North Carolina, two men with Ku Klux Klan ties attack Isaiah Edgerton, his wife, and their two-year-old daughter in their home. The men, both in their twenties, are charged with a hate crime. Police suspect that the local chapter of the American Knights of the KKK ordered the shooting.

May 20 A cross is burned in front of a Jewish family's home in Huntington Beach, California. It is the second anti-Jewish crime committed against the family; in an earlier incident, someone stamped a swastika on their front lawn.

June 7 James Byrd Jr., a 49-year-old black man, is chained to a pickup truck in Jasper, Texas, and dragged along an asphalt road for almost two miles. His head, neck, and right arm are later found on the road. His attackers, who claimed membership in the white supremacist group Aryan Nations, reportedly said to Byrd, "We're starting the *Turner Diaries* early." This book, widely disseminated among white racists and neo-Nazis, advocates the murder of African Americans and Jews. President Bill Clinton issues a statement condemning the grisly murder.

September 20 In the South Ozone Park neighborhood of Queens, New York, Rishi Maharaj, the 21 year-old son of Trinidadian immigrants of Indian descent, is beaten by three young men who utter anti-Indian slurs. He suffers severe head trauma, facial fractures, and other injuries. The Queens district attorney condemns the incident as an unprovoked hate crime and charges the assailants with attempted murder.

October 6 Matthew Shepard, a gay college student in Laramie, Wyoming, is tied to a fence and savagely beaten with a gun by two men he met in a bar. Left for dead, he is found by a passerby 18 hours later. He remained in a coma for several days and died October 12. His funeral is protested by the Reverend

Fred Phelps and his followers from the Westboro Baptist Church in Topeka, Kansas, who carry signs saying "God hates fags" and "Fags deserve to die."

October 12–15   President Clinton condemns the murder of Matthew Shepard; the U.S. House of Representatives passes a resolution condemning the murder as a hate crime.

1999

February 19   In Sylacauga, Alabama, Billy Jack Gaither is bludgeoned to death with an ax handle and his body is burned. Steven Eric Mullins and Charles Monroe Butler murdered Gaither because he allegedly propositioned the two men.

May 16   James Longenbach deliberately drives his car into Austin Hansen-Tyler and Dontrell Langston, two African American teenagers who are riding bicycles in Kenosha, Wisconsin. Longenbach was sentenced to 176 years in prison for this racially motivated hate crime.

June 18   Congregation B'nai Israel and Knesset Israel Torah Center in Sacramento and Congregation Beth Shalom in Carmichael, California, are set ablaze, causing an estimated $3 million in damage.

July 1   Gary Matson and Winfield Scott Mowder, a gay couple, are shot to death in their Happy Valley home, outside Redding, California, in an antigay hate crime.

July 2–4   Benjamin Nathaniel Smith, a 21-year-old white supremacist involved with the World Church of the Creator, goes on a murderous rampage in Illinois and Indiana, killing Ricky Birdsong, a black coach at Northwestern University, and Won-Joon Yoon, a graduate student at Indiana University. He also shot at Orthodox Jews, African Americans, and Asians, leaving nine people injured. He shoots and kills himself in Indiana during a car chase with local police.

August 10   Buford O. Furrow Jr., a self-professed white supremacist, shoots and wounds five people at the North Valley

Jewish Community Center in Los Angeles and murders Joseph Santos Ileto, a Filipino-American postal worker.

2000

April 28   Richard Baumhammers, a white immigration attorney who professed hatred of minorities, murders Anil Thakur and paralyzes Sandip Patel at the India Grocers store in Pittsburgh. He begins his rampage by killing Anita Gordon, a Jewish neighbor, and later goes to a Chinese restaurant and kills Thao Q. Pham and Ji-Ye Sun. His last victim is Garry Lee, a 25-year-old African American. On May 11, 2001, a jury deliberated for three hours and convicted Baumhammers of killing five people and paralyzing a sixth. He was on death row in a Pennsylvania prison for more than a decade but Pennsylvania governor Tom Wolf issued a moratorium on state executions during February 2015.

May 17   Thirty-seven years after the crime, Thomas Blanton Jr. and Bobby Frank Cherry are charged with planting a bomb at the Sixteenth Street Baptist Church in Montgomery, Alabama, that killed four black schoolgirls. They are both later sentenced to life imprisonment for the murders by mixed-race juries. (*See* 1963: September)

2001

April 19   Leo V. Felton and Erica Chase, members of a white supremacist group, are arrested for passing counterfeit money in Boston and are later indicted for plotting to blow up major Jewish and African American monuments in the Boston area. (They were also plotting the assassinations of Steven Spielberg and Jesse Jackson.) On July 26, 2003, Felton is convicted and sentenced to twenty years in prison; Chase, who is repentant, receives a five year sentence. The *Boston Globe* (November 3, 2002) publishes a feature story revealing that Felton had a black father and a white mother.

September 12   Three hundred men and women chanting "U.S.A., U.S.A." try to storm a mosque in the Chicago suburb of Bridgeview, Illinois. More than 100 police restrain the demonstrators and arrest three people.

September 15   Balbir Singh Sodhi, a Sikh gas station owner, is murdered by Frank Roque in Mesa, Arizona, who vows vengeance for the September 11 terrorist attacks.

September 30   Swaran Kaur Bhullar, a Sikh woman, is stabbed twice in the head by two men when she stops her car at a red light in San Diego. The attackers, who are never caught, probably assumed she was a Muslim.

December 11   Federal prosecutors charge Irv Rubin, the head of the Jewish Defense League, and his associate Earl Krugel with plotting to blow up the King Fahd Mosque in Culver City, California, and bomb the office of Congressman Darrell Issa (R-CA), a Lebanese American. Rubin reportedly commits suicide in prison in November 2002.

2002

May 18   Stephen J. Kinney attacks a group of three Chinese families at Harrah's casino in Lake Tahoe, Nevada, shouting racial epithets and injuring three people. Kinney is charged with aggravated assault and committing a hate crime. The sentence will be suspended for three years, however, if Kinney completes 56 hours of community service with the Chinese Historical Society and pays the costs of the prosecution in this case.

August 10   Mizanor Rahman, a 37-year-old Bangladeshi photojournalist, is beaten to death in his Brooklyn neighborhood. Although Michael Gabriel, the inspector with the New York City Police Department, reportedly says the murder may have been motivated by racial bias, no hate crime statute is invoked against the murderers, Rafael Santos and Hardy Marston.

November 11   Mohammed Sakawat Hossain, a 19-year-old Bangladeshi immigrant, is beaten to death in his Brooklyn neighborhood by Javier Amigan and Charles Durante. Police do not charge the perpetrators with a hate crime, but some members of the Bangladeshi community feel the attack is racially motivated. Dr. Iftekhar Ahmed Chowdhury, a Bangladeshi diplomat, joins with community leaders, charging that this incident, along with the August 10, 2002, murder of Mizanor Rahman (*see* August 10, above), are hate crimes.

2003

March 27   James Tyler Williams, the killer of gay couple Gary Matson and Winfield Scott Mowder (*see* 1999: July 1), is sentenced to 29 years to life in prison for the murders. Williams also receives a 19-year sentence for the firebombing of three Sacramento-area synagogues (*see* 1999: June 18). His brother, Benjamin Williams, who is an accomplice, commits suicide in his Shasta County jail cell on November 17, 2002. Benjamin Williams reportedly says that the murder of the gay couple was "God's will."

May 1   The Carbondale Islamic Center near Southern Illinois University is spray-painted with graffiti in English and Hindi. The FBI investigates the vandalism as a hate crime.

May 1   Sen. Edward Kennedy (D-MA) and Sen. Gordon Smith (R-OR) reintroduce the Local Law Enforcement Enhancement Act, formerly called the Hate Crimes Prevention Act, which died in congressional committee in 2001. This legislation, which has 49 cosponsors, provides additional federal support to local law enforcement agencies to prosecute hate crimes. The law would also add sexual orientation, gender, and disability as hate crime categories; current statutes cover only race, national origin, and religion.

May 11   Sakia Gunn, 15, is fatally stabbed in the chest at a bus stop in Newark, New Jersey. She and her two friends were being harassed by three men and attempted to rebuff their advances by claiming to be lesbians.

June 11   A jury finds Aaron Price, a 19-year-old sophomore at Morehouse College in Atlanta, Georgia, guilty of aggravated assault and aggravated battery in the November 3, 2002, beating of his fellow student Gregory Love in a dorm shower. Price, who thought that Love was gay and was making a pass at him, attacked Love with a baseball bat. Price receives ten years on each count, to be served concurrently. Price is acquitted of a hate crime after prosecutors fail to convince jurors that his actions were motivated by antigay feelings. Love testified that he was not gay. This trial is the first case involving Georgia's recently passed hate crimes enhancement penalty statute.

November 13   An arson fire destroys the CANDLES Holocaust Museum in Terre Haute, Indiana. (CANDLES stands for Children of Auschwitz Nazi Deadly Experiments Survivors.) The museum was founded in 1995 by Holocaust survivor Eva Kor and housed artifacts from Auschwitz and documents relating to Dr. Josef Mengele, the infamous Nazi doctor who experimented on human beings. "Remember Timothy McVeigh" is scrawled on a nearby wall. McVeigh, the Oklahoma City bomber, was executed at a prison near Terre Haute.

December 17   Raussi Uthman, a U.S. citizen born to Palestinian parents, is convicted of hate crimes for burglarizing and burning down Temple Beth El in Syracuse, New York, on October 13, 2000. He is sentenced to 25 years in prison for the fire, which caused more than $700,000 in damage but no injuries. His accomplice, Ahed Shehadeh, is sentenced to five years for aiding and abetting the arson.

2004

April 5   The library of the United Talmud Torah elementary school in Montreal is firebombed. Sleiman Elmerhebi, is charged with throwing six kerosene canisters, which destroyed the library. In December 2004, Sleiman Elmerhebi pleaded guilty and was later sentenced to forty months in prison; his mother Rouba Elmerhebi Fahd was found to be an accessory after the fact. Judge Robert Marchi, of Quebec Court, ruled that his mother tried to arrange for her son to fly to Brazil to avoid prosecution for torching the United Talmud Torah school, causing $500,000 in damage. The judge sentenced the woman to one year's probation, acknowledging that a mother might act in such a way for her child. But he noted his disappointment that Rouba Elmerhebi Fahd had shown no remorse for her son's criminal act.

June 9   Brian Williamson, a leading gay rights activist in Jamaica, is murdered in his home in the capital city of Kingston. A crowd soon gathered outside the murder scene and chanted, "boom, bye bye," a lyric from a popular Jamaican song advocating the murder of gay people.

June 22   A California judge declared a mistrial for the three men accused of the brutal murder of seventeen year-old Eddie Araujo, a transgendered male, in Newark, California, on October 4, 2002. The jury was deadlocked but prosecutors plan again to try the accused men for first degree murder.

September 2   Thousands of demonstrators in Kathmandu, Nepal riot, burn down a mosque, and attack local Muslims after 12 Nepalese hostages are executed in Iraq.

September 29   Fanny Ann Eddy, the 30-year-old founder of the Sierra Leone Lesbian and Gay Association, is found dead in her office in the capital, Freetown. According to the organization Human Rights Watch, she had been repeatedly raped and stabbed, and her neck was broken.

November 2   Theo Van Gogh, a Dutch filmmaker who produced a controversial movie on the treatment of Muslim women, was murdered while cycling through Amsterdam. Police later arrested a 26-year-old man who had dual Dutch–Moroccan nationality and was suspected of having links to radical Islamic groups. The murder evoked a furious backlash among some Dutch citizens and several mosques were burned down in the following weeks. In retaliation, a few Dutch churches were later destroyed.

November 26   The ABC television newsmagazine program *20/20* features an investigative report claiming that the murder of Matthew Shepard, a gay Wyoming college student (see

1998: October 6), was not a hate crime, but a botched robbery committed by men high on drugs. Some gay rights organizations denounce the show and question the veracity and motives of the perpetrators who were interviewed on the show from their prison cells.

December 20   The Mississippi Religious Leadership Conference offers a $100,000 reward for information leading to the arrest and conviction of the murderers of three civil rights workers—James Chaney, Andrew Goodman, and Michael Schwerner—killed in Philadelphia, Mississippi on June 21, 1964.

2005

January 15   In Jersey City, New Jersey, four Copt Christians immigrants from Egypt—Hossam Armanious, his wife, Amal Garas, and their daughters, Sylvia and Monica—are murdered in their home. The killings enrage Copts in Jersey City—a community with a large Egyptian Copt and Muslim population—who blame the local Egyptian Muslims for the crime. Many Copts fled Egypt because of religious persecution.

March 11   A Santa Fe, New Mexico, grand jury issued indictments against six men in the severe beating of 21-year-old James Maestas, a gay man, outside a local hotel on February 27. His companion, 23-year-old Joshua Stockham, received minor injuries. The perpetrators reportedly shouted antigay epithets during the assault. New Mexico Attorney General Patricia Madrid announced that the accused perpetrators would be prosecuted under the state hate crimes penalty enhancement statute—the first such prosecution since the law went into effect in July 2003.

2006

June 1   Donna Jean Hubbard, a Fresno, California high school teacher was charged with a hate crime more than a year after she allegedly pushed a Jewish woman to the ground, pulled her hair, kicked her and told her, "You should have burned in the oven with the rest of the Jews." Asked whether the hate crime case is unusual to the district, Fresno Unified School District spokeswoman replied that "to my knowledge"—in 30 years— "I've never encountered a case like this."

2007

January 11   Four black girls in Portland, Oregon—Chelsea Rivers,14, Rinita Low and Brianna Streeter, both 13 and Mary Michelle Blackshear, 16—were charged with robbery, intimidation and assault for allegedly attacking and robbing a 16-year-old white girl because of her race.

January 27   In Elk Creek, California, Christopher Wayne Fisher, 22, was charged with battery with serious injury and threatening with intent to terrorize for punching Gaurav Kumar Sharma and yelling racial slurs when Sharma's father began to speak in his native language, Punjabi.

February 1   Eric Hunt, 22, attacked Holocaust survivor and Nobel Laureate Elie Wiesel in a San Francisco elevator. A jury later found Hunt guilty of one felony charge with a hate crime allegation. He was also convicted of two misdemeanor counts, one for battery and one for elder abuse.

February 16   Patrick John Dizon Solis, 22, and Michael Douglas Rama, 24, were charged in Fullerton, California with committing hate crimes as well as civil rights violations for allegedly beating disabled men who were in their care.

March 14   William David Brown Jr., 20, and Joseph Bearden, 21, murdered Ryan Keith Skipper, a gay man in Wahneta, Florida. Filmmakers Vicki Nantz and Mary Meeks produced and filmed a documentary about Skipper's murder titled *Accessory to Murder: Our Culture's Complicity in the Death of Ryan Skipper*, which was shown during the Tampa International Gay and Lesbian Film Festival in January 2008.

April 3   Jacob Albert Laskey, of Springfield, Ore., was sentenced to serve 11 years and three months in federal prison for his role in the October 25, 2002, racially motivated attack on Temple Beth Israel, in Eugene, Ore. In August 2006, Laskey pleaded guilty to conspiracy to deprive individuals of their civil rights, damaging religious property, solicitation to murder witnesses, soliciting a bomb threat against the federal courthouse in Eugene, among other charges.

April 23   James Anthony McGillis, 18, was charged with potential felony aggravated assault as a hate crime after he and another person allegedly beat a man with a baseball bat in Provo, Utah, because the victim is a member of the Church of Jesus Christ of Latter-day Saints.

July 6   A Bosnian American immigrant family was the victim of a hate crime in Sarasota, Florida. Although Hasib Sejfovic, his wife and two children fled to the United States to escape the 1992–1995 Serbian–Bosnian war, criminals burned down their Florida home and spray painted anti-Islamic slurs on the outside and inside of the house.

September 1   Sean MacArthur, 20, Nicholas James, 18, David Townsend, 21, and Adam Casey, 24, all of Baileyville, Maine were charged with assault in connection with an attack on two Native American youths in this rural Maine community.

September 8   Philip Hale, 18, and an unidentified male were arrested in Antioch, California in connection with an assault on a deaf person at a party. The two are said to have taunted and mimicked a group of deaf partygoers before allegedly attacking one of them with a brick, a stick, and a hoe. The 23-year-old male victim sustained minor injuries after being struck in the head.

2008

January 3   Jared Horne, a self-described drug addict, and Anthony "Tony" Cascio, 21, were charged with attempted second-degree murder and a hate crime in the Monroe Louisiana Fourth Judicial District Court in connection to an unprovoked assault on a homeless black man, Walter Ford. Mr. Ford was beaten and stabbed after he asked Horne and Cascio for money and was then assaulted because of his race.

February 9   Swastikas were spray-painted on a mosque and Molotov cocktails were thrown at the building in Columbia, Tennessee. Michael Golden, 23, Eric Baker, 32, and Jonathan Stone, 19, were arrested on federal charges of unlawful possession of a destructive device and state charges of arson of a religious building.

February 15   Early in the morning a non-student was assaulted on North Broad St. on Temple University's Main Campus in Philadelphia. The assault included anti-Jewish language aimed at the student who was seriously injured. The assailants were all Temple University students and were suspended in connection with the incident.

March 18   Hussein Ali, 19, was charged with grand larceny as a hate crime and aggravated harassment after he allegedly yanked a skullcap off a rabbi's head in Brooklyn, New York and shouted an Arabic phrase for "God is great."

April 10   Caleb Lussier, 21, was sentenced to 14 years in federal prison after he pleaded guilty to third-degree arson and committing a hate crime for setting fire to Christ Episcopal Church in May 2006 and to New Testament Church in Plymouth, Massachusetts, in December 2005.

May 3   A group approaches two teens in a park in Gilbert, Arizona and asks if they are Mormon. When the teens reply yes, the group begins to shoot them with a pellet gun and to beat them, yelling anti-Mormon slurs during the assault. One of the Mormon teens is taken to the hospital.

June 9   Mahmoud Alkhazaleh, 53, was charged with a hate crime, aggravated battery and vehicle invasion in Chicago after he and his three sons allegedly pulled a white man out of a car, hit him and called the white man, a "blue-eyed devil." His sons, Ala Alkhazaleh, 27; Ali Alkhazaleh, 23; and Ahmad Alkhazaleh, 20, were charged with aggravated battery and vehicle invasion.

July 12   Pichardo Dearmas, 49, was charged with assault with prejudice in Miami Beach, Florida, for allegedly slapping Rabbi Abraham S. Mann while making a racist remark against Jews.

August 15   A Plymouth County, Massachusetts grand jury indicted seven people charged in connection with a racial beating of a black man in Marshfield. Plymouth County District Attorney Timothy Cruz says the court action shows that racism "will not be tolerated and that those charged will be held accountable for their actions."

September 9   Steven Sandstrom, 23, and Gary L. Eye, 22, both of Kansas City, Missouri were sentenced to multiple life sentences for the racially-motivated murder of William L. McCay, an African American, on March 9, 2005.

October 1   Muhidin Mumin, a 42-year-old Somali Muslim man, was fatally beaten in a downtown alley in Rochester, Minnesota. Adam Brandrup and Joshua Lee, both 25, were charged with second-degree unintentional murder, classified by police as a bias crime. In April 2012, Brandrup was sentenced to five years in prison.

November 5   Prosecutors said Thomas Gleason, Benjamin Haskell and Michael Jacques burned down the predominantly black Macedonia Church of God in Christ in Springfield, Massachusetts, hours after Obama was elected as the nation's first black president. Thomas Gleason was ordered to pay $1.7 million in restitution and sentenced to four and a half years in prison. He expressed remorse for what prosecutors called a racially-motivated crime. His companions were sentenced to 9 and 14 years. All three perpetrators are white.

2009

March 2   Thanh Hong, a Vietnamese American student at the University of California at Santa Barbara, and his Asian

American friend walked in front of the Pi Kappa Alpha fraternity house when four men emerged from inside the fraternity
house, approached Thanh and his friend, and began yelling
racial epithets at them. They punched Thanh's friend in the
face, and then attacked Thanh, who suffered a facial laceration
requiring several stitches and his friend suffered a concussion
resulting in partial memory loss.

July 22 Three men were sentenced to prison after being
convicted in July of committing a hate crime in connection
with the July 4, 2008, beating of a black man in Boise, Idaho.
Michael Bullard, 23, was sentenced to more than four years,
Richard Armstrong, 24, to more than three years and James
Whitewater, 23, to a year and a half. Evidence revealed that
the three men using racial slurs ambushed, chased and beat
a 24-year-old African American man as he walked out of a
Wal-Mart store in Nampa, Idaho. Witnesses testified that Bullard, Armstrong and Whitewater all participated in the assault,
while a fourth person, a girlfriend of one of the defendants,
held their belongings and cheered them on.

2010

April 20 Rocks with derogatory messages about Mormons
were thrown through windows at the Church of Jesus Christ of
Latter-day Saints in Idaho Falls, Idaho.

October 14 A federal jury in Scranton, Pa., convicted Brandon Piekarsky and Derrick Donchak, both of Shenandoah, Pa.,
of a hate crime arising out of the fatal beating of Luis Ramirez on
July 12, 2008. The jury found the defendants guilty of violating
the criminal component of the federal Fair Housing Act, which
makes it a crime to use a person's race, national origin or ethnicity as a basis to interfere, with violence or threats of violence,
with a person's right to live where he chooses to live. During the
trial, the jury heard evidence from multiple eyewitnesses that
the defendants, aided and abetted each other and some of their
friends in fatally beating Luis Ramirez because he was Latino
and because they did not want Latinos living in Shenandoah.

2011

September 27   Sean Popejoy, 20, was sentenced to four years in prison for his part in a 2010 racially motivated attack where Popejoy was a passenger in a truck that rammed a car with five Latino men inside, forcing it to overturn and burn, injuring all the men in Harrison, Arkansas. Popejoy was the first person convicted under the Matthew Shepard and James Byrd Jr. Hate Crimes Prevention Act of 2009.

September 30   Francisco Vasquez, 34, and Anthony Gonzales, 19, were convicted of a hate crime and attempted murder in San Fernando, California for yelling a racial slur and opening fire on two black men in May 2010.

September 30   Thomas Frank Ross, a 19-year-old student at the University of Colorado in Boulder, was arrested on suspicion of second-degree assault and bias-motivated crime after allegedly making derogatory remarks about Asian food, then breaking the nose of a half-Asian student who objected.

2012

January 2   Luis Alberto Gonzalez, 50, was charged with two counts of second-degree attempted murder and one count of falsely reporting a crime for allegedly trying to run down two black men and then falsely claiming they tried to rob him on January 2, in Hialeah, Florida.

January 16   A Hillard, Ohio residence occupied by the son of an Egyptian native was set afire. The house had been painted with anti- Arab and anti-Islamic slurs several months earlier.

January 24   Paul Beebe, 27, and Jesse Sanford, 25, were both sentenced to prison for branding a swastika on the arm of disabled Navajo man in Santa Fe, New Mexico in 2010. Beebe was sentenced to 8 1/2 years in prison followed by three years' supervised release and Sanford was sentenced to five years in prison followed by three years' supervised release.

February 17   Chad Martin Jurjaks was sentenced to 16 months in prison on two counts of hate crime battery for attacking two Latino men outside a convenience store in Costa Mesa, California in March 2011.

March 3   Ray Lazier Lengend was charged with one count of arson as a hate crime, four counts of arson and five counts of criminal possession of a weapon for allegedly firebombing a convenience store, two residences in Elmont Queens, a home in Nassau County and an Islamic center on New Year's Day.

March 4   Aakash Dalal, 19, was arrested in connection with the Jan. 3 firebombing of a synagogue in Paramus and the January 11 firebombing of a synagogue in Rutherford, New Jersey. An indictment accuses Dalal of bias intimidation at a Maywood synagogue, criminal mischief for allegedly spray-painting anti-Semitic graffiti on a Hackensack synagogue, three counts of conspiracy to commit aggravated arson, two counts of aggravated arson, three counts of bias intimidation, possession of a destructive device, a Molotov cocktail, attempted arson, hindering apprehension and terrorism, the report said.

March 27   Ivan Alquicira, a 19-year-old Los Angeles Latino man, was charged with three counts of assault with a deadly weapon, two counts of making terrorist threats and enhancements for hate crimes, gang involvement and firearms possession after he allegedly yelled racial epithets and pointed a shotgun at three black people on the street.

April 29   In Oakland, California, Brandy Martell, a 37-year-old transgender woman, was fatally shot in a car parked in an area frequented by transgender women.

May 15   Myles Burton, 21, a former basketball player at Elmhurst College in Illinois, was convicted of a felony hate crime for etching the letters "KKK" and racist remarks on the home of the school's only black dorm supervisor in November.

May 22   In Nyack, New York, a Latino man was allegedly attacked by a black man who made anti-Latino remarks while wielding a baseball bat. Wendy Jean, 17, was charged with felony assault as a hate crime and fourth-degree criminal possession of a weapon.

June 5   Nicholas Velasquez, 29, was charged with elder abuse and committing a hate crime after allegedly yelling "I hate white people" while punching a woman in a wheelchair.

June 12   A storage building in Dearborn, Michigan owned by the American Muslim Center was set afire and graffiti that included the word "Arabs" was found at the scene.

June 21   Javier Correa was charged with interfering with the religious freedom of members of a mosque in Murfreesboro, Tennessee by threatening to use force against them when he allegedly left a racist message threatening to bomb the building in 2011. Correa was also charged with threatening to use an explosive device to interfere.

June 27   Jeremiah Leo 'Smurf' Hernandez, 33, was sentenced to 11 years in prison for his role in a March 2011 cross burning near a black teen's residence in San Luis Obispo, California.

July 12   Two white teens, ages 17 and 16, were charged with committing a hate crime, aggravated unlawful restraint, intimidation, aggravated battery and battery in connection with a December 2011 incident in Chicago. The teenagers, along with Matthew Herrmann, 18, allegedly put a noose around a black high school student's neck, threatened him with a knife and used racial slurs while holding him captive.

July 14   A white man armed with a steak knife allegedly burst into an apartment, screamed anti-Latino epithets and struck a child in the face in Congers, New York. Thomas Cheviot, 53, was charged with three counts of first-degree burglary, assault on a child less than 11 as a hate crime, assault as a hate crime, criminal possession of a weapon, resisting arrest and endangering the welfare of a child.

July 25   Five people allegedly yelled racial epithets, destroyed property and shot paintballs at campers at a Jewish summer camp in Waymart, Pennsylvania several times in July. Mark Trail, 21; Tyler Spencer and Cassandra Robertson, both 18; and two juveniles face numerous charges including ethnic intimidation, terroristic threats and riot.

August 5   Wade Michael Page, a white supremacist and U.S. Army veteran, fatally shot six people and wounded four others at a Sikh Temple in Oak Creek, Wisconsin. Page took his life by shooting himself in the head after he was shot in the stomach by a responding police officer. Apart from the shooter, all of the dead were members of the Sikh faith. The incident drew responses from President Barack Obama ordered American flags flown at half-staff and Indian Prime Minister Manmohan Singh, himself a Sikh. The six victims killed included one woman: Paramjit Kaur, 41; and five men: Satwant Singh Kaleka, 65, the founder of this Sikh temple (gurdwara; Prakash Singh, 39, an assistant priest; Sita Singh, 41; Ranjit Singh, 49; and Suveg Singh, 83. All of the male victims wore turbans as part of their Sikh faith Four of the victims were Indian nationals, while the rest were Americans.

August 23   A reported self-proclaimed white supremacist allegedly yelled "white pride," threatened to kill an 18-year-old Native American and his two cousins and then punched the teen in Shasta, California. The man allegedly later threatened the teen's mother with a gun.

September 19   A U.S. congressional hearing addressed hate crimes in response to the tragic murder of Sikh worshippers in Wisconsin, before the Senate Judiciary Committee's Subcommittee on the Constitution, Civil Rights and Human Rights convened by Senator Dick Durbin.

October 3   The Wynne School Board has expelled two junior varsity football players who were accused of placing a noose around the neck of a black student. The board met in executive session Wednesday and decided to expel the two students for the rest of the semester. Family members have said the white students placed a noose around the 14-year-old black student's neck.

October 12   A white Bay City, Michigan man has been charged with committing a hate crime in the racially motivated beating of a black man. The intimidation charge carries up to two years in prison.

October 17   A Utah man was arrested for assaulting two people after finding them in a same-sex romantic encounter. Summit County deputies say they responded to reports of a fight in Kamas on Wednesday evening. They found three people with cuts and bruises, and ended up arresting 40-year-old Travis Gentry on suspicion of a hate crime assault.

December 14   Ventura County sheriff's deputies in Upper Ojai, California said they arrested four people Wednesday in connection with hate crimes that occurred three months ago at two campgrounds in Rose Valley. Authorities also arrested a suspect in September, about two weeks after the incident. Detectives said they also seized a large quantity of illegal ammunition.

December 18   Federal agents on Tuesday arrested a Waretown man and an East Windsor man, both purported to be white supremacists, and charged them with hate crimes in connection with an attack on three Egyptian men in Sayreville, New Jersey. They were picked up by FBI agents after being charged in an indictment handed down by a federal grand jury sitting in Newark.

2013

January 4   A Mississippi man pleaded guilty Thursday to a federal hate crime charge in connection with a group of young men and teenagers who carried out racial attacks against African Americans in 2011.

January 6   Two men who were with a female friend outside a bar in St. Charles, Illinois were allegedly attacked by a woman and two men who called the victims antigay slurs during the attack. On Jan. 28, Christopher M. Miner, 30, and Stephan C. Bolt and Susan V. Patton, both 31, were charged with aggravated battery, battery, mob action, and hate crimes.

February 21   A black student at Full Sail University in Winter Park, Florida was allegedly stabbed in the neck by another student who yelled racial slurs. Xavier Nunez, 29, was charged with aggravated battery with a deadly weapon.

March 10   Clayton Daniel Garzon, 19, brutally beat and shouted antigay slurs at Lawrence "Mikey" Partida outside a house party in Davis, California. In March 2014, Garzon was sentenced to a five-year prison sentence.

August 15   Islan Nettles, a 21-year-old transgender woman, was beaten, allegedly by a man shouting antigay slurs in Harlem, New York. Nettles died of her injuries on Aug. 23. A 20-year-old man was arrested in connection with the incident.

September 17   Antonio Lanier, 23, was charged with aggravated harassment and assault as a hate crime for allegedly participating in the Aug. 14 beating of two Manhattan men who were holding hands on the street.

October 26   Dylan Grall, 23, was arrested on battery and hate crime charges in Madison, Wisconsin for allegedly punching two men who were speaking Hebrew. Grail allegedly thought the men were speaking Spanish and yelled at them to speak in English.

October 30   Jamie Hebert, 20, pled guilty to second-degree battery and to violating Louisiana's hate crime statute for shouting antigay slurs and punching a man who was holding hands with another man in the French Quarter in February 2013. Hebert was sentenced to two years on the battery charge and three years on the hate crime charge but the sentences were suspended. Instead, Hebert will spend three years on probation.

November 1   Tavares Spencer, 16, was convicted of attempted first-degree felony murder, attempted second-degree murder and robbery for the April shooting of a transgender man in Tampa, Florida.

November 8   Eric Hyland and Hayden Grom, both 19, were charged with ethnic intimidation, criminal mischief and disorderly conduct after they allegedly spray-painted anti-Semitic, sexual and graphic words and images on 12 cars, a dumpster and a garage near a predominantly Jewish fraternity at Penn State University.

December 9   Justin Baker, 25, pleaded guilty to violating the civil rights of students of a Jewish school for defacing the school's Torah scroll and prayer books before a January 2013 worship service held at a Jackson, Tenn., hotel where Baker was working as a security guard.

December 23   In Turlock, California, two men allegedly called a black woman a racial epithet while beating her unconscious in a bar. Eddie Taylor, 53, and Eddie Taylor Jr., 25, were charged with aggravated assault and a hate crime.

2014

January 6   A 35-year-old New York man has been charged with hate crimes in connection with seven "knockout" assaults, including attacks on two elderly women and a mother walking with her daughter. Barry Baldwin, a Brooklyn resident, was charged with six counts of assault as a hate crime, six counts of aggravated harassment as a hate crime, and other crimes for a spate of attacks between November 9 and December 27 in predominantly Jewish sections of Brooklyn.

March 11   In Portland, Oregon, white supremacist Holly Ann Grigsby pled guilty to racketeering in connection with a 2011 road trip that allegedly culminated in the murders of four people. Grigsby and her boyfriend, fellow white supremacist David Pedersen, allegedly killed Pedersen's father and step mother, a black man and a 19-year-old stranger who was singled out because they thought he was Jewish.

March 25   White supremacist Billy James Hammett, 30, was sentenced to 87 months in prison for a 2011 racially motivated attack against a white man and a black woman in Marysville, California. Hammett was also ordered to pay $175 in restitution and serve three years of supervised release following his prison sentence.

April 9 A 16-year-old black Detroit youth was charged with assault and a hate crime for allegedly brutally beating a white motorist who stopped to help a boy he accidentally hit with his pickup truck.

April 13 Frazier Glenn Miller, a neo-Nazi and former Ku Klux Klan member, killed three people at the Jewish Community Center of Greater Kansas City and Village Shalom, a Jewish retirement community, both located Overland, Kansas.

The victims were a 14-year-old boy, Reat Griffin Underwood, and his 69-year-old grandfather, Dr. William Lewis Corporon, were killed at the Jewish Community Center. Both were Christians and attendants at the United Methodist Church of the Resurrection A 53-year-old woman, Terri LaManno, also a Christian was killed at the parking lot of Village Shalom, where her mother resides. LaManno was also a Christian who attended St. Peter's Catholic Church in Kansas City. Only one person targeted by gunfire was Jewish.

April 15 Perry Germano, 50, was charged with attempted assault, aggravated harassment, and menacing in an April 7 assault on a 15-year-old girl riding a New York City bus. He allegedly made statements attacking Islam, spat on the girl, and threatened to punch her.

May 1 Anthony Merrell Tyler, 33, pleaded guilty to violating the Matthew Shepard and James Byrd Jr. Hate Crimes Prevention Act for his role in a racially motivated attack (see 2014; March 25) in Marysville, California.

May 2 Former New York City police officer Michael Setiawan, 36, was arrested for spray-painting anti-Semitic graffiti on 15 vehicles and four buildings near a synagogue and Jewish school.

May 8 Two Montgomery County, Maryland high school students, ages 16 and 17, were charged with hate crimes and vandalism for allegedly painting anti-Semitic graffiti on the sign of a synagogue; an anti-Jewish slur and swastika on two buses at a child care facility; and a swastika and a SS Nazi symbol on the windshield of a car at a nearby residence.

June 13   Bernhard Laufer, awaiting trial for attempted murder at a mosque in 2012, was arrested on charges of threatening to kill leaders of a Muslim civil rights organization, the Council on American-Islamic Relations.

June 15   Michael Phillips, 36, was sentenced to 28 months in prison after pleading guilty to assault with a dangerous weapon, enhanced as a hate crime, for pistol-whipping a transgender woman in January in Washington, DC.

June 19   David Malcolm Strickland, 27, was charged with capital murder, aggravated assault with a weapon, and aggravated sexual assault in Heliotes, Texas, for the 2012 attack on a 19-year-old lesbian, Mollie Olgin, because of her sexual orientation.

2015

February 5   Two men were arrested for the hate-crime assault of a transgender woman who, with the help of dozens of supporters, took her case this week to the Spokane City Council in the state of Washington. Adam R. Flippen, 45, faces charges of second-degree assault and malicious harassment. Marc A. Fessler, 42, is charged with one count of malicious harassment, a felony hate crime charge in Washington State. The victim, Jacina Scamahorn, who is homeless, told investigators she was on a public sidewalk when two men began making negative, unsolicited comments about her gender identity. Scamahorn said she was punched in the face and kicked, causing a blackened eye and broken facial bones.

June 17   Six women and three men were shot dead at the Emanuel African Methodist Episcopal Church in Charleston, South Carolina. Among the victims was the Reverend Clementa Pinckney, 41, who was also a South Carolina state senator. The others were Tywanza Sanders, 26, Sharonda Singleton, 45, DePayne Middleton, 49, Cynthia Hurd, 54, Myra Thompson,

59, Ethel Lee Lance, 70, Daniel Simmons, 76, and Susie Jackson, 87. The gunman was a 21-year-old white supremacist Dylann S. Roof, who reportedly shouted racial epithets before opening fire inside this historic black church that traces its roots to the slave-holding days before the Civil War.

American Indian or Alaska Native: A person having origins in any of the original peoples of North and South America (including Central America) and who maintains tribal affiliation or community attachment. This category includes persons from the following tribal affiliations: Navajo, Blackfeet, Inupiat, Yup'ik, or Central American Indian groups or South American Indian groups.

Anti-Semitism: The "longest hatred" in human history has been defined in many ways to describe prejudice, discrimination and violence aimed at Jewish people. Anti-Semitism may denote hatred against Jews because of their religious beliefs, their group membership (ethnicity) and sometimes the erroneous belief that Jews are a "race." The term is a misnomer because "Semitic" refers to a language group and not a religious or ethnic identity; the term is exclusively used about Jews and not Arabs or others who speak Semitic languages.

Arab: A person having origins, and/or ancestry, in any of the Arabic speaking peoples of Lebanon, Syria, Palestine, Jordan, Iraq, Saudi Arabia, Yemen, Oman, United Arab Emirates, Qatar, Bahrain, Kuwait, Egypt, Libya, Tunisia, Comoros, Algeria, Morocco, Sudan, Djibouti, Mauritania, and Somalia.

Asian American: According to the U.S. Census Bureau, this demographic category includes Americans of Chinese, Filipino, Japanese, Asian Indian, Korean, Vietnamese, Cambodian, Hmong, Laotian, Thai, Bangladeshi, Burmese, Indonesian, Pakistani, Sri Lankan, Amerasian, or Eurasian descent.

Bias Crime: See "hate crime."

Black or African American: A person having origins in any of the black racial groups of Africa, according to the Office of Management and Budget (OMB) category definitions on race and ethnicity.

Disability: An individual with a disability is defined by the Americans with Disability Act (ADA) as a person who has a physical or mental impairment that substantially limits one or more major life activities, a person who has a history or record of such an impairment, or a person who is perceived by others as having such an impairment. The ADA does not specifically name all of the impairments that are covered.

Disability bias: A preformed negative opinion or attitude toward a group of persons based on their physical or mental impairments, whether such disability is temporary or permanent, congenital or acquired by heredity, accident, injury, advanced age, or illness.

Gay: The adjective used to describe people whose emotional, romantic, and/or physical attraction is to people of the same sex. The term "lesbian" is often the preferred term for women. Individuals who are gay need not have had any sexual experience—the attraction determines orientation.

Gender Identity: A person's internal sense of being male, female, or a combination of both; this sense of a person's gender may be different from the person's gender as determined at birth.

Hate Crime: A criminal offense that is motivated, in whole or in part, by the offender's bias(es) against a race, religion, disability, sexual orientation, ethnicity, gender, or gender identity. Also known as a "bias crime."

Hate Crime victimization: Refers to a single victim or household that experienced a criminal incident believed by the victim to be motivated by prejudice based on race, gender or gender identity, religion, disability, sexual orientation, or ethnicity.

Hate Group: An organization whose primary purpose is to promote animosity, hostility, and malice against persons of or with a race, religion, disability, sexual orientation, ethnicity, gender, or gender identity which differs from that of the members of the organization (e.g., the Ku Klux Klan, American Nazi Party, Nation of Islam).

Hispanic or Latino: A person of Cuban, Mexican, Puerto Rican, South or Central American, or other Spanish culture or origin, regardless of race. Includes people from Hispanic or Latino groups such as: Dominican Republic; Central American (excludes Mexican) Costa Rican, Guatemalan, Honduran, Nicaraguan, Panamanian, Salvadoran, Other Central American; South America and South American. Argentinian, Bolivian, Chilean, Columbian, Ecuadorian, Paraguayan, Peruvian, Uruguayan, Venezuelan, Other South American; Spaniard

Homophobia: An aversion to lesbian or gay people that often manifests itself in the form of prejudice and bias.

Homosexual: An outdated clinical term, which is now considered derogatory, as opposed to the preferred terms, "gay" and "lesbian."

Islamophobia: The term was first introduced as a concept in a 1991 Runnymede Trust Report (an independent "race equality" British think tank) and defined as "unfounded hostility towards Muslims, and therefore fear or dislike of all or most Muslims." The term was coined in the context of attitudes toward Muslims in the UK in particular and Europe in general, and formulated based on the more common "xenophobia" framework.

LGBT: An acronym for lesbian, gay, bisexual and transgender which refers to these individuals collectively.

Lynching: The term is derived from the vigilante justice practiced by Captain William Lynch and his neighbors in Pittsylvania County, Virginia in the late 18th century. In the 19th century, lynching was usually associated with hanging but also feathering, burning and killing, among other violent activities which were mostly directed against African Americans.

National Incident-Based Reporting System (NIBRS): The NIBRS is an incident-based reporting system in which agencies collect data on each single crime occurrence. NIBRS data come from local, state, and federal automated records' systems.

Sikh: A person who follows the monotheistic religion founded by Guru Nanak in the Punjab region of South Asia. Sikhs follow the teachings of 10 gurus; study from the religion's primary sacred text (i.e., the Guru Granth Sahib) and worship in Gurdwaras. Some members of the Sikh faith may be distinguished by the *dastarr* (Sikh turban) and five religious articles: *kesh* (unshorn hair, including a beard), *kanga* (wooden comb), *kara* (steel bracelet), *kachera* (short trousers), and *kirpan* (religious sword).

Transgender: A general term for people whose gender identity and/or gender expression differs from what is conventionally associated with the sex they were assigned at birth. A transgender man is a person who was born as a biological female but identifies and lives as a man, also known as a *trans man*; a transgender woman was born as a biological male but identifies and lives as a woman, also known as a *trans woman*.

Undocumented Immigrant: A person who is residing in the United States without the permission of the U.S. government. Undocumented immigrants enter the United States either illegally, without being inspected by an immigration officer or by using false documents, or legally, with a temporary visa and then remain in the United States after the visa has expired. The term "illegal alien" is considered pejorative.

advocates of hate crime
legislation, 4–5
African Americans, 46–51,
354
church arsons and, 47–48
examples of hate crimes
against, 48–51
hate crime statistics, 46
police officer murders of
unarmed, 47
violent rampages against,
5–6, 46–47
Ahmed, Abdo Ali, 77
Alaska Native, 353. *See also*
Native Americans
Alden, Matt, 127
Al-Suwaij, Zainab, 135–136
American Civil Liberties
Union (ACLU), 121
American Indian, 353.
See also Native Americans
American Islamic Congress
(AIC), 83, 135, 155–157
American Jewish Committee
(AJC), 82, 157
American Knights, 194
American Renaissance, 193

Americans with disabilities,
58–59
Angry Aryans, 196
Anti-Arson Act, 1982, 9
Anti-Defamation League
(ADL), 6–7, 11, 22,
30–31, 60–61, 81, 84,
97, 120, 158–159
Audit of Anti-Semitic
Incidents, 60
FBI and, 181
Hate on the Internet
manual, 191–204
Anti-Hispanic Immigrant
Hate Crimes (Stacey,
Carbone-Lopez, and
Rosenfeld), 112–115
anti-Semitism, 59, 108–110,
353
Apprendi, Charles C., Jr., 23
Apprendi v. New Jersey, 23–24
Arab Americans, 76–84, 353
Islamophobia and, 83–84
sympathetic reactions to,
80–83
violent incidents against,
77–80, 87–88

About the Author

Donald Altschiller is a librarian at Boston University. He has written eight reference books and his articles have been published in the *Wall Street Journal*, *Chronicle of Higher Education*, the *Boston Globe*, and the *Los Angeles Times*. His most recent book is *Animal-Assisted Therapy* published by Greenwood, and he has written two earlier editions of *Hate Crimes: A Reference Handbook*. Altschiller has contributed essays to almost a dozen encyclopedias, including *The Historical Encyclopedia of World Slavery* and the *Encyclopedia of the American Civil War*, both published by ABC-CLIO. He regularly reviews reference books for library journals and was a longtime contributor to the ALA online *Guide to Reference Sources*.